Presented to

_____

By

_____

On the Occasion of

_____

Date

_____

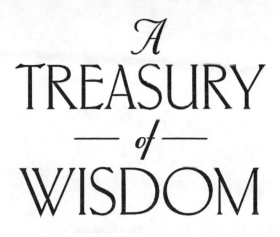

A TREASURY — of — WISDOM

*Daily Inspiration
from Favorite Christian Authors*

Compiled by
Ken and Angela Abraham

BARBOUR
PUBLISHING, INC.
Uhrichsville, Ohio

©MCMXCVIII by Barbour Publishing, Inc.

ISBN 1-57748-204-2

All Scripture quotations (unless otherwise noted) are taken from The Authorized King James Version of the Bible.

All Scripture quotations marked (NIV) are taken from the HOLY BIBLE, NEW INTERNATIONAL VERSION®. Copyright 1973, 1978, 1984 by International Bible Society. Used by permission of Zondervan Publishing House. All rights reserved.

All Scripture quotations marked (NAS) are taken from the New American Standard Bible, ©1960, 1962, 1963, 1968, 1971, 1972, 1973, 1975, 1977 by The Lockman Foundation. Used by permission.

Published by Barbour Publishing, Inc.
      P.O. Box 719
      Uhrichsville, OH 44683
      http://www.barbourbooks.com

Member of the
Evangelical Christian
Publishers Association

Printed in the United States of America.

"*Lord. . .teach us to number our days, that we may apply our hearts unto wisdom. For. . .happy is the man that findeth wisdom, and the man that getteth understanding. For the merchandise of it is better than the merchandise of silver, and the gain thereof than fine gold.*"

PSALM 90:12; PROVERBS 3:13, 14

A Treasury of Wisdom is a collection of spiritual insights borrowed from well-known men and women who have walked closely with God. Each selection has been carefully chosen to challenge, encourage, and inspire you as you continue your daily walk with the Lord.

These timeless and relevant Scriptures and insights are a breath of fresh air in the midst of difficult times, an inviting spring of unknown depth when you desire to know more.

Wisdom is a gift from God, freely given to all who seek Him sincerely and in earnest.

JANUARY

GOD'S CALENDAR *by William A. Quale*

"And God said, Let there be lights in the firmament of the heaven to divide the day from the night; and let them be for signs, and for seasons, and for days, and years."

GENESIS 1:14

*H*ours and minutes are man's invention. Weeks and days and nights and the month and the year are God's inventions. A seventh day for rest, God said; and the week was put in the calendar. One daylight and one dark; and the day was created. One advent and exit of the silvery moon; and the month was included in its silvery circuit. The planet's panting journey around the sun; and the year became a terrestrial and celestial fact. Twelve comings and goings of the moon, with a few days excess thrown in for good measure, as is customary with God; and God's calendar is an accomplished loveliness.

TIME IS A GIFT *by Elisabeth Elliot*

"To every thing there is a season, and a time to every purpose under the heaven."　　　　　　　　ECCLESIASTES 3:1

*T*ime is a creature—a created thing—and a gift. We cannot make any more of it. We can only receive it and be faithful stewards in the use of it.

"I don't have time" is probably a lie more often than not, covering "I don't want to." We have time—twenty-four hours in a day, seven days in a week. All of us have the same portion. "If the president can run the country on twenty-four hours a day, you ought to be able to get your room cleaned" is what one mother said to her teenage son. Demands on our time differ, of course, and it is here that the disciple must refer to his Master. What do You want me to do, Lord? There will be time, depend upon it, for everything God wants us to do.

THE LIGHT WITHIN *by Charles H. Spurgeon*

"And God saw the light."　　　　　　　　GENESIS 1:4

*T*his morning we noticed the goodness of the light, and the Lord's dividing it from the darkness. We now note the special eye which the Lord had for the light. "God saw the light"—He looked at it with complacency, gazed upon it with pleasure, saw that it "was good." If the Lord has given you light, dear reader, He looks on that light with peculiar interest; for not only is it dear to Him as His own handiwork, but because it is like Himself, for "He is light." Pleasant it is to the believer ever to know that God's eye is thus tenderly observant of that work of grace which He has begun. He never loses sight of the treasure which He has placed in our earthen vessels. Sometimes we cannot see the light, but God always sees the light, and that is much better than our seeing it. Better for the judge to see my innocence than for me to think I see it. It is very comfortable for me to know that I am one of God's people—but whether I know it or not, if the Lord knows it, I am still safe. This is the foundation, "The Lord knoweth them that are His." You may be sighing and groaning because of inbred sin, and mourning over your darkness, yet the Lord sees "light" in your heart, for He has put it there, and all the cloudiness and gloom of your soul cannot conceal your light from His gracious eye. You may have sunk low in despondency, and even despair; but if your soul has any longing towards Christ, and if you are seeking to rest in His finished work, God sees the "light." He not only sees it, but He also preserves it in you. "I, the Lord, do keep it." This is a precious thought to those who, after anxious watching and guarding of themselves, feel their own powerlessness to do so. The light thus preserved by His grace, He will one day develop into the splendor of noonday, and the fulness of glory. The light within is the dawn of the eternal day.

SAIL ON! *by Mrs. Charles E. Cowman*

"Hitherto hath the Lord helped us."   1 SAMUEL 7:12

*S*o now into another year we sail and something of what we may expect as we continue our voyage we may infer from the past. Without doubt storms will come as they came in the bygone days. But we will give them firm and courageous welcome, for we have already weathered so many storms that we are unafraid of the wind and the tide, the lightning and the snow.

And so we shall—when the Voyage is completed drop anchor where no storms come, but where the green swell is at last in the haven dumb, and we are forever out of the swing of the Sea.

> We have come very safely—hitherto;
>   And sometimes seas were calm, and skies were blue;
> Sometimes the wild waves rose—the tempest roared;
>   But never barque went down with Christ on board.
>
> And so it shall be to the very end—
>   Through ebb or flow, the one unchanging Friend,
> Ruling the waves which sink at His command,
>   Holding them in the hollow in His hand.
>
> There comes an hour, when, every tempest o'er
>   The harbour lights are reached, the golden shores:
> Never, oh nevermore to fret or fear—
>   Christ, give us faith to praise Thee even here!
>   Mary Gorges

DAY BY DAY *compiled by Mary W. Tileston*

"Thy servants are ready to do whatsoever my lord the king shall appoint." 2 SAMUEL 15:15

*I*f we are really, and always, and equally ready to do whatsoever the King appoints, all the trials and vexations arising from any change in His appointments, great or small, simply do not exist. If He appoints me to work there, shall I lament that I am not to work here? If He appoints me to wait indoors today, am I to be annoyed because I am not to work out-of-doors? If I meant to write His messages this morning, shall I grumble because He sends interrupting visitors, rich or poor, to whom I am to speak them, or show kindness for His sake, or at least obey His command, Be courteous? If all my members are really at His disposal, why should I be put out if today's appointment is some simple work for my hands or errands for my feet, instead of some seemingly more important doing of head or tongue?

THE UNKNOWN JOURNEY *by John Henry Jowett*

"He went out, not knowing whither he went." HEBREWS 11:8

*A*bram began his journey without any knowledge of his ultimate destination. He obeyed a noble impulse without any discernment of its consequences. He took "one step," and he did not "ask to see the distant scene." And that is faith, to do God's will here and now, quietly leaving the results to Him. Faith is not concerned with the entire chain; its devoted attention is fixed upon the immediate link. Faith is not knowledge of a moral process; it is fidelity in a moral act. Faith leaves something to the Lord; it obeys His immediate commandment and leaves to Him direction and destiny.

And so faith is accompanied by serenity. "He that believeth shall not make haste"—or, more literally, "shall not get into a fuss." He shall not get into a panic, neither fetching fears from his yesterdays nor from his tomorrows. Concern-ing his yesterdays Faith says, "Thou hast beset me behind." Concerning his tomorrows Faith says, "Thou hast beset me before." Concerning his today Faith says, "Thou hast laid Thine hand upon me." That is enough, just to feel the pressure of the guiding hand.

JANUARY 7TH

DESERT SANDS OR DEEP SEAS *by Hannah Hurnard*

"I will instruct thee and teach thee in the way which thou shalt go."   PSALM 32:8

*T*he Shepherd and Much-Afraid walked together through the burning desert sands, then one day, quite unexpectedly a path crossed the main track which they were following. "This," said the Shepherd quietly, "is the path which you are now to follow." So they turned westward with the High Places right behind their backs and came in a little while to the end of the desert. They found themselves on the shore of a great sea.

The Shepherd said to Much-Afraid, "Remember, even

though you seem to be farther away than ever from the High Places and from me, there is really no distance at all separating us. I can cross the desert sands as swiftly as I can leap from the High Places to the valleys, and whenever you call for me, I shall come. This is the word I now leave with you. Believe it and practice it with joy. My sheep hear my voice and they follow me.

"Whenever you are willing to obey me, Much-Afraid, and to follow the path of my choice, you will always be able to hear and recognize my voice, and when you hear it you must always obey. Remember also that it is always safe to obey my voice, even if it seems to call you to paths which look impossible."

JANUARY 8TH

IN HIS TIME *by R.T. Kendall*

"Choosing rather to suffer affliction with the people of God, than to enjoy the pleasures of sin for a season."
HEBREWS 11:25

*W*hen God shows us that he is going to use us (and he can do that), we usually tend to think that we are going to see this happen in the next week or two. What often happens is that it is a long time before God gets around to using us as he has in mind. Take Moses. When Moses grew up, he refused to be called the son of Pharaoh's daughter, "choosing rather to suffer affliction with the people of God, than to enjoy the pleasures of sin for a season" (Heb. 11:25). Moses thought that when he left the palace and identified himself with his brethren, they would clap their hands and say, "Welcome. We've been waiting for you to come." The truth

15

is they rejected him, and Moses needed another forty years of preparation.

It may be a good while indeed before God's greater purpose in us will be realized. It could be that you too are in a similar situation. Perhaps you are older and you have yet to see what God's greater purpose in your own life is. Perhaps you have just about given up. You thought at one time that God was going to use you. You were convinced of it, but it didn't work out. God's message to you right now is: the end is not yet. The story isn't over.

JANUARY 9TH

VALLEYS OF WAITING *by Lloyd John Ogilvie*

"But if we hope for that which we see not, then do we with patience wait for it."   ROMANS 8:25

*L*ife does have its mountain peaks of triumph and delight—and its valleys of impatient waiting for our prayers to be answered. I've discovered three things about those valleys. The first two are now firm convictions. The third I have to relearn constantly.

First, it has been in the valleys of waiting for answers to my prayers that I have made the greatest strides in growing in the Lord's grace.

Second, it's usually in retrospect, after the strenuous period is over, that I can look back with gratitude on what I've received of the Lord Himself. I wouldn't trade the deeper trust and confidence I experienced from the valley for a smooth and trouble-free life.

Third, I long to be able to remember what the tough times provide in my relationship with the Lord, so that when new valleys occur, my first reaction will be to thank and praise the Lord in advance for what is going to happen in and through me as a result of what happens to me. I really want my first thought to be, *Lord, I know You didn't send this, but You have allowed it and will use it as a part of working all things together for good. I trust You completely, Lord!*

What I need is to be more myopic in being able to see and interpret the deeper meaning of problems close at hand, to live more fully in the present challenges, trusting that the Lord who has been so faithful in the past will guide me through the present.

JANUARY 10TH

TRUSTING IN THE DARKNESS *by D. L. Moody*

"Now faith is the substance of things hoped for, the evidence of things not seen."　　　　　HEBREWS 11:1

*S*uppose I have a sick boy. I know nothing about medicine; but I call in the doctor, and put that boy's life and everything into his hands. I do not fail to believe in him; and I do not interfere at all. Do you call that trusting in the dark? Not at all! I used my best judgment and I put that boy's life into the hands of a good physician.

You have a soul diseased. Put it into the hand of the Great Physician! Trust Him, and He will take care of it. He has had some of the most hopeless cases. He was able to heal all that came to Him while on earth. He is the same today.

Take another illustration. Suppose you have one thousand dollars, and there are forty thieves who want to rob you of it. I tell you that there is a bank here, and that I will introduce you to the president so that you can deposit the money.

17

You do not know anything of the bank, save by repute; you know nothing about how the books are kept but you take my word, and you believe my testimony, that if you deposit the money it will be safe; and you go in and place the thousand dollars there.

We must trust God in time of trouble, in time of bereavement. You can trust Him with your soul until your dying day, if you will. Will you not do it?

JANUARY 11TH

IMPOSSIBLE PROOFS *by Andrew Murray*

"For with God nothing shall be impossible."   LUKE 1:37

Your religious life is every day to be a proof that God works impossibilities; your religious life is to be a series of impossibilities made possible and actual by God's almighty power. That is what the Christian needs. He has an almighty God that he worships, and he must learn to understand: I do not want a little of God's power, but I want—with reverence be it said—the whole of God's omnipotence to keep me right, and to live like a Christian.

IRRESISTIBLE TRUST *by Hannah Whitall Smith*

"And I, if I be lifted up from the earth, will draw all men unto me."   JOHN 12:32

If you are an uncomfortable Christian, then the only thing to give you a thoroughly comfortable religious life is to know God. The psalmist says that they that know God's name will put their trust in Him, and it is, I am convinced, impossible for anyone really to know Him and not to trust Him. A trustworthy person commands trust, not in the sense of ordering people to trust him, but by irresistibly winning their trust by his trustworthiness.

What our Lord declares is eternally true, "And I, if I be lifted up, will draw all men unto me." When once you know Him, Christ is absolutely irresistible. You can no more help trusting Him than you can help breathing. And could the whole world but know Him as He is, the whole world, sinners and all, would fall at His feet in adoring worship. They simply could not help it. His surpassing loveliness would carry all before it.

How then can we become acquainted with God?

There are two things necessary: first, God must reveal Himself; and second, we must accept His revelation and believe what He reveals.

FAITH APPEARS WHERE LEAST EXPECTED
by Philip Yancey

"So then faith cometh by hearing, and hearing by the word of God."   ROMANS 10:17

I once read through all the miracle stories together and found they reveal remarkably different degrees of faith. A few people demonstrated bold, unshakable faith, such as a centurion who told Jesus he need not bother with a visit—just a word would heal his servant long-distance. "I tell you the truth, I have not found anyone in Israel with such great faith," Jesus remarked, astonished.

Another time, a foreign woman pursued Jesus as he was seeking peace and quiet. At first Jesus answered her not a word. Then he replied sharply, telling her he was sent to the lost sheep of Israel, not to "dogs"—referring to her status as a Gentile. But nothing could deter this Canaanite woman, and her perseverance won Jesus over. "Woman, you have great faith!" he said.

These stories threaten me, because seldom do I have such outstanding faith. Unlike the Canaanite woman, I am easily discouraged by the silence of God. When my prayers do not seem to be answered, I am tempted to give up, and not ask again. I identify more readily with the wavering man who declared to Jesus, "I do believe; help me overcome my unbelief!" All too often I find myself echoing these words, dangling somewhere between belief and unbelief, wondering how much I miss out on by my lack of faith.

To my surprise, I noticed as I read through the stories that the people who knew Jesus best sometimes faltered in their faith. It was his own neighbors who doubted him. John the Baptist, who had proclaimed, "Look, the Lamb of God!" and had heard a voice from heaven at Jesus' baptism, later questioned him. And several times Jesus remarked with astonishment on the twelve disciples' faithlessness.

A curious law of reversal seems to be at work in the Gospels: Faith appears where least expected and falters where it should be thriving.

JANUARY 14TH

HOW MUCH FAITH? *by Elisabeth Elliot*

"In the beginning God created the heaven and the earth."
GENESIS 1:1

Time magazine once reported the discovery of the most massive object ever detected in the universe. The odd thing is nobody knows what it is. Something called a "gravitation lens" seemed to be bending the light. . .in such a way as to produce two identical images. The great question is just exactly *what* is acting as a gravitational lens. Whatever it is, it has to have the mass of a thousand (1,000) galaxies. If it's a black hole, it is "at least a thousand times as large as the Milky Way. . . ." I was bemused by the statement, "Astrophysicists find it difficult to explain how so tremendous a black hole could have formed."

The most numbing of the facts of this story for me is that people go to such elaborate lengths to avoid mentioning one vastly prior fundamental possibility that (surely?) stares them in the face: creation.

How much faith does it take to believe in God? Less, I venture to say—a great deal less—than to believe in the Unconscious generating the Conscious, Mindlessness creating

Mind, Nothing giving birth to Something.

What we know of God we have seen in His Son. He in whom we are asked to trust is Love, creative Love; thinking of us, I suppose, before He thought of gravitational lenses; giving Himself in sacrificial love long before He gave us His own breath of life—for the Lamb was slain *before the foundations of the world.*

My Lord and my God. Forgive my faithlessness.

JANUARY 15TH

GOD'S TIMING *by Mrs. Charles E. Cowman*

"By faith Moses. . .choosing rather to suffer."
HEBREWS 11:24, 25

"*B*y faith Moses refused." Faith rests on promise; to faith the promise is equivalent to fulfillment; and if only we have the one, we may dare to count on the other as already ours. It matters comparatively little that the thing promised is not given; it is sure and certain because God has pledged His word for it, and in anticipation we may enter on its enjoyment. Had Moses simply acted on what he saw, he had never left Pharaoh's palace. But his faith told him of things hidden from his contemporaries; and these led him to act in a way which to them was perfectly incomprehensible.

It was a rude surprise when he essayed to adjust a difference between two Hebrews to find himself repulsed from them by the challenge, "Who made thee a prince and a judge over us?" "For he supposed his brethren would have understood how that God by His hand would deliver them" (Acts 7:25). Evidently, God's time had not arrived; nor could it come until the heat of his spirit had slowly evaporated in the desert air, and he had learned the hardest of all lessons, that "by strength shall no man prevail."

Faith is only possible when we are on God's plan, and stand on God's promise. It is useless to pray for increased faith until we have fulfilled the conditions of faith. It is useless to waste time in regrets and tears over the failures which are due to our unbelief. "Wherefore liest thou thus upon thy face?" Faith is as natural to right conditions of soul, as a flower is to a plant.

Ascertain your place in God's plan, and get on to it. Feed on God's promises. When each of these conditions is realized, faith comes of itself; and there is absolutely nothing which is impossible. The believing souls will then be as the metal track along which God travels to men in love, grace and truth.

JANUARY 16TH

A DREAM COME TRUE *by R. T. Kendall*

"For whosoever will save his life shall lose it: but whosoever will lose his life for my sake, the same shall save it."

LUKE 9:24

*W*hen the time came for God to fulfill Joseph's dreams, Joseph himself had virtually no interest at all in it. Jesus said, "For whosoever will save his life shall lose it: but whosoever will lose his life for my sake, the same shall save it" (Luke 9:24). God wants to teach us a different set of values so that the kind of thing we start out wanting becomes secondary. God has something in mind for us far greater than the interest we began with.

Joseph's day of exaltation had arrived. And yet, through it all, a very real humiliation had to take place. We know

23

about the humiliation Joseph had experienced for thirteen years before—sold by his brothers into slavery, then taken to Egypt. We know how he was falsely accused and cast into prison.

But then came a different situation. Joseph had had a triumph and been given an exaltation, but the kind he really never asked for. He did not appear to be all that interested in what was about to happen. He watched as the Pharaoh took his ring off his finger and put it on Joseph's finger. Joseph never asked for that. All he wanted was to go home. He longed to go back to Canaan, to see his father, and to have his dreams fulfilled.

And so here we find an extraordinary incongruity: a humiliation in the heart of vindication. A triumph that was the opposite of everything he himself could have envisaged. Joseph wanted to go home, but a one way ticket to Canaan wasn't on. Before he knew it, he had Egypt in his hip pocket. He had never prayed for that. But God wanted Egypt. What God wanted is what Joseph got.

Joseph was given something that he could be trusted with because it didn't mean that much to him.

JANUARY 17TH

RESTORER *by T. C. Horton & Charles E. Hurlburt*

"He restoreth my soul; he leadeth me in the paths of righteousness for his name's sake." PSALM 23:3

We wander from God and from the paths of righteousness—from following Him beside the still waters—till we lose the way, lose joy, lose the sound of His voice. Then the Master "restoreth (the only use of this form in the Old

24

Testament) our soul," "brings us back into His Way," into
the paths of righteousness. *Oh, gracious "RESTORER," bring
back my wandering soul as a straying sheep, and lead me
on in the paths of righteousness "for Thy name's sake."
Amen.*

OBEDIENCE WITHOUT DELAY *by Elisabeth Elliot*

*"Servants, be obedient to them that are your masters accord-
ing to the flesh, . . .as unto Christ."*   EPHESIANS 6:5

S aint Benedict's rule for Monasteries states that the first
degree of humility is obedience without delay.

But this very obedience will be acceptable to God and
pleasing to men only if what is commanded is done without
hesitation, delay, lukewarmness, grumbling, or objection. For
the obedience given to superiors is given to God, since He
Himself has said, "He who hears you, hears Me." And the disciples should offer their obedience with a good will, for "God
loves a cheerful giver." For if the disciple obeys with an ill
will and murmurs, not necessarily with his lips but simply in
his heart, then even though he fulfills the command yet his
work will not be acceptable to God, who sees that his heart is
murmuring.

THE MODEL PRAYER *by Andrew Murray*

"After this manner therefore pray ye: Our Father which art in heaven."   MATTHEW 6:9

*E*very teacher knows the power of example. He not only tells the child what to do and how to do it, but shows him how it really can be done. In condescension to our weakness, our Heavenly Teacher has given us the very words we are to take with us as we draw near to our Father. We have in them a form of prayer in which there breathes the freshness and fullness of the Eternal Life. So simple that the child can lisp it, so divinely rich that it comprehends all that God can give. A form of prayer that becomes the model and inspiration for all other prayer, and yet always draws us back to itself as the deepest utterance of our souls before our God.

"Our Father which art in heaven!" To appreciate this word of adoration aright, I must remember that none of the saints in Scripture had ever ventured to address God as their Father.

BRINGING EVERYTHING TO HIM *by A. B. Simpson*

"In every thing. . .let your requests be made known unto God."   PHILIPPIANS 4:6

*A*n important help in the life of prayer is the habit of bringing everything to God, moment by moment, as it comes to us in life. This may become habit the same way all habits are formed: repeated and constantly attended, moment by moment, until that which is at first an act of will becomes spontaneous and second nature.

If we will watch our lives, we shall find that God meets the things that we commit to Him in prayer with special blessing. He often allows the best things that we have not committed to Him to be ineffectual, simply to remind us of our dependence upon Him for everything. It is very gracious and thoughtful of God to compel us gently to remember Him. He would hold us so close to Himself that we cannot get away for a single minute from His all-sustaining arms.

Let us bring our least petitions,
    Like the incense beaten small,
All our cares, complaints, conditions
    Jesus loves to bear them all.

JANUARY 21ST

THE PROMISE-KEEPER *by Andrew Murray*

". . .For if I go not away, the Comforter will not come unto you; but if I depart, I will send him unto you."   JOHN 16:7

*I*n all our prayer let us remember the lesson the Saviour would teach us this day, that if there is one thing on earth we can be sure of, it is this, that the Father desires to have us filled with His Spirit, that He delights to give us His Spirit.

And when once we have learned thus to believe for ourselves, and each day to take out of the treasure we hold in heaven, what liberty and power to pray for the outpouring of the Spirit on the Church of God, on all flesh, on individuals,

27

or on special efforts! He that has once learned to know the Father in prayer for himself, learns to pray most confidently for others too. The Father gives the Holy Spirit to them that ask Him, not least, but most, when they ask for others.

LORD, TEACH US TO PRAY.

JANUARY 22ND

CALL TO WORSHIP *by Jack Hayford*

"O come, let us worship and bow down: let us kneel before the LORD our maker. For he is our God; and we are the people of his pasture, and the sheep of his hand."

PSALM 95:6,7

*W*e have a national disposition to emphasize our right to worship "in our own way." While I'm grateful for that freedom, of course, it misses an essential fact about true worship: biblical worship is on *God's* terms, not ours. Psalm 95, in calling us to worship, says nothing about our rights. Instead, it summarily calls us to *bow down,* to *kneel* before this One whose creatures we are, sheep of His pasture. And make no mistake—the call to bowing and kneeling is more than merely to bodily postures. It focuses the surrender of our will and way to Him. It means that we are granting supreme authority to God; that in worship and in life we are giving up our will in favor of His. It notes a foundational fact about true worship: Once I choose the Living God as my God, *I give up the right to worship "in my own way."* In the very act of naming God *God,* you and I are granting to Him alone the right to prescribe how He wishes to be worshiped.

ESCAPE FROM ABOVE *by A. B. Simpson*

"Cast down, but not destroyed."   2 CORINTHIANS 4:9

*H*ow did God bring about the miracle of the Red Sea? By shutting His people in on every side so that there was no way out but the divine way. The Egyptians were behind them, the sea was in front of them, the mountains were on both sides of them. There was no escape but from above.

Someone has said that the devil can wall us in, but he cannot roof us over. We can always get out at the top. Our difficulties are but God's challenges, and many times He makes them so hard that we must get above them or go under.

In the Providence of God, such an hour furnishes us with the highest possibilities for faith. We are pushed by the very emergency into God's best.

Beloved, this is God's hour. If you will rise to meet it you will get such a hold upon Him that you will never be in extremities again; or if you are, you will learn to call them not extremities, but opportunities. Like Jacob, you will go forth from that night at Peniel, no longer Jacob, but victorious Israel. Let us bring to Him our need and prove Him true.

NO LIMITS *by Ken Abraham*

"He said unto them, 'Have ye received the Holy Ghost since ye believed?' "   ACTS 19:2

*S*urrender completely every area of your life to the Lordship of Christ. Hold nothing back. Give Him all the keys. There's no time for hypocrisy now. You cannot attempt to bargain with God ("I'll give you this area, God, if You will give me that gift") if you hope to enter into holiness. As you obey Christ and allow Him to have absolute control in your life, He will fill you with His Spirit. He will then continue to expand your capacity to be filled for the rest of your life, producing more and more of His character—the fruit of the Spirit—in you.

This is a never-ending process. You can never plumb the depths of God's love. You will never exhaust His fresh supply of resources in your life. There is no height, nor depth, no limit at all to how deeply you can grow in Christ. His Spirit will continue to extend your horizons.

Maybe that explains why truly holy people rarely become bored. Just about the time you say, "Okay, God, I think I've got a handle on this Christian life; I think I've gone as far as I can go," He says, "Oh, really? Well, open wide, because I am going to do something more in your heart, something your mind has not even yet conceived!" What an exciting way to live! And it begins the moment you wholeheartedly place your life in His hands.

William Booth, the founder of the Salvation Army, was often asked the secret to his spiritual success. In his later years, the great General would respond, "The secret of my success is that God had all there was of William Booth."

DELIGHT IN THE LORD *compiled by Mary W. Tileston*

"Delight thyself also in the LORD; and he shall give thee the desires of thine heart."   PSALM 37:4

> Though today may not fulfil
>   All thy hopes, have patience still;
> For perchance tomorrow's sun
>   Sees thy happier days begun.

P. GERHARDT

*H*is great desire and delight is God; and by desiring and delighting, he hath Him. Delight thou in the Lord, and He shall give thee thy heart's desire,—HIMSELF; and then surely thou shall have all. Any other thing commit it to Him, and He shall bring it to pass.

R. LEIGHTON

All who call on God in true faith, earnestly from the heart, will certainly be heard, and will receive what they have asked and desired, although not in the hour or in the measure, or the very thing which they ask; yet they will obtain something greater and more glorious than they had dared to ask.

MARTIN LUTHER

SHE DIDN'T KNOW THEIR VALUE *by D. L. Moody*

"Whereby are given unto us exceeding great and precious promises: that by these ye might be partakers of the divine nature." 2 PETER 1:4

A poor old widow, living in the Scottish Highlands, was called upon one day by a gentleman who had heard that she was in need. The old lady complained of her condition, and remarked that her son was in Australia and doing well.

"But does he do nothing to help you?" inquired the visitor.

"No, nothing," was the reply. "He writes me regularly once a month, but only sends me a little picture with his letter."

The gentleman asked to see one of the pictures that she had received, and found each one of them to be a draft for ten pounds.

That is the condition of many of God's children. He has given us many "exceeding great and precious promises," which we either are ignorant of or fail to appropriate. Many of them seem to be pretty pictures of an ideal peace and rest, but are not appropriated as practical helps in daily life. And not one of these promises is more neglected than the assurance of salvation. An open Bible places them within reach of all, and we may appropriate the blessing which such a knowledge brings.

ABIDING IN CHRIST *by Oswald Chambers*

"If ye abide in me, and my words abide in you, ye shall ask what ye will, and it shall be done unto you."   JOHN 15:7

"*I* AM the true vine, and my Father is the husbandman. Every branch in me that beareth not fruit he taketh away: and every branch that beareth fruit, he purgeth it, that it may bring forth more fruit" (John 15:1, 2).

The only reliable way to be truly guided by God is to assimilate the Word of God to your character. Yet even that spiritual truth will damage instead of help you, if the Holy Spirit is not present.

Have you ever noticed that the most hardened people are not the backsliders, but preachers or teachers who thunder out the truth of Scripture, yet make no application of it to themselves? Scripture reveals God's will only if we allow His Holy Spirit to apply it to our circumstances.

The Bible is not a book that you can open and say, "Now, Lord, put some magic into my soul that will open up the meaning of this book." There is only one way really to understand the Word, and that is through wrestling with the circumstances and happenings of life. God will take His servants through things no one else seems to endure, because He wants them to understand the deep secrets of His Word.

When I complain, Lord Jesus, about the circumstances of life, allow me to realize that You are sharing the truth with me.

THE BEAUTY OF THE DEEP *by F. B. Meyer*

"Deep calleth unto deep."　　　　　　　　PSALM 42:7

*W*e need to dwell deep, to have a life beneath a life, to
have windows in our heart that look across the river into the
unseen and eternal. The pictures that fascinate are those that
suggest more than they reveal, in which the blue distance
fades into the heavens, and the light mist veils mountain,
moorland, and sea. Oh, for the peace that passeth understanding, the joy that is unspeakable and full of glory, the
deep things which eye hath not seen, nor ear heard, nor the
heart of man conceived!

ARTIST AT WORK *by R. T. Kendall*

". . .To be conformed to the image of his Son."
　　　　　　　　　　　　　　　　　ROMANS 8:29

A sculptor was going to make a horse out of a big block
of marble and somebody came along to him and said, "How
are you going to do that?"

He replied, "It's simple. I just start chipping away, and
I chip away anything that doesn't look like a horse!"

And so with us. God takes the big block we give Him.
He begins to chip away anything that is not just like His
Son. We have been predestined "to be conformed to the
image of his Son" (Rom. 8:29). The day will eventually

come when He can begin to use us.

The reason God lets us suffer is to chip away what isn't like Jesus, otherwise we will keep on making the same old mistakes. We may say, "Why do I do that all the time?" Perhaps it is because we haven't yet submitted ourselves to God's refining fires. This is why James said, "Count it all joy when ye fall into divers temptations" (James 1:2). May I suggest this: the next time a trial comes, rather than battle it out, rather than try to be rid of it and grumble the whole time, accept it graciously. See what God does.

JANUARY 30TH

THE LAW OF LOVE *by Brennan Manning*

"The law of the Spirit of life in Christ Jesus hath made me free from the law of sin and death."   ROMANS 8:2

*F*or the Christian, there is no law but the Spirit. There is no need to law; a child doesn't have to be told to love his Father. How well St. Augustine put it: "Love, and do what you please." Freedom from law means freedom for others.

The disciple of Christ may know the Ten Commandments, the six traditional precepts of the church, the whole network of rules and regulations governing moral behavior, in the way that a good lawyer knows his law books, but he does not live by these laws. He lives by the life of the Master. Christianity is not an ethical code. It is a love affair, a Spirit-filled way of living aimed at making us professional lovers of God and people. To continue to eye God primarily in terms of laws, obligations, and town ordinances represents a retreat to a pre-Christian level of thought and a rejection of Jesus Christ and the total sufficiency of His redeeming work.

HIS WITNESS *by J. I. Packer*

"For he dwelleth with you, and shall be in you."

JOHN 14:17

*T*he truth we must grasp is that our exercise of spiritual gifts is nothing more nor less than Christ himself ministering through His body to His body, to the Father, and to all mankind. From heaven Christ uses Christians as His mouth, His hands, His feet, even His smile; it is through us, His people, that He speaks and acts, meets, loves, and saves here and now in this world. This seems (though the point is disputed) to be part of the meaning of Paul's picture of the church as Christ's body, in which every believer is a "member" in the sense of a limb or organ: The head is the command center for the body, and the limbs move at the head's direction.

FEBRUARY

WINTER RELENTING *by William A. Quale*

". . .For I have learned, in whatsoever state I am, therewith to be content." PHILIPPIANS 4:11

*F*ebruary is Winter losing heart and sitting down for a breathing spell. Even Winter relents. February is Winter relenting. After the perfect jubilation of harshness in January, February grows tenderhearted. The sleet melts: the snow turns to slush: the creeks are swollen and noisy: the snow fields become tattered like an ill-kept child: the black ground shows in patches: cattle huddle around and near the friendly haystack and chew cud in a mild way as to say, "We knew your weather would moderate." Cattle are your genuine philosophers. They never fuss. They take what comes. They hump up when snow falls and the wind is piercing; but they use no bad words that I ever heard, and sleep out in the snow without cover uncomplaining as a soldier trained to hard campaigns. When February comes, with its temporary geniality, the cattle kick up some and frisk as to say, "Bully for the weather! We are tickled!" But a frisky disposition when there is anything to frisk at, and an indisposition to kick when there is something to kick at, are worthy of consideration. People might learn from the critters if they would only take them as schoolmasters, and chew their cud more and their grievances less.

37

A HEART THAT SINGS *by A. B. Simpson*

'These things have I spoken unto you, that my joy might remain in you, and that your joy might be full."

JOHN 15:11

*T*here is a joy that springs spontaneously in the heart without any external or even rational cause. It is like an artesian fountain. It rejoices because it cannot help it. It is the glory of God; it is the heart of Christ; it is the joy divine of which He says, "These things have I spoken unto you, that my joy might remain in you, and that your joy might be full" (John 15:11). And your joy no man can take from you. Those who possess this fountain are not discouraged by surrounding circumstances. Rather, they are often surprised at the deep, sweet gladness that comes without apparent cause—a joy that frequently is strongest when everything in their condition and circumstances would tend to fill them with sorrow and depression.

It is the nightingale in the heart that sings at night because it is its nature to sing.

It is the glorified and incorruptible joy that belongs with heaven and anticipates already the everlasting song. *Lord, give us Thy joy under all circumstances this day, and let our full hearts overflow in blessing to others.*

LEARNING LOVE *by Henry Drummond*

". . .God is love; and he that dwelleth in love dwelleth in God, and God in him."   1 JOHN 4:16

*T*hat is the supreme work to which we need to address ourselves in this world, to learn Love. Is life not full of opportunities for learning Love? Every man and woman every day has a thousand of them. The world is not a playground; it is a schoolroom. Life is not a holiday, but an education. And the one eternal lesson for us all is how better we can love. What makes a man a good cricketer? Practice. What makes a man a good artist, a good sculptor, a good musician? Practice. What makes a man a good linguist, a good stenographer? Practice. What makes a man a good man? Practice. Nothing else.

There is nothing suspicious about religion. We do not get the soul in different ways, under different laws, from those in which we get the body and the mind. If a man does not exercise his arm, he develops no biceps muscle; and if a man does not exercise his soul, he acquires no muscles in his soul, no strength of character, no vigor of a moral fiber, nor beauty of spiritual growth. Love is not a thing of enthusiastic emotion. It is a rich, strong, manly, vigorous expression of the whole round Christian character—the Christ-like nature in its fullest development. And the constituents of this great character are only to be built up by ceaseless practice.

TREASURES OF THE HEART *by Brother Lawrence*

"For where your treasure is, there will your heart be also."
LUKE 12:34

$\mathcal{W}$e cannot escape the dangers which abound in life without the actual and continual help of God. Let us, then, pray to Him for it continually. How can we pray to Him without being with Him? How can we be with Him but in thinking of Him often? And how can we often think of Him but by a holy habit which we should form of it? You will tell me that I am always saying the same thing. It is true, for this is the best and easiest method I know; and as I use no other, I advise all the world to do it. We must know before we can love. In order to know God, we must often think of Him; and when we come to love Him, we shall also think of Him often, for our heart will be with our treasure. This is an argument which well deserves your consideration.

FEBRUARY 5TH

LOVING THE LORD *by John Henry Jowett*

"He that loveth not knoweth not God; for God is love."
1 JOHN 4:8

$\mathcal{T}$he secret of life is to love the Lord our God, and our neighbours as ourselves. But how are we to love the Lord? We cannot manufacture love. We cannot love to order. We cannot by an act of will command its appearing. No, not in these ways is love created. Love is not a work, it is a fruit. It grows in suitable soils, and it is our part to prepare the soils. When the conditions are congenial, love appears, just as the crocus and the snowdrop appear in the congenial air of the spring.

What, then, can we do? We can seek the Lord's society. We can think about Him. We can read about Him. We can fill our imaginations with the grace of His life and service. We can be much with Him, talking to Him in prayer, singing to Him in praise, telling Him our yearnings and confessing to Him our defeats. And love will be quietly born. For this is how love is born between heart and heart. Two people are "much together," and love is born! And when we are much with the Lord, we are with One who already loves us with an everlasting love. We are with One who yearns because He first loved us. And when we truly love God, every other kind of holy love will follow. Given the fountain, the rivers are sure.

FEBRUARY 6TH

THE ROYAL LAW OF LOVE *by Hannah Hurnard*

"...*Thou shalt love the Lord thy God with all thy heart, and with all thy soul, and with all thy strength, and with all thy mind; and thy neighbour as thyself.*" LUKE 10:27

*L*ove is the one basic law on which the whole universe is founded, and by obeying that law, everything abides in harmony, perfect joy and perfect fruitfulness. But when it is broken, disharmony immediately results and then come miseries and evils of every kind.

Righteousness is the condition of everything which is in harmony with the law of the universe and therefore right. Unrighteousness is everything which is out of harmony with the

41

law of love and therefore unright. Love which worketh no ill to her neighbor is the fulfillment of the whole law on which the universe is founded. Holiness and happiness and health are the result of complete separation from everything which breaks the law of love, and a holy people are those who are set apart to love.

CHARITY *by C. S. Lewis*

"He that despiseth his neighbour sinneth: but he that hath mercy on the poor, happy is he." PROVERBS 14:21

*D*o not waste time bothering whether you "Love" your neighbour; act as if you did. As soon as we do this we find one of the great secrets. When you are behaving as if you loved someone, you will presently come to love him. If you injure someone you dislike, you will find yourself disliking him more. If you do him a good turn, you will find yourself disliking him less. There is, indeed, one exception. If you do him a good turn, not to please God and obey the law of charity, but to show him what a fine forgiving chap you are, and to put him in your debt, and then sit down to wait for his "gratitude," you will probably be disappointed. (People are not fools: they have a very quick eye for anything like showing off, or patronage.) But whenever we do good to another self, just because it is a self, made (like us) by God, and desiring its own happiness as we desire ours, we shall have learned to love it a little more or, at least, to dislike it less.

Some writers use the word charity to describe not only Christian love between human beings, but also God's love for man and man's love for God. About the second of these two, people are often worried. They are told they ought to love God. They cannot find any such feeling in themselves. What are they to do? The answer is the same as before. Act as if you did. Do not sit trying to manufacture feelings. Ask yourself, "If I were sure that I loved God, what would I do?" When you have found the answer, go and do it.

FEBRUARY 8TH

PRAISE WITH THE MIND *by Jack Hayford*

"I will extol thee, my God, O king; and I will bless thy name for ever and ever. . .Great is the LORD, and greatly to be praised; and his greatness is unsearchable. PSALM 145:1,3

*T*he Bible insists that worship includes our entire being. In Romans 12:1, the apostle Paul says that serving God involves our "reasonable" faculties, and he uses the very Greek term from which we derive our word "logic." He challenges us to *renew our minds* (vs. 2); to worship not only in spirit but in *truth* (John 4:24).

Thinking carefully about the attributes of God as we praise Him is a way of offering Him our minds. When we hear the psalmist say that God is "above all gods," (Psalm 135:5) let's try to wrap our minds around His *omnipotence* —the fact that He is all powerful. What a staggering intellectual concept! Employ your mind also to contemplate God's *omnipresence* —that He is everywhere present. He's inescapably, marvelously near, all at once. And think further on *our* God—the *one* God, who alone is *omniscient*—knowing all there is to know, now or forever. What an absolutely mind-boggling thought, as are all these attributes which thinking on His greatness brings to mind.

43

THE FRESH EYE *by John Henry Jowett*

". . .His compassions fail not. They are new every morning."
Lamentations 3:22, 23

*W*e have not to live on yesterday's manna; we can gather it fresh today. Compassion becomes stale when it becomes thoughtless. It is new thoughts that keep our pity strong. If our perception of need can remain vivid, as vivid as though we had never seen it before, our sympathies will never fail. The fresh eye insures the sensitive heart. And our God's compassions are so new because He never becomes accustomed to our need. He always sees it with an eye that is never dulled by the commonplace; He never becomes blind with much seeing! We can look at a thing so often that we cease to see it. God always sees a thing as though He were seeing it for the first time. "Thou, God, seest me," and "His compassions fail not."

And if my compassions are to be like a river that never knows drought, I must cultivate a freshness of sight. The horrible can lose its horrors. The daily tragedy can become the daily commonplace. My neighbour's needs can become as familiar as my furniture, and I may never see either the one or the other. And therefore must I ask the Lord for the daily gift of discerning eyes, "Lord, that I may receive my sight." And with an always newly awakened interest may I reveal "the compassions of the Lord"!

THE STRENGTH OF MY HEART
by Mrs. Charles E. Cowman

"Whosoever drinketh of the water that I shall give him shall never thirst." JOHN 4:14

*M*y heart needs Thee, O Lord, my heart needs Thee! No part of my being needs Thee like my heart. All else within me can be filled by Thy gifts. My hunger can be satisfied by daily bread. My thirst can be allayed by earthly waters. My cold can be removed by household fires. My weariness can be relieved by outward rest. But no outward thing can make my heart pure. The calmest day will not calm my passions. The fairest scene will not beautify my soul. The richest music will not make harmony within. The breezes can cleanse the air, but no breeze can cleanse a spirit. This world has not provided for my heart. It has provided for my eye; it has provided for my ear; it has provided for my touch; it has provided for my taste; it has provided for my sense of beauty but it has not provided for my heart.

Lift up your eyes unto the hills! Make haste to Calvary, "Calvary's awful mountainclimb" and on the way there visit the slopes of Mount Olivet, where grow the trees of Gethsemane. Contemplate there the agony of the Lord, where He already tasted the tremendous cup which He drank to the dregs the next noontide on the Cross. There is the answer to your need.

Provide Thou for my heart, O Lord. It is the only unwinged bird in all creation. Give it wings! O Lord, give it wings! Earth has failed to give it wings; its very power of loving has often drawn it into the mire. Be Thou the strength of my heart. Be Thou its fortress in temptation, its shield in

45

remorse, its cover in the storm, its star in the night, its voice in the solitude. Guide it in its gloom; help it in its heat; direct it in its doubt; calm it in its conflict; fan it in its faintness; prompt it in its perplexity; lead it through its labyrinth; raise it from its ruins.

FEBRUARY 11TH

COMMUNION *by Hannah Hurnard*

"My soul waiteth for the Lord more than they that watch for the morning: I say, more than they that watch for the morning." PSALM 130:6

*G*race and Glory looked up into the face of the King and said, "My soul waiteth for the Lord more than they that watch for the morning: I say, more than they that watch for the morning" (Psalm 130:6).

He took her by the hand and they went leaping and bounding over the heights towards the Mountain of Pomegranates. As they went she sang a little song:

THE MOUNTAIN PEAKS AT DAWN

As in the early morning
    The snowy mountain peaks
Look up to greet the dawning,
    So my heart longs and seeks
To see thy face
    And glow with grace.
Here like the peaks at sunrise
    My mind to thee I raise;
Clothe me with glory likewise
    Make me to burn with praise

In love's attire
    Of flaming fire.
In robes of snowy whiteness
    They greet their lord the sun;
I too, await thy brightness,
    On winged feet I run.
Give, now we meet,
    Communion sweet.

FEBRUARY 12TH

A MIND RESOLVED *by Brother Lawrence*

"Keep yourselves in the love of God, looking for the mercy of our Lord Jesus Christ unto eternal life."   JUDE 21

Having found in many books different methods of going to God, and diverse practices of the spiritual life, I thought this would serve rather to puzzle me than facilitate what I sought after, which was nothing but how to become wholly God's. This made me resolve to give the all for the all; so after having given myself wholly to God, that He might take away my sin, I renounced, for the love of Him, everything that was not He, and I began to live as if there was none but He and I in the world. Sometimes I considered my self before Him as a poor criminal at the feet of his judge, at other times I beheld Him in my heart as my Father, as my God. I worshipped Him the oftenest that I could, keeping my mind in His holy presence, and recalling it as often as I found it wandered from Him. I found no small pain in this exercise, and yet I continued it, notwithstanding all the difficulties that occurred, without troubling or disquieting myself when my mind had wandered involuntarily.

I made this my business as much all the day long as at the appointed times of prayer; for at all times, every hour, every minute, even in the height of my business, I drove away from my mind everything that was capable of interrupting my thought of God.

FEBRUARY 13TH

PARDONING FORGIVENESS *by Andrew Murray*

" '. . .Lord, how oft shall. . .I forgive him?. . .' Jesus saith unto him. . .'Until seventy times seven.' "   MATTHEW 18:21, 22

*W*e pray, "Forgive, even as we have forgiven." Scripture says, "Forgive one another, even as God also in Christ forgave you." God's full and free forgiveness is to be the rule of ours with men. Otherwise our reluctant, half-hearted forgiveness, which is not forgiveness at all, will be God's rule with us. Every prayer rests upon our faith in God's pardoning grace. If God dealt with us after our sins, not one prayer could be heard. Pardon opens the door to all God's love and blessing: because God has pardoned all our sin, our prayer can prevail to obtain all we need. The deep sure ground of answer to prayer is God's forgiving love. When it has taken possession of the heart, we pray in faith. But also, when it has taken possession of the heart, we live in love. God's forgiving disposition, revealed in His love to us, becomes a disposition in us; as the power of His forgiving love shed abroad and dwelling within us, we forgive even as He forgives.

LOVE ONE ANOTHER *compiled by Mary W. Tileston*

"If we love one another, God dwelleth in us, and his love is perfected in us."   1 JOHN 4:12

Abide in me; o'ershadow by Thy love
        Each half-formed purpose and
        dark thought of sin;
Quench, ere it rise, each selfish, low desire,
        And keep my soul as Thine,
        calm and divine.

H. B. STOWE

*T*he Spirit of love must work the works, and speak the tones, of Love. It cannot exist and give no sign, or a false sign. It cannot be a spirit of Love, and mantle into irritable and self-ish impatience. It cannot be a spirit of Love, and at the same time make self the prominent object. It cannot rejoice to lend itself to the happiness of others, and at the same time be seeking its own. It cannot be generous, and envious. It cannot be sympathizing, and unseemly; self-forgetful, and vain-glorious. It cannot delight in the rectitude and purity of other hearts, as the spiritual elements of their peace, and yet unnecessarily suspect them.

J. H. THOM

THE MEASURE OF HIS LOVE *by J. I. Packer*

"He that spared not his own Son, but delivered him up for us all, how shall he not with him also freely give us all things?"
ROMANS 8:32

*T*he Spirit's way of witnessing to the truth that as believers we are sons and heirs of God (Romans 8:15–17) is first to make us realize that as Christ on earth loved us and died for us, so in glory now he loves and lives for us as the Mediator whose endless life guarantees us endless glory with him. The Spirit makes us see the love of Christ toward us, as measured by the cross, and to see along with Christ's love the love of the Father who gave his Son up for us (Romans 8:32). The line of thought is given in Romans 5:5–8, and as the Spirit leads us along it, over and over, "God's love [is] poured into our hearts."

FROM LITTLE FAITH TO GREAT FAITH
by Charles H. Spurgeon

"Have faith in God."
MARK 11:22

*F*aith is the foot of the soul by which it can march along the road of the commandments. Love can make the feet move more swiftly; but faith is the foot which carries the soul. Faith is the oil enabling the wheels of holy devotion and of earnest piety to move well; and without faith the wheels are taken from the chariot, and we drag heavily. With faith I can do all things; without faith I shall neither have the inclination nor the power to do anything in the service of God. If you would find the men who serve God the best, you must look for the men of the most faith. Little faith will save a man, but little faith cannot defeat things for God. Poor Little-Faith could not have fought "Apollyon"; it needed "Christian" to do that. Poor Little-Faith could not have slain "Great Despair"; it required "Great-heart's" arm to knock that monster down. Little-Faith will go to heaven most certainly, but it often has to hide itself in a nut-shell, and it frequently loses all but its jewels. Little-Faith says, "It is a rough road, beset with sharp thorns, and full of dangers; I am afraid to go"; but Great-heart remembers the promise, "Thy shoes shall be iron and brass; as thy days, so shall thy strength be"; and so he boldly ventures. Little-Faith stands desponding, mingling his tears with the flood; but Great-heart sings, "When thou passest through the waters, I will be with thee; and through the rivers, they shall not over-flow thee": and he fords the stream at once. Would you be comfortable and happy? Would you enjoy religion? Would you have the religion of cheerfulness and not that of gloom? Then "have faith in God." If you love darkness, and are satisfied to dwell in gloom and misery, then be content with little faith; but if you love the sunshine, and would sing songs of rejoicing, covet earnestly this best gift, "great faith."

HEREIN IS LOVE *by Dietrich Bonhoeffer*

"But I say unto you that hear, Love your enemies, do good to them which hate you."   LUKE 6:27

*B*y our enemies Jesus means those who are quite intractable and utterly unresponsive to our love, who forgive us nothing when we forgive them all, who requite our love with hatred and our service, with derision, "For the love that I had unto them, lo, they now take my contrary part: but I give myself unto prayer" (Psalm 109:4). Love asks nothing in return, but seeks those who need it. And who needs our love more than those who are consumed with hatred and are utterly devoid of love? Who in other words deserves our love more than our enemy? Where is love more glorified than where she dwells in the midst of her enemies?

GOD IS A CONSUMING FIRE *by George MacDonald*

"For our God is a consuming fire."   HEBREWS 12:29

*A*ll that is not beautiful in the beloved, all that comes between and is not of love's kind, must be destroyed. God is a consuming fire. If this be hard to understand, it is as the simple, absolute truth is hard to understand. It may be centuries of ages before a man comes to see a truth—ages of strife, of effort, of aspiration. But when once he does see it, it is so plain that he wonders how he could have lived without seeing it. That he did not understand it sooner was simply and only that he did not see it. To see a truth, to know what it is, to understand it, and to love it, are all one.

Let us look at the utterance of the apostle which is crowned with this lovely terror: "Our God is a consuming fire."

"Therefore, let us be grateful for receiving a kingdom that cannot be shaken, and thus let us offer to God acceptable worship, with reverence and awe; for our God is a consuming fire." We have received a kingdom that cannot be moved—whose nature is immovable. Let us have grace to serve the Consuming Fire, our God, with divine fear; not with the fear that cringes and craves, but with the bowing down of all thoughts, all delights, all loves before Him who is the life of them all, and will have them all pure. The kingdom He has given us cannot be moved, because it has nothing weak in it. It is of the eternal world, the world of being, of truth. We, therefore, must worship Him with a fear pure as the kingdom is unshakable. He will shake heaven and earth, that only the unshakable may remain (v. 27).

He is a consuming fire, that only that which cannot be consumed may stand forth eternal. It is the nature of God, so terribly pure that it destroys all that is not pure as fire, which demands like purity in our worship.

BENT ON KINDNESS *by Hannah Whitall Smith*

"For I know the thoughts that I think toward you, saith the Lord, thoughts of peace, and not of evil, to give you an expected end."   JEREMIAH 29:11

A great many people are afraid of the consuming fire of God, but that is only because they do not understand what it is. It is the fire of God's love, that must in the very nature of things consume everything that can harm His people; and if our hearts are set on being what the love of God would have us to be, His fire is something we shall not be afraid of, but shall warmly welcome.

> Implacable is love.
>   Foes may be bought or teased
> From their malign intent;
>   But he goes unappeased,
> Who is on kindness bent.

BEAUTIFUL DISCOVERIES *by St. Augustine*

"O the depth of the riches both of the wisdom and knowledge of God! how unsearchable are his judgments, and his ways past finding out!"   ROMANS 11:33

Not with doubting, but with assured consciousness, do I love Thee, Lord. Thou has stricken my heart with Thy word, and I loved Thee. Yea also heaven and earth, and all that therein is behold on every side they bide me love Thee; nor cease to say so unto all, that they may be without excuse. But more deeply wilt Thou have mercy on whom Thou wilt have mercy, and wilt have compassion on whom Thou hast had compassion, else in deaf ears do the heaven and the earth speak Thy praises. But what do I love, when I love Thee? not beauty of bodies, nor the fair harmony of time, nor the brightness of the light, so gladsome to our eyes, nor sweet melodies of varied songs, nor the fragrant smell of flowers, and ointments, and spices, not manna and honey, not limbs acceptable to embracements of flesh. None of these I love, when I love my God; and yet I love a kind of light, and melody, and fragrance, and meat, and embracement when I love my God, the light, melody, fragrance, meat, embracement of my inner man: there shineth unto my soul what space cannot contain and there soundeth what time beareth not away, and there smelleth what breathing desperseth not, and there tasteth what eating dimenisheth not. This is it which I love when I love my God.

FEBRUARY 21ST

HIS OWN SPIRIT *by Andrew Murray*

". . .How much more shall your heavenly Father give the Holy Spirit to them that ask him?" LUKE 11:13

*O*ur Father in heaven desires to educate us as His children for the holy, heavenly life in which He dwells, and for this gives us, from the depths of His heart, His own Spirit. It was that which was the whole aim of Jesus when, after having made atonement with His own blood, He entered for us into God's presence, that He might obtain for us, and send down to dwell in us, the Holy Spirit. As the Spirit of the Father, and of the Son, the whole life and love of the Father and the Son are in Him; and, coming down into us, He lifts us up into their fellowship. As Spirit of the Father, He sheds abroad the Father's love, with which He loved the Son, in our hearts, and teaches us to live in it. As Spirit of the Son, He breathes in us the childlike liberty, and devotion, and obedience in which the Son lived upon earth. The Father can bestow no higher or more wonderful gift than this: His own Holy Spirit, the Spirit of sonship.

FEBRUARY 22ND

A LOVING SPIRIT *by D. L. Moody*

"By this shall all men know that ye are my disciples, if ye have love one to another."　　　　JOHN 13:35

*I*n the late Professor Drummond's *The Greatest Thing in the World,* he tells of meeting with natives in the interior of Africa who remembered David Livingstone. They could not understand a word he uttered, but they recognized the universal language of love through which he appealed to them. It had been many years since that Christian hero had passed their way, but the very remembrance of his presence among them would kindle a friendly smile.

It is this very selfsame universal language of love, divine, Christlike love, that we must have if we are going to be used of God. The world does not understand theology or dogma, but it understands love and sympathy. A loving act may be more powerful and far reaching than the most eloquent sermon.

TRUST *by Jill Briscoe*

". . .Christ in you, the hope of glory."   COLOSSIANS 1:27

*T*he King of Hearts in the Book of Proverbs trusted his queen. So would our King of Hearts in heaven trust us!

This is what really blows my mind. God trusts us! Yes, He does. He trusts us to come through for Him. He looks to us. Think about it for a minute. He trusts us with the Holy Spirit. He has not only sent His Spirit into our hearts crying, "Abba, Father," He has sent Him knowing our hearts are unholy. He trusts us then to be obedient to His holy promptings and hate the sin He hates, and repent of the selfishness He abhors. He trusts us to clean our spiritual house, just as diligently as the Proverbs woman cleaned her physical house.

Not only does our King of Hearts trust us with His Spirit, He trusts us with His Son! "Christ in you," Paul says in wonder, "the hope of glory" (Colossians 1:27). What does this mean? It means Christ comes to live within our hearts when we invite Him to. It means the second Person of the Trinity is present with us. It means that we, like Mary, can say, "Behold the handmaiden of the Lord," and nurture as she did the new life of Christ within till "He be fully formed in us" (*see* Galatians 4:19). He trusts us to bid Him welcome, make Him feel at home, and settle Him down. Paul prayed the strangest prayer one day. He prayed for some new converts that "Christ may dwell in your hearts by faith. . ." (Ephesians 3:17). Was not Christ already dwelling in their hearts? Surely, but the secret lies on the word that the apostle used—the word dwell. The meaning is clear in the original language. It means to "settle down and feel at home."

TRANSPARENT *by Gail and Gordon MacDonald*

"Lord, thou hast heard the desire of the humble: thou wilt prepare their heart, thou wilt cause thine ear to hear."
PSALM 10:17

*I*n a relationship where there is transparency there can be enormous growth. For as the windows become unshaded, we permit others to offer light to our opinions, our concerns, and our dreams. They help complete our thoughts, balance our extremes, and correct our miscalculations. We are reminded of parallel situations that we may have forgotten and that now bring encouragement, direction, or prevention. They may have shared with us the very keys of life, which may escalate our maturity or protect us from destruction. But transparency has to happen first.

When the architect first came to Plato with his offer to build a very private house, he thought he had a special thing to offer. But Plato saw it all differently. A healthy life in a home is a transparent one, he believed. And that demands more windows than walls. What Plato knew about homes, we must learn about relationships. The question is: Are we building walls or opening windows?

Each time you take a look, Jesus seems to have been one step ahead of every one else, because He saw what virtually no one else saw. Why? Because Jesus was the most sensitive person who ever lived.

DROPS OF GREATNESS *by Edith Schaeffer*

"And God said, Let us make man in our image, after our likeness. . . . And God saw every thing that he had made, and, behold, it was very good."　　　GENESIS 1:26, 31

*W*hat is the difference between good, mediocre, and great? The beauty of work well done, the attention to detail and meticulously careful workmanship, combined with a flair and taste that affects all the small choices—plus something that can't be taken apart and described or analyzed and copied—are what goes into making a work great or an artist outstanding throughout history. Greatness is the "leftover beauty" of what human beings were meant to be in the first place. I'm sure that as with the diversity of snowflakes, there would have been (without the Fall) diversity in talents but not the great differences and the abnormality which result from the Fall.

HEAVENLY DESIGNERS *by James Allen*

"Them hath he filled with wisdom of heart, to work all manner of work, of the engraver, . . .the embroiderer, . . .the weaver, . . .and of those that devise cunning work."
　　　EXODUS 35:35

*T*he dreamers are the saviors of the world. As the visible world is sustained by the invisible, so men, through all their trials and sins and sordid vocations, are nourished by the beautiful visions of their solitary dreamers. Humanity cannot forget its dreamers; it cannot let their ideals fade and die; it lives in them; it knows them as the realities which it shall one day see and know.

Composer, sculptor, painter, poet, prophet, sage, these are the makers of the after-world, the architects of heaven. The world is beautiful because they have lived; without them, laboring humanity would perish.

FEBRUARY 27TH

RESULTS GUARANTEED! *by A. B. Simpson*

"...The effectual fervent prayer of a righteous man availeth much."   JAMES 5:16

*S*top praying so much for yourself; begin to ask unselfish things, and see if God will not give you faith. See how much easier it will be to believe for another than for your own concerns.

Try the effect of praying for the world, for definite things, for difficult things, for glorious things, for things that will honor Christ and save mankind. After you have received a few wonderful answers to prayer in this direction, see if you will not feel stronger to touch your own little burden with a divine faith and then go back again to the high place of unselfish prayer for others.

Have you ever learned the beautiful art of letting God take care of you and giving all your thought and strength to pray for others and for the kingdom of God? It will relieve you of a thousand cares. It will lift you up into a noble and lofty sphere and teach you to live and love like God. *Lord, save us from our selfish prayers; give us the faith that works through love and the heart of Christ for a perishing world.*

A LARGER BLESSING *by A. B. Simpson*

"Nay, in all these things we are more than conquerors through him that loved us."　　　ROMANS 8:37

I once heard an old man say something that I have never forgotten. "When God tests you it is a good time for you to test Him by putting His promises to the proof. Claim from Him just as much as your trials have made necessary."

There are two ways of getting out of a trial. One is simply to try to get rid of the trial, and be thankful when it is over. The other is to recognize the trial as a challenge from God to claim a larger blessing that we have ever had. We should greet it with delight as an opportunity of obtaining a larger measure of divine grace.

Thus even the adversary becomes an auxiliary, and the things that seem to be against us turn out to be for the furtherance of our way. Surely, we are to be "more than conquerors through him that loved us" (Romans 8:37).

FRIENDSHIP WITH JESUS *by Oswald Chambers*

"Ye are my friends, if ye do whatsoever I command you."
JOHN 15:14

*C*ome unto me, all ye that labour and are heavy laden, and I will give your rest. Take my yoke upon you, and learn of me; for I am meek and lowly in heart: and ye shall find rest unto your souls. For my yoke is easy, and my burden is light (Matthew 11:28–30).

We long for perennial freshness in our Christian lives. It is indeed a blessing to enjoy spiritual freshness at camp meeting, during a revival meeting, and in our prayer meetings; but what we yearn to know is the secret source of abiding freshness.

Friendship with Jesus is the first source of abiding freshness in our Christian lives. What is a friend? A "friend" is one in agreement and attachment to the deepest and most fundamental things of a person's life. In order to be a friend of Jesus, I must be born again of the Spirit of God. Only then will I have a disposition like His.

It is an experience of perennial delight to any man or woman to now that he or she has a friend "that sticketh closer than a brother"! Jesus is this kind of friend. He understands the heart so thoroughly that He satisfies the last aching abyss of the heart. Jesus is ready to be your friend, if you will but come to Him. This attachment in holy friendship will bring freshness to your heart and life.

Thank You, Jesus, for being my personal friend.

MARCH

THE JUBILANT MONTH *by William Quale*

". . .Weeping may endure for a night, but joy cometh in the morning."   PSALM 30:5

*M*arch is the trumpet month, the jubilant month. March winds do not blow trumpets for fun. That is their business which they stick to with astonishing fidelity which every looker on can testify. Let us not be grumpy with March winds. They have a Herculean task on hand. They are trying to blow the moored ship of Winter into the open sea. Blow, ye March winds, and the winter ship will break anchor and will dash out to sea. March winds are spring's Rough Riders. Stormy winds come not without blessing. There is music in the blast if we listen closely. Watch the winds transform into a boisterous lover of flowers and the spring leaf.

BE STILL AND KNOW *by Oswald Chambers*

"Be of good cheer: it is I; be not afraid."　　　MARK 6:50

*A*nd he saw them toiling in rowing; for the wind was contrary unto them: and about the fourth watch of the night he cometh unto them, walking upon the sea, and would have passed by them. But when they saw him walking upon the sea, they supposed it had been a spirit, and cried out: For they all saw him, and were troubled. And immediately he talked with them, and saith unto them, "Be of good cheer: it is I; be not afraid" (Mark 6:48–50).

A sudden storm arose on the Sea of Galilee. Apparently, Jesus Christ permitted this crisis to enter the lives of His disciples. The uproar of nature threatened to overthrow their boat. They were isolated in the terror of a storm. Why would the Lord God permit such an astonishing set of circumstances?

Whatever the reasons for our trouble, we must not allow our souls to become so overwhelmed that we think we have committed some "unpardonable sin." For out of all the terror comes the soothing voice of our Lord Himself, "Be of good cheer: it is I; be not afraid."

Too many disciples have faith in their faith, or in their joy in the Lord; and when a spiritual storm comes, they have neither faith nor joy. Only one thing can endure, and that is love for God. If such love is not there, we will not recognize the living voice of God when He cries out to us that He is our refuge and strength, a very present help in trouble.

". . .be still, and know that I am God. . ."(Psalm 46:1, 10a). You are my God, and I seek strength and shelter in Your love and goodness.

FEAR NOT *by Mrs. Charles E. Cowman*

"Stormy wind fulfilling his word."   PSALM 148:8

*S*tormy winds come not without mercy and blessing. There is music in the blast if we listen aright. Is there no music in the heart of sorrow that the Lord of all has chosen for His own? Are you not nearer to the Master, have you not grown in faith, in patience, in prayerfulness, in thankful hope, since the time the storm winds first sighed across your life?

Do not tremble because of the winds of the future; your Lord will be living and loving tomorrow, even as He lives and loves today, and no storm waits in your path but shall leave behind another record that your Heavenly Father is stronger than the tempest, nearer than the grief.

We are traveling home to that beauteous shore where the chill winds never sweep, the hurricane makes no moan; yet, amid the rest of the painless Homeland, shall we not love the Lord a thousandfold more for every storm of earth in which He drew near to us, saying, "Fear not," and held us by the hand, and tenderly bore us through the hour that seemed the darkest? We shall glorify Him then that He has been to us, again and again, a cover from the blast; but let us not wait to glorify Him till the blast is over. Even now let us give thanks that all the winds of life—the rough ones as well as those that blow from the south—are of His appointing.

Set your thoughts, not on the storm, but on the Love that rules the storm; then the winds of trouble shall no longer seem as sad and restless voices, but as an Aeolian harp attuned to peace, to hope, to everlasting victory.

THE POTENCY OF PRAYER *by E. M. Bounds*

"The righteous cry, and the Lord heareth, and delivereth them out of all their troubles." PSALM 34:17

> *"The potency of prayer hath subdued the strength of fire; it hath bridled the rage of lions, hushed the anarchy to rest, extinguished wars, appeased the elements, expelled demons, burst the chains of death, expanded the gates of heaven, assuaged diseases, rescued cities from destruction, stayed the sun in its course, and arrested the progress of the thunderbolt. Prayer is an all-efficient panoply, a treasure undiminished, a mine which is never exhausted, a sky unobscured by clouds, a heaven unruffled by the storm. It is the root, the fountain, the mother of a thousand blessings."*
>
> JOHN CHRYSOSTOM

It was said of the late C. H. Spurgeon, that he glided from laughter to prayer with the naturalness of one who lived in both elements. With him the habit of prayer was free and unfettered. He lived in constant fellowship with his Father in Heaven. He was ever in touch with God, and thus it was as natural for him to pray as it was for him to breathe.

That is the attitude with regard to prayer that ought to mark every child of God. There are, and there ought to be, stated seasons of communication with God when, everything else is shut out, we come into His presence to talk to Him and to let Him speak to us; and out of such seasons springs that beautiful habit of prayer that weaves a golden bond between earth and heaven.

In every circumstance of life, prayer is the most natural out-pouring of the soul, the unhindered turning to God for communion and direction. Whether in sorrow or in joy, in defeat or in victory, in health or in weakness, in calamity or in success, the heart leaps to meet with God.

MARCH 5TH

FOCUS ON CHRIST—CLAIM CHRIST'S VICTORY
by Lloyd John Ogilvie

"And I will give unto thee the keys of the kingdom of heaven: and whatsoever thou shalt bind on earth shall be bound in heaven: and whatsoever thou shalt loose on earth shall be loosed in heaven."   MATTHEW 16:19

*O*ur great concern is to focus on Christ and not evil. The more we allow the Lord to fill us with Himself, the more powerful we become in facing the trials of life. We are not helpless victims.

Nor are we powerless in our ministry to one another in times of need. After Jesus had declared the power of faith over the government of evil, He said, "And I will give unto thee keys of the kingdom of heaven: and whatsoever thou shalt bind on earth shall be bound in heaven: and whatsoever thou shalt loose on earth shall be loosed in heaven" (Matthew 16:19). That awesome challenge tells us that we can bind Satan and loose people from their bonds of fear, doubt, unbelief, and crippling limitations.

So often it's just the opposite. We bind people up with our negative judgments, attitudes, and actions. In so doing we loose Satan to influence them. The same is true of families, schedules, and the groups of which we are a part. What we say and how we act can debilitate prayers and frustrate growth. Instead, we are to claim our ministry of loosing people and groups. We are to do that by binding Satan in the name of Jesus. The same power Jesus exercised in liberating people during His ministry on earth is given to us. So let's claim Christ's victory!

The ministry of loosing people includes listening, loving, and liberating prayer in Christ's powerful name. In our private prayers about those who are sick, we should dare to say, "Christ, You are all-powerful. You are more powerful than evil, sickness, or the demons of doubt and discouragement. In Your name I ask you to bind Satan and loose this person." A version of that prayer can be prayed in the sick person's presence after we've talked with him or her about Christ's supremacy over all.

MARCH 6TH

JESUS IS VICTOR *by Corrie ten Boom*

"Put on the whole armour of God. . ." EPHESIANS 6:11

*J*esus is Victor. Calvary is the place of victory. Obedience is the pathway of victory, Bible study and prayer the preparation. Courage, faith, the spirit of victory—every temptation is a chance for victory, a signal to fly the flag of our Victor, a chance to make the tempter know anew that he is defeated. Roy Hession writes in Calvary Road: "Jesus is always victorious. We have only to keep the right relationship with Him and His victorious life will flow through us and touch other people."

Thank You, Lord Jesus, that You have won the victory for us.

MARCH 7TH

PLACE OF PRIVILEGE *by Hannah Whitall Smith*

"The Lord is my rock, and my fortress, and my deliverer; my God, my strength, in whom I will trust; my buckler, and the horn of my salvation, and my high tower."　　PSALM 18:2

*B*etter and sweeter than health, or friends, or money, or fame, or ease, or prosperity, is the adorable will of our God. It gilds the darkest hours with a divine halo, and sheds brightest sunshine on the gloomiest paths. He always reigns who has made it his kingdom, and nothing can go amiss to him. Surely, then, it is only a glorious privilege that is opening before you when I tell you that the first step you must take in order to enter into the life hid with Christ in God is that of entire consecration. I beg of you not to look at it as a hard and stern demand. You must do it gladly, thankfully, enthusiastically. You must go in on what I call the privilege side of consecration; and I can assure you, from the universal testimony of all who have tried it, that you will find it the happiest place you have ever entered yet.

A CLOUD OF WITNESSES *compiled by Mary W. Tileston*

"Wherefore seeing we also are compassed about with so great a cloud of witnesses, let us lay aside every weight, and the sin which doth so easily beset us, and let us run with patience the race that is set before us."   HEBREWS 12:1

When the powers of hell prevail
    O'er our weakness and unfitness,
Could we lift the fleshly veil,
    Could we for a moment witness
Those unnumbered hosts that stand
    Calm and bright on either hand;

Oh, what joyful hope would cheer,
    Oh, what faith serene would guide us!
Great may be the danger near,
    Greater are the friends beside us.

ANONYMOUS

*W*e are compassed about by a cloud of witnesses, whose hearts throb in sympathy and who thrill with joy at every success. How should this thought check and rebuke every worldly feeling and unworthy purpose, and enshrine us, in the midst of a forgetful and unspiritual world, with an atmosphere of heavenly peace! They have overcome—have risen—are crowned, glorified; but still they remain to us, our assistants, our comforters, and in every hour of darkness their voice speaks to us: "So we grieved, so we struggled, so we fainted, so we doubted; but we have overcome, we have obtained, we have seen, we have found,—and in our victory behold the certainty of thy own."

H. B. STOWE

MIST AND CLOUDS *by Hannah Hurnard*

*"Though I walk in the midst of trouble, thou wilt revive me;
thou shalt stretch forth thine hand. . .and thy right hand shall
save me. The LORD will perfect that which concerneth me: thy
mercy, O LORD, endureth forever. . ."* PSALM 138:7, 8

*O*n one such occasion the Shepherd said to Much-Afraid,
"When you continue your journey there may be much mist
and cloud. Perhaps it may even seem as though everything
you have seen here of the High Places was just a dream, or the
work of your own imagination. But you have seen reality and
the mist which seems to swallow it up is the illusion.

"Believe steadfastly in what you have seen. Even if the
way up to the High Places appears to be obscured and you are
led to doubt whether you are following the right path, remember the promise, 'Thine ears shall hear a word behind thee,
saying, This is the way, walk ye in it, when ye turn to the right
hand and when ye turn to the left.' Always go forward along
the path of obedience as far as you know it until I intervene,
even if it seems to be leading you where you fear I could
never mean you to go.

"Remember, Much-Afraid, what you have seen before
the mist blotted it out."

A GUIDE FOR THE JOURNEY *by Tim Hansel*

"For this God is our God for ever and ever: he will be our guide. . ."   PSALM 48:14

A map is not the same as being there. A map shows you where to go and how to get there. It shows you where the high places are and what they will be like. But it is no substitute for the wilderness itself.

The Bible is a map and a survival manual for the Christian life. The Holy Spirit is the compass and our personal guide. But we still have to put our boots on and explore the wilderness ourselves. We can't get there by taxi.

None of us knows exactly what we will find. There will be difficult places as well as awesome beauty. There will be hard grinds and oases. There will be moving experiences, and some experiences we would like to avoid altogether.

But the more time we spend in the wilderness, the more comfortable we become there. The rugged terrain turns into veritable adventure. The unique beauty is an invitation to the mystery of living, and we begin to appreciate the gift of each day.

HEARING THE VOICE OF GOD
by Loren Cunningham/Janice Rogers

"The LORD is nigh unto them that are of a broken heart; and saveth such as be of a contrite spirit. Many are the afflictions of the righteous: but the LORD delivereth him out of them all."   PSALM 34:18, 19

*I*f you know the Lord, you have already heard His voice —it is that inner leading that brought you to Him in the first place. Jesus always checked with His Father (John 8:26–29) and so should we; hearing the voice of the heavenly Father is a basic right of every child of God.

1. Don't make guidance complicated. It's actually hard not to hear God if you really want to please and obey Him! If you stay humble, He promises to guide you (Proverbs 16:9).
2. Allow God to speak to you in the way He chooses. Don't try to dictate to Him concerning the guidance methods you prefer. He is Lord—you are His servant (1 Samuel 3:9). So listen with a yielded heart; there is a direct link between yieldedness and hearing. He may choose to speak to you: Through His Word: this could come in your daily reading, or He could guide you to a particular verse (Psalm 119:105). Through an audible voice (Exodus 3:4). Through dreams (Matthew 2) and visions (Isaiah 6:1, Revelation 1:12–17). But probably the most common of all means is through the quiet, inner voice (Isaiah 30:21).
3. Confess any unforgiven sin. A clean heart is necessary if you want to hear God (Psalm 66:18).
4. Use The Axehead Principle—a term coined from the story in 2 Kings 6. If you seem to have lost your way, go back

to the last time you knew the sharp, cutting edge of God's voice. Then obey. The key question is, Have you obeyed the last thing God told you to do?

MARCH 12TH

THE GREAT SHEPHERD *by Kay Arthur*

"Now the God of peace, that brought again from the dead our Lord Jesus, that great shepherd of the sheep, through the blood of the everlasting covenant."   HEBREWS 13:20

*I*f you are ever going to know the Shepherd's care, you must first realize your great need for a shepherd. If any animal God created ever needed a shepherd, it is sheep! And I truly believe that God created sheep so we could see what we are like.

Learning about sheep can be very humbling and very eye-opening! To learn about sheep is to see how greatly we, as sheep, need our Shepherd. It makes you cast yourself on Him in total dependence, and that is where we are meant to live!

Sheep are the dumbest of all animals. Because of this they require constant attention and meticulous care. They are helpless, timid, feeble animals that have little means of self-defense. If they do not have the constant care of a shepherd they will go the wrong way, unaware of the dangers at hand. If they are not led to proper pastures, they will obliviously eat or drink things that are disastrous to them. Not only that, they will literally live their lives in a rut if the shepherd does not lead them to new pastures. Sheep easily fall prey to other animals, and, when they do, they are virtually defenseless without their shepherd to protect them. Sheep can also become cast down and, in that state, panic and die. And so because sheep are sheep, they need shepherds to care for them.

You, beloved, are the sheep of His pasture. It was for you that God ". . .brought up from the dead the great Shepherd of the sheep through the blood of the eternal covenant, even Jesus our Lord" (Hebrews 13:20 NAS) and through Him, beloved, He will "equip you in every good thing to do His will, working in us that which is pleasing in His sight. . ." (Hebrews 13:21 NAS).

Oh, precious sheep, take a good look at your life. How can you make it on your own? Can you see your need for a Shepherd?

MARCH 13TH

MY OWN SHEPHERD *by John Henry Jowett*

"The Lord is my shepherd; I shall not want." PSALM 23:1

*H*ow shall we touch this lovely psalm and not bruise it? It is exquisite as "a violet by a mossy stone"! Exposition is almost an impertinence, its grace is so simple and winsome.

There is the ministry of rest. "He maketh me to lie down in green pastures." The Good Shepherd knows when my spirit needs relaxation. He will not have me always "on the stretch." The bow of the best violin sometimes requires to have its strings "let down" and so my Lord gives me rest.

And there is the discipline of change. "He leadeth me in the paths of righteousness." Those strange roads in life, unknown roads, by which I pass into changed circumstances and surroundings! But the discipline of the change is only to bring me into new pastures, that I may gain fresh nutriment for my soul. "Because they have no changes they fear not God."

And there is "the valley of the shadow," cold and bare!

What matter? He is there! "I will fear no evil." What if I see "no pastures green"? "Thy rod and thy staff they comfort me!" The Lord, who is leading, will see after my food. "Thou preparest a table before me in the presence of mine enemies." I have a quiet feast while my foes are looking on!

MARCH 14TH

GUIDANCE IS NOT A GAME
by Loren Cunningham/Janice Rogers

"A man's heart deviseth his way: but the LORD directeth his steps."   PROVERBS 16:9

*O*ne key test for true guidance: does your leading follow principles of the Bible? The Holy Spirit never contradicts the Word of God.

Every follower of Jesus has a unique ministry (1 Corinthians 12; 1 Peter 4:10–11; Romans 12; Ephesians 4). The more you seek to hear God's voice in detail, the more effective you will be in your own calling. Guidance is not a game—it is serious business where we learn what God wants us to do in ministry and how He wants us to do it. The will of God is doing and saying the right thing in the right place, with right people, at the right time and in the right sequence, under the right leadership, using the right method with the right attitude of heart.

Practice hearing God's voice and it becomes easier. It's like picking up the phone and recognizing the voice of your best friend. . .you know his voice because you have heard it so much. Compare young Samuel with the older man Samuel (1 Samuel 3:4–7; 8:7–10; 12:11–18).

Relationship is the most important reason for hearing the

voice of the Lord. God is not only infinite but personal. If you don't have communication, you don't have a personal relationship with Him. True guidance is getting closer to the Guide. We grow to know the Lord better as He speaks to us and, as we listen to Him and obey, we make His heart glad.

MARCH 15TH

GODLY PERCEPTION *by Gail & Gordon MacDonald*

"Open thou mine eyes. . ."   PSALM 119:18

*O*ne wonders how many people could be touched, how many relationships healed, if many of us were to set out to acquire sensitivity. And if we did, where would we begin?

1. Pray for it. Sensitivity is in part a gift of God's Spirit. No more beautiful picture of sensitivity is seen in the Bible than that of the shepherd who cares for the sheep. He knows when they need the coolness and refreshment of green pastures and quiet streams. He is aware when the flock requires a "table" set in the presence of feared enemies. Shepherds sense when there is the necessity for guidance through a dark valley or when it is time to go out to seek a lost lamb. They understand the vulnerability of the sheep and therefore stand at the door of the sheepfold, turning away predators.

It is those qualities that Jesus willed to His people. But they are gained by prayer, by reflection and meditation, by careful and consistent practice.

2. Study sensitivity in the Bible, in the lives of great saints, and in the performance of mature people about you. Among the most sensitive people in the Bible are David, John, and Mary, the mother of the Lord. Timothy was a sensitive person; so was Luke.

We learn sensitivity by watching mature men and women who are remarkably perceptive in groups, in marriages and families, in friendships. If we develop a curiosity about the way they respond to situations, the things they listen and look for, the conclusions to which they come when they are dealing with people, we will learn fast. It's important to ask sensitive people questions about how they have come to discern things the way that they do.

MARCH 16TH

THE SHEPHERD'S STAFF *by Kay Arthur*

". . .For thou art with me; thy rod and thy staff they comfort me."   PSALM 23:4

*A*lthough Louis XIV had condemned her to prison, Madame Guyon knew that, like Paul, she was the Lord's prisoner, not the king's. In her tenth year of imprisonment, taking pen in hand, she wrote by candlelight:

"My cage confines me round; abroad I cannot fly; but though my wing is closely bound, my heart's at liberty. My prison walls cannot control, the flight, the freedom of my soul. Ah', it is good to soar these bolts and bars above, to Him whose purpose I adore, whose Providence I love; and in Thy mighty will to find the job, the freedom of the mind."

Oh, beloved, have you ever wondered how people in circumstances such as these "can soar these bolts and bars above"? How can they be imprisoned and still sing?

There is no fear; there is contentment, rest, comfort not only because of the Shepherd, but also because of the Shepherd's rod and His staff.

The staff is the extension between the shepherd's hand

and his sheep. It is used to rescue and restore sheep when they fall into the water or are caught in a thicket. The staff is also used to draw the sheep together and to restore lambs to their ewes. The shepherd will many times guide his sheep with his staff. And last, but most precious, the shepherd uses his staff to touch his sheep so that he can have intimate contact with them while he walks towering above them.

The staff is a picture of the Holy Spirit—the extension between our Shepherd's hand and us. "I will not leave you as orphans; I will come to you." "And I will ask the Father, and He will give you another Helper [Comforter], that He may be with you forever" (John 14:18, 16 NAS).

So remember, beloved, wherever you are, His staff, His Spirit is your Comforter.

THROUGH HIM THAT LOVED US
by Mrs. Charles E. Cowman

". . .We are more than conquerors through him that loved us."   ROMANS 8:37

It is better that we should not sing of sadness. There are sad notes enough already in the world's air. We should sing of cheer, of joy, of hope. We do not need to be defeated in our battles, to sink under our loads, to be crushed beneath our sorrows. We may be victorious. Sorrow comes into every life; we cannot shut it away, but we can be conquerors in it. When the snow melts away in the springtime, I have often seen under it sweet flowers in bloom. The very drifts are like warm blankets to keep them safe. So it is with sorrow: under the cold snows of grief the flowers of the Christian graces grow unhurt. We can overcome in sorrow. This does not mean that we should not shed tears. The love of Christ does not harden the heart; it really makes it more sensitive. The grace of Christ does not save us from suffering in bereavement; yet we are to be conquerors. Our sorrow must not crush us: we must go through it victoriously, with sweet submission, and joyous confidence. Let us keep in mind that it is "through Him that loved us."

Then nestle your hand in your Father's,
    And sing if you can as you go;
Your song may cheer some one behind you
    Whose courage is sinking low;
And if your lips do quiver,—
    God will love you the better so.

MARCH 18TH

WHY THE WILDERNESS? *by Tim Hansel*

"And he saw the Spirit of God descending like a dove, and lighting upon him: And lo a voice from heaven, saying, 'This is my beloved Son, in whom I am well pleased.' Then was Jesus led up of the Spirit into the wilderness. . ."

MATTHEW 3:16, 17; 4:1

*T*his passage of Scripture has always been slightly confusing for me. Jesus has just been baptized. A holy dove has descended from heaven to endorse Him as the Son of God. The heavens have opened. The place is in awe. Folks are stunned. Excited. Expectant. The Messiah they've been awaiting for centuries has just been announced. Jesus is ready to begin His public ministry. What will God do next?

What God did next is unexpected, to say the least. He said,

"This is my beloved Son in whom I'm well pleased." And then He immediately sent Him into the wilderness to undergo loneliness, hunger, hardship, and temptation.

Isn't it interesting that the way the Father showed His love for Jesus, His only Son, was to put Him in the desert, so that at the critical beginning of His ministry He would learn to depend on the Father. . .alone?

Perhaps one of the reasons God nudges each of us into a desert of some kind is so that we will learn to depend on Him in new ways.

C. S. Lewis said that God whispers to us in our joys, speaks to us in our conscience, and shouts to us in our pain. In our joys, it is as though He is whispering in a crowded auditorium of His immense, outrageous love for us—but we can't hear. We're too busy.

He tries again to speak to us through our conscience, but we don't slow down enough to listen. Our hearing aid is on low, because we're engaged with so many things. Without purposeful listening, the communication process is not complete.

But God is persistent in His love and concern, so He shouts. . .through our pain. He finally has our attention.

MARCH 19TH

FEELING OUR INFIRMITIES *by R. T. Kendall*

"We have not an high priest which cannot be touched with the feeling of our infirmities; but was in all points tempted like as we are, yet without sin."   HEBREWS 4:15

*G*od feels a thousand times more deeply than we do for ourselves. This is the way Jesus feels behind the scenes. "We have not an high priest which cannot be touched with the feeling of our infirmities; but was in all points tempted like as we are, yet without sin" (Heb. 4:15). Our Lord is touched with the feeling of our weaknesses. It doesn't only mean that He used to be touched when He was on earth, as if that was the only time He could sympathize. It describes how Jesus feels right now. He yearns to reveal Himself now. And yet He is bound to certain principles. One of those principles is described in Acts 14:22, "We must through much tribulation enter into the kingdom of God." But in the meantime He feels what we feel—only a thousand times more. Our Lord weeps with us now. He weeps because of what He sees that we don't see; for He has much more to feel deeply about than we have.

> Standing somewhere in the shadows you'll find Jesus,
>   He's the Friend who always cares and understands.
> Standing somewhere in the shadows you will find Him,
>   And you'll know Him by the nailprints in His hands.

MARCH 20TH

DON'T FORFEIT YOUR PEACE *by Elisabeth Elliot*

"Be careful for nothing; but in every thing by prayer and supplication with thanksgiving let your requests be made known unto God. And the peace of God, which passeth all understanding, shall keep your hearts and minds through Christ Jesus."   PHILIPPIANS 4:6,7

*J*t would not be possible to exaggerate the importance hymns and spiritual songs have played in my spiritual growth. One of the latter, familiar to most of you, has this line: "O what peace we often forfeit, O what needless pain we bear, all because we do not carry everything to God in prayer" (Joseph Scriven). Prayerlessness is one of the many ways by which we can easily forfeit the peace God wants us to have.

> *Grant, O Lord my God, that I may never fall away in success or failure; that I may not be prideful in prosperity nor dejected in adversity. Let me rejoice only in what unites us and sorrow only in what separates us. May I strive to please no one or fear to displease anyone except Yourself. May I seek always the things which are eternal and never those that are only temporal.*
>
> ST. THOMAS AQUINAS

MARCH 21ST

PEACE LIKE A RIVER *by Sallie Chesham*

"And let the peace of God rule in your hearts, to the which also ye are called in one body; and be ye thankful."

COLOSSIANS 3:15

*S*amuel Logan Brengle believed the key to living a victorious Christian life was keeping a peaceful heart. The peaceful heart has a single initial requisite: desire for God.

A peaceful heart is: the self freed of self will, put under the complete control of God. It is the soul captured and captivated by Divinity, who is apprehended as personal and all-loving; the soul eager only to do and be what glorifies God, characterized by creative love that has for its object, God. The overflow of such lives is the "living water" that helps cleanse and sustain our lives. It denotes the true conservation approach to life—cherishing all life because all life is of God.

83

The peaceful heart becomes such when God as Spirit is perceived as Personal and allowed to become a great Friend in the most intimate manner. Listening for God's direction and following is all-important, but it is imperative here to note that God's voice of revelation will never oppose the recorded ordinances of God.

Brengle said of the holy men in the Bible: "When Jesus came, a body was prepared for Him and through the body He wrought wondrous works; but when the other Comforter comes, he takes possession of those bodies that are freely presented to Him, and He touches their lives with grace; He shines peacefully and gloriously on their faces. He flashes beams of pity and compassion and heavenly affection from their eyes; He kindles a fire of love in their hearts, and lights the flame of truth in their minds. They become His temple, and their hearts are a holy of holies in which His blessed Presence abides. From that central citadel He works, enduing the man who has received Him with power. . . "

MARCH 22ND

SHOWERS UPON THE EARTH
by T. C. Horton & Charles E. Hurlburt

"He shall come down like rain upon the mown grass: as showers that water the earth."　　　PSALM 72:6

*O*ur lives grow dusty, dry and desert in our earthly pilgrimage, but He who seeks a love that is fresh and pure and strong comes down upon us as "THE SHOWERS UPON THE EARTH." Have you turned to Him today and found that cool, refreshing, cleansing blessing which He seeks to give?

There shall be showers of blessing,
   Oh, that today they might fall!
Now, as to God we're confessing,
   Now, as on Jesus we call.

GIVE AND IT SHALL BE GIVEN
by Charles H. Spurgeon

"He that watereth shall be watered also himself."
                                                    PROVERBS 11:25

*W*e are here taught the great lesson, that to get, we must give; that to accumulate, we must scatter; that to make ourselves happy, we must make others happy; and that in order to become spiritually vigorous, we must seek the spiritual good of others. In watering others, we are ourselves watered. How? Our efforts to be useful bring out our powers for usefulness. We have latent talents and dormant faculties which are brought to light by exercise. Our strength for labour is hidden even from ourselves until we venture forth to fight the Lord's battles, or to climb the mountains of difficulty. We do not know what tender sympathies we possess until we try to dry the widow's tears and soothe the orphan's grief. We often find in attempting to teach others, that we gain instruction for ourselves. Oh, what gracious lessons some of us have learned at sick beds! We went to teach the Scriptures; we came away blushing that we knew so little of them. In our converse with poor saints, we taught the way of God more perfectly for ourselves and get a deeper insight into divine truth. So that watering others makes us humble. We discover how much grace there is where we had not

85

looked for it; and how much the poor saint may outstrip us in knowledge. Our own comfort is also increased by our working for others. We endeavour to cheer them, and the consolation gladdens our own heart. Like the two men in the snow; one chafed the other's limbs to keep him from dying, and in so doing kept his own blood in circulation, and saved his own life. The poor widow of Sarepta gave from her scanty store a supply for the prophet's wants, and from that day she never again knew what want was. Give then, and it shall be given unto you, good measure, pressed down, and running over.

MARCH 24TH

GOD—MY STRENGTH AND SONG
by John Henry Jowett

"The Lord is my strength and my song." PSALM 118:14

Yes, first of all "my strength" and then "my song"! For what song can there be where there is languor and fainting? What brave music can be born in an organ which is short of breath? There must first be strength if we would have fine harmonies. And so the good Lord comes to the songless, and with holy power He brings the gift of "saving health."

"And my song"! For when life is healthy it instinctively breaks into song. The happy, contented soul goes about the ways of life humming its satisfactions to itself, and is now and again heard by the passer-by. The Lord fills the life with instinctive music. When life is holy it becomes musical with His praise.

So here I see the appointed order in Christian service. It is futile to try to make people joyful unless we do it by seeking first to make them strong. First the good, and then the truly happy! First the holy, and then the musical. First God, and the breath of His Holy Spirit, and "the new song."

MARCH 25TH

THE STRENGTH OF JOY *by Andrew Murray*

". . .The joy of the LORD is your strength." NEHEMIAH 8:10

*W*hen we speak of the quickening or the deepening or the strengthening of the spiritual life, we are thinking of something that is feeble and wrong and sinful; and it is a great thing to take our place before God with the confession: O God, our spiritual life is not what it should be! May God work that in every heart.

As we look around about on the Church we see so many indications of feebleness, and of failure, and of sin, and of shortcoming, that we are compelled to ask, Why is it? Is there any necessity for the Church of Christ to be living in such a low state? Or is it actually possible that God's people should be living always in the joy and strength of their God? Every believing heart must answer, *It is possible.*

KEEP YOUR EYES ON JESUS *by Ken Abraham*

"For I know the thoughts that I think toward you, saith the Lord, thoughts of peace, and not of evil, to give you an expected end."   JEREMIAH 29:11

You may be disillusioned. You may be experiencing terribly difficult days. Perhaps God is putting the pressure on your most sensitive spot. He may be bringing you through a desperately demanding period in your life or through a dry, dusty wilderness. Possibly you have been humiliated as you have struggled to hold onto your faith in an entirely new or unfamiliar set of circumstances.

Keep your eyes on Jesus! You've probably been tempted to stick your head up, gawk around and say, "Lord, what about him (or her)? God, this is not fair! You know I love You. Now, what's all this about?"

Perhaps you have been tempted to look across the aisle at church, or across the street from where you live, or maybe even across your dining room table, and think, *Lord, why aren't You dealing with that person the way You are turning the heat up on me? Why do they have it so cozy and comfortable?*

If you listen carefully, you will probably hear the Spirit of Jesus say, "What is that to you? You follow Me!"

Understand, God is not calling everyone to do what He has called you to do. He is not asking everyone to endure what He has allowed you to endure. He is working in each one of our lives in wonderfully different ways, so each of us can magnify and glorify the name of Jesus.

BREATHING LIFE *by Malcolm Smith*

"Thou wilt show me the path of life: in thy presence is fulness of joy; at thy right hand there are pleasures for evermore.
PSALM 16:11

A person is healed of burnout when he receives a fresh revelation of Who God is. This does not make sense to human reasoning. We think that we would be healed if we could see God judging all the people who have disappointed us or, at least, making them come and tell us how wrong they were! We would be satisfied if there was a demonstration of power that ordered life in the way we feel it would show God's glory the best.

We come to God and demand a formula, a series of steps we can tell others we followed to get out of the pit of spiritual exhaustion. But God frustrates us, He doesn't give us a formula. . .He gives us Himself! Understand Who He is, and everything begins to fall into place. The answer to spiritual burnout is to respond to God afresh, and discover a new relationship with Him.

The "sound of a gentle blowing" has become flesh and lived among us in Jesus. The Gospel is that He has risen out of death and is now alive and, by His Spirit, is breathing His life into our weary, tattered spirits and making us whole.

THE ROCK OF MY SALVATION
by T. C. Horton & Charles E. Hurlburt

"The Lord liveth; and blessed be my rock; and exalted be the God of the rock of my salvation."   2 SAMUEL 22:47

*N*o graver danger threatens the believer than that of forgetting that he was redeemed—forgetting even in the joy of realized life what our salvation cost, and what is the rock foundation of our faith. To meet this need our Saviour pictures Himself not merely as the Rock of Ages, and our Strong Rock of Refuge, but the Rock of our Salvation. Here, in Him and upon His merit and atoning grace, we were saved from among the lost. Let us glory in this precious name and never forget that He was "wounded for our transgressions" and "that He bore our sins in His own body on the tree."

TOTAL FORGIVENESS *by R. T. Kendall*

"And we know that all things work together for good to them that love God, to them who are the called according to his purpose."   ROMANS 8:28

*T*he only forgiveness that is worth anything is that which makes it possible for us to forgive ourselves. It is one thing to say, "God forgives." It is another to forgive ourselves. There are many people walking around who claim to have God forgiving them of all their sins, yet they are not living in the present. They are living in the past. They cannot forgive themselves.

What is God saying to you? Forgive yourself. He's trying to show you right now how you can do it. Our gracious God comes from behind to shape your past so that, if you will believe Him and give Him time, you will come to see that His hand was with you even at your worst moment. Total forgiveness shows God's sovereign plan in everything. If you really do forgive someone, show that you mean it by bringing in God's total sovereignty. This will convince them.

The principle is in Romans 8:28, my favorite verse in the Bible: "And we know that all things work together for good to them that love God, to them who are the called according to his purpose." Think of all that you have done that is wrong. All that is bad. All that is wicked. Can anything be better than this—that all things "work together" for good? This is what Joseph was saying to his brothers in Genesis 50, the very ones who had been so wicked, so jealous and so cowardly. "You didn't do it. God did it. It wasn't you that sent me here. God did it." Oh, the relief I feel—to think that God was with me in my worst moment! But this is the sovereign grace of God. Only a God like that can do it. He can shape your past and take your worst moment and, in time, so redeem your past that you can look back and not wish to change anything. This is the God of the Bible.

THE UNGODLY MAN'S BIBLE *by Corrie ten Boom*

"How are they to believe in him of whom they have never heard? And how are they to hear without a preacher?"

ROMANS 10:14 RSV

*H*ow do you think of yourself—as owner or as captain of what you possess? Are you delivering the goods? The world does not read the Bible—it reads you and me. The godly man is the ungodly man's Bible. Are you growing like Peter? Are you glowing like Stephen? Are you going like Paul?

People will ask: "Why was I not told back at the crossroads of this Jesus?"

Thank You, Lord, that You will strengthen us by a dying Saviour's love, a risen Saviour's power, an ascended Saviour's prayer, and an eternal Saviour's glory.

MARCH 31ST

WHERE IS THE CHURCH WHEN IT HURTS?
by Philip Yancey

"Is it not to deal thy bread to the hungry, and that thou bring the poor that are cast out to thy house? when thou seest the naked, that thou cover him; and that thou hide not thyself from thine own flesh?" ISAIAH 58:7

*R*eaching out to the needy is not an option for the Christian. It is a command. I wrote a book entitled *Where Is God When It Hurts?* The real answer to that question, the answer implicit in the New Testament, is another question: Where is the church when it hurts? We followers of Jesus are God's primary response to the massive needs of the world. We are literally Christ's body.

When Jesus lived here in a physical body, He spent time among the poor, the widowed, the paralyzed, and even those with dreaded diseases. People with leprosy, for example—the AIDS patients of ancient times. We in the church, God's body on earth, are likewise called to move toward those who suffer. We are, after all, God's means of expressing His love to the world.

We must remember that all of us are needy beggars, sustained each moment by the mercy of a sovereign God. Only as we experience God's grace as pure grace, not something we earned or worked for, can we offer love with no strings attached to another person in need. There is but one true Giver in the universe; all else are debtors.

APRIL

A GENTLE MAIDEN *by William A. Quale*

"He hath made every thing beautiful in his time. . . "
ECCLESIASTES 3:11

April is a gentle maiden with eyes sky blue and clad in a green kirtle braided with wild flowers. She has smiling lips; and her smile is warm though her hands are cold. April's stiff fingers thaw out as to pick the first violet. Her voice is the blue bird's voice. She sings with her lips closed as singers who hum a minor in an accompaniment to vocalization and then trills like surprise, "Bermuda! Bermuda!" What a lyrist she is. She sings with those sweet shut lips meant for kisses, as the south wind knows full well. April is the willow's greening and the elm in bloom and the adventurous brass blades' surprising emerald in places sheltered from the winds but open to the sun. April is singing. . .and her voice is like rapture and her song is "Spring!"

SUNRISE *by Catherine Marshall*

"Give ear to my words, O LORD, consider my meditation. Hearken unto the voice of my cry. . .My voice shalt thou hear in the morning, O LORD; in the morning will I direct my prayer unto thee, and will look up."   PSALM 5:1–3

> Awake my soul, and with the sun
>   Thy daily stage of duty run;
> Shake off dull sloth, and joyful rise
>   To pay the morning sacrifice!
>
> Shine on me, Lord, new life impart,
>   Fresh ardors, kindle in my heart;
> One ray of Thine all-quickening light
>   Dispels the clouds and dark of night.

THOMAS KEN

I find the above verses help move me from "dull sloth" to "fresh ardors." Then in Psalm 5, I read: "Give ear to my words, O Lord, consider my meditation. Hearken unto the voice of my cry. . . My voice shalt thou hear in the morning, O Lord; in the morning will I direct my prayer unto thee, and will look up." Psalm 5:1–3 KJV

God, who created heaven and earth, will hear my voice? The King of the universe will consider my meditation? *Oh, thank You, Lord, for the undreamed-of opportunity of this audience with the King!* Anyone who has a favor to ask of an earthly monarch has no chance of having his request granted until he makes his wish known to the king. What a privilege to have an audience in person! *Yet this is the status and the honor You allow each of us, Lord.*

95

Even more privileged is he so in favor with the King that he is allowed as long as he wishes to be with the One he loves, listen to Him, watch Him, bask in His presence. In earthly courts, such a one would be considered favored indeed, and the courts we're invited to enter are of an "infinite majesty." Just to say "Thank You" seems inadequate. This morning I make it a willing, swelling gratitude!

APRIL 3RD

THE MINUTES OF OUR HOURS *by Elisabeth Elliot*

". . .Forget not my law; but let thine heart keep my commandments: For length of days, and long life, and peace, shall they add to thee."   PROVERBS 3:1, 2

Lover of All, I hold me fast by Thee,
      Ruler of time, King of Eternity
There is no great with Thee, there is no small,
      For Thou art all, and fillest all in all.
The newborn world swings forth at Thy command,
      The falling dewdrop falls into Thy hand.
God of the firmament's mysterious powers
      I see Thee thread the minutes of my hours.

A my Carmichael has beautifully bound together in her poem the two ancient concepts of time. One, expressed by the Greek word *chronos,* refers to "the minutes of our hours," or the notion of duration and succession. The other, *kairos,* is called "time evaluated," signifying instrumentation and purpose. "Man needs to see himself significant, in the light of events, of kairos, seeing himself hopefully in the context of a greater reality than his own temporality, of chronos."

"I hold me fast by Thee, Ruler of time, King of Eternity" is the expression of faith that my temporality is understood only in the infinite context of eternity. Not even the tiny dewdrop lacks the care and attention of the Lover of all. Shall I then think of any detail of my earthly life, even so little a thing as a minute of one of my hours, as without meaning?

APRIL 4TH

UNION WITH CHRIST *by Andrew Murray*

". . .Behold, now is the day of salvation."

2 CORINTHIANS 6:2

Let any Christian begin, then, and he will speedily experience how the blessing of the present moment is passed on to the next. It is the unchanging Jesus to whom he links himself; it is the power of a divine life, in its unbroken continuity, that takes possession of him. The do it now of the present moment—a little thing though it seems —is nothing less than the beginning of the ever-present now, which is the mystery and the glory of eternity. Therefore, Christian, abide in Christ: do it now.

THE JOY OF THE LORD *compiled by Mary W. Tileston*

"Let the heart of them rejoice that seek the LORD."
PSALM 105:3

Be Thou my Sun, my selfishness destroy,
    Thy atmosphere of Love be all my joy;
Thy Presence be my sunshine ever bright,
    My soul the little mote that lives but in Thy
    light.

GERHARD TERSTEEGEN

I do not know when I have had happier times in my soul, than when I have been sitting at work, with nothing before me but a candle and a white cloth, and hearing no sound but that of my own breath, with God in my soul and heaven in my eye. . . . I rejoice in being exactly what I am,—a creature capable of loving God, and who, as long as God lives, must be happy. I get up and look for a while out of the window, and gaze at the moon and stars, the work of an Almighty hand. I think of the grandeur of the universe, and then sit down, and think myself one of the happiest beings in it.

A POOR METHODIST WOMAN
18TH CENTURY

THE SKYLARK *by Corrie ten Boom*

"For as the heaven is high above the earth, so great is his mercy toward them that fear him."   PSALM 103:11

*O*nce, while we were on roll call, a cruel guard kept us standing for a long, long time. Suddenly a skylark began to sing in the sky, and all the prisoners looked up to listen to that bird's song. As I looked at the bird I saw in the sky, I thought of Psalm 103:11. O love of God, how deep and great; far deeper than man's deepest hate. God sent that skylark daily for three weeks, exactly during roll call, to turn our eyes away from the cruelty of men to the ocean of His love.

Thank You, Lord, that You are always willing to turn our eyes in the right direction unto You.

BEAUTY FROM UGLINESS *by Mrs. Charles E. Cowman*

"For we which live are alway delivered unto death for Jesus' sake, that the life also of Jesus might be made manifest in our mortal flesh."   2 CORINTHIANS 4:11

*E*very phase of nature about us is a wonder. Beauty from ugliness, good out of evil, everywhere. The rose sucks its life from some festering death beneath the sod. The white pond-lily climbs up out of the muddy waters, and lifts its pure petals above slime and corruption. The fleece-cloud of the upper heaven is the evaporation of stagnant pools and swamps.

And in the human sphere, the most beautiful lives are the outcome of anguish and tears. Then may we not say, "We glory in tribulations; knowing that tribulation worketh patience; and patience, experience; and experience, hope." The rose of life as well as of the garden, the sweet-scented flowers though they climb up to such a height as to overrun the jasper walls, and bloom fairest from the root of some death or loss, and grow strong as they are shaken by the sharp winds of sorrow.

REGENERATION *by Charles H. Spurgeon*

"Ye must be born again."   JOHN 3:7

*R*egeneration is a subject which lies at the very basis of salvation, and we should be very diligent to take heed that we really are "born again," for there are many who fancy they are, who are not. Be assured that the name of a Christian is not the nature of a Christian; and that being born in a Christian land, and being recognized as professing the Christian religion is of no avail whatever, unless there be something more added to it—the being "born again" by the power of the Holy Spirit. To be "born again" is a matter so mysterious that human words cannot describe it. "The wind bloweth where it listeth, and thou hearest the sound thereof, but canst not tell whence it cometh, and whither it goeth: so is every one that is born of the Spirit" (John 3:8). Nevertheless, it is a change which is known and felt: known by works of holiness, and felt by a gracious experience. This great work is supernatural. It is not a change of my name, but a renewal of my nature, so that I am not the man I used to be, but a new man in Christ Jesus. To wash and dress a corpse is a far different thing from making it alive; man can do the one, God alone can do the other. If you have then, been "born again," your acknowledgment will be, *O Lord Jesus, the everlasting Father, Thou art my spiritual Parent; unless Thy Spirit has breathed into me the breath of a new, holy, and spiritual life, I had been to this day "dead in trespasses and sins." My heavenly life is wholly derived from Thee, to Thee I ascribe it. "My life is hid with Christ in God." It is no longer I who live, but Christ who liveth in me.* May the Lord enable us to be well assured on this vital point, for to be unregenerate is to be un-saved, unpardoned, without God, and without hope.

THE COMMUNION OF FAITH *by Brother Lawrence*

". . .That ye, being rooted and grounded in love, May be able to comprehend with all saints what is the breadth, and length, and depth, and height; and to know the love of Christ, which passeth knowledge. . . ." EPHESIANS 3:17–19

The elevating and perfecting of character come largely through sorrow. This is the "mystery of the Cross." All process is by crucifixion. Experiences sad and dark, seemingly cruel, press upon us. The past is tear-worn and furrowed, and the future glooms with shapes of trial. Like Paul, we "know not what shall befall us there." Only the Holy Spirit witnessed to him, and experience witnesses to us, that "afflictions abide" us. I murmured at this, until I saw the crosses and stakes and racks and scaffolds of all ages, and the white feet of those who made these the stairways up which they climbed to light, to truth, to God. Light breaks when I see Jesus, scarred with whipping, thorn-crowned, staggering up Calvary beneath His Cross. I falter sometimes when I try to say, "It is good for me that I have been afflicted." But I can now and then catch a glimpse of the truth of it, when the light of some suffering and conquering hero breaks through the blinding mist of my tears. Gethsemanes have deeper and grander meanings than Canas.

APRIL 10TH

BOUGHT WITH A PRICE *by Corrie ten Boom*

". . .While they beheld, he was taken up; and a cloud received him out of their sight."   ACTS 1:9

*A*bout His death, resurrection and ascension:

"What is it all about?" they asked.

"The redemption of the world," He replied.

"But You have come back here. How will the world know about it?"

"I have trained My men."

"To evangelize the whole world?"

"Yes, indeed, every corner of it."

"How many men did You train for such a mammoth task?"

"A handful."

"A handful? But what if they fail?"

"If they fail, I have made no other plans."

"But is that not a great risk to take?"

"No, they will not fail."

POWER TO STAY *by Andrew Murray*

"Can a woman forget her sucking child. . .yea, they may forget, yet will I not forget thee. . .I have graven thee upon the palms of my hands. . ."　　　　ISAIAH 49:15, 16

O God, make me as holy as a pardoned sinner can be made. And, if every heart here will say that, and say it earnestly, if that prayer is in your heart, come today, and let us enter into a covenant with the everlasting and omnipotent Jehovah afresh, and not in great helplessness, but in great restfulness, place ourselves in His hands. And then as we enter into our covenant, let us go away with the one prayer—that we may believe fully that the everlasting God is going to be our Companion, holding our hand every moment of the day; our Keeper, watching over us without a moment's interval; our Father, delighting to reveal Himself in our souls always. He has the power to let the sunshine of His love be with us all the day. Do not be afraid because you have got your business that you cannot have God with you always. Learn the lesson that the natural sun shines upon you all the day, and you enjoy its light, and wherever you are you have got the sun; God takes care that it shines upon you. And God will take care that His own divine light shines upon you, and that you shall abide in that light, if you will only trust Him for it. Let us trust God to do that with a great and entire trust.

DAILY CLEANSING *by Charles H. Spurgeon*

"He. . .began to wash the disciples' feet." JOHN 13:5

The Lord Jesus loves His people so much, that every day He is still doing for them much that is analogous to washing their soiled feet. Their poorest actions He accepts; their deepest sorrow He feels; their slenderest wish He hears, and their every transgression He forgives. Humbly, patiently, He yet goes about among His people with the basin and the towel. He does this when He puts away from us day by day our constant infirmities and sins. Last night, when you bowed the knee, you mournfully confessed that much of your conduct was not worthy of your profession, and even tonight, you must mourn afresh that you have fallen again into the selfsame folly and sin from which special grace delivered you long ago; and yet Jesus will have great patience with you; He will hear your confession of sin; He will say, "I will, be thou clean;" He will again apply the blood of sprinkling, and speak peace to your conscience, and remove every spot. It is a great act of eternal love when Christ once for all absolves the sinner, and puts him into the family of God; but what condescending patience there is when the Saviour with much long-suffering bears the oft recurring follies of His wayward disciple; day by day, and hour by hour, washing away the multiplied transgressions of His erring but yet beloved child! To dry up a flood of rebellion is something marvelous, but to endure the constant dropping of repeated offenses—to bear with a perpetual trying of patience, this is divine indeed! While we find comfort and peace in our Lord's daily cleansing, its legitimate influence upon us will be to increase our watchfulness, and quicken our desire for holiness. Is it so?

IN GETHSEMANE *by John Henry Jowett*

"And when he was at the place, he said unto them, 'Pray that ye enter not into temptation.' "　　　　LUKE 22:40

*S*urely this is the very Holy of Holies! It were well for us to fall on our knees and "be silent unto the Lord." I would quietly listen to the awful words, "Remove this cup from Me!" and I would listen again and again until never again do I hold a cheap religion. It is in this garden that we learn the real value of things, and come to know the price at which our redemption was bought. No one can remain in Gethsemane and retain a frivolous and flippant spirit.

"And there appeared unto Him an angel from heaven, strengthening Him." I know that angel! He has been to me. He has brought me angel's food, even heavenly manna. Always and everywhere when my soul has surrendered itself to the Divine will, the angel comes, and my soul is refreshed. The laying down of self is the taking up of God. When I lose my will I gain the Infinite. The moment of surrender is also the moment of conquest. When I consecrate my weakness I put on strength and majesty like a robe.

"And when He rose up from His prayer"—what then? Just this, He was quietly ready for anything, ready for the betraying kiss, ready for crucifixion. "Arise, let us be going."

THE CHOICES OF BARABBAS *by John Henry Jowett*

"And they cried out all at once, saying, 'Away with this man, and release unto us Barabbas. . .' Pilate therefore, willing to release Jesus, spake again to them. But they cried, saying, 'Crucify him, crucify him.' " LUKE 23:18, 20–21

*B*arabbas rather than Christ! The destroyer of life rather than the Giver of life! This was the choice of the people; and it is a choice which has often stained and defiled my own life.

When I choose revenge rather than forgiveness, I am preferring Barabbas to Christ. For revenge is a murderer, while forgiveness is a healer and saviour of men. But how often I have sent the sweet healer to the cross, and welcomed the murderer within my gate!

When I choose carnality before holiness, I am preferring Barabbas to Christ. For is there any murderer so destructive as carnality? And holiness stands waiting, ready to make me beautiful with the wondrous garments of grace. But I spurn the angel, and open my door to the beast.

The devil is always soliciting my service, and the devil "is a murderer from the beginning." Have I never preferred him, and sent my Lord to be "crucified afresh," and "put Him to an open shame"?

Again let me pray.

THE FEAR OF MEN *by John Henry Jowett*

"And Simon Peter stood and warmed himself. They said therefore unto him, 'Art not thou also one of his disciples?' He denied it, and said, 'I am not.' " JOHN 18:25

And this is the disciple who had been surnamed "The Rock"! Our Lord looked into the morrow, and He saw Simon's character, compacted by grace and discipline into a texture tough and firm as granite. But there is not much granite here! Peter is yet loose and yielding; more like a bending reed than an unshakable rock. A servant girl whispers, and his timid heart flings a lie to his lips and he denies his Lord.

Peter denied the Master, not because he coveted money, but because he feared men. He was not seeking crowns, but escaping frowns. He was not clutching at a garland, but avoiding a sword. It was not avarice but cowardice which determined his ways. He shrank from crucifixion! He saw a possible cross, and with a great lie he passed by on the other side.

But the Lord was not done with Peter. He is still "in the making." Some day he will justify his new name. Some day we shall find it written: "When they saw the boldness of Peter, they marvelled"! Once a maid could make him tremble. Now he can stand in high places, "steadfast and unmovable"!

From the spirit of cowardice and from all temporising, and from the unholy fear of man, deliver me, good Lord!

THE PRICE OF SIN *by Charles H. Spurgeon*

"With his stripes we are healed."   ISAIAH 53:5

*P*ilate delivered our Lord to the lictors to be scourged. The Roman scourge was a most dreadful instrument of torture. It was made of the sinews of oxen, and sharp bones were intertwisted every here and there among the sinews so that every time the lash came down these pieces of bone inflicted fearful laceration, and tore off the flesh from the bone. The Saviour was, no doubt, bound to the column, and thus beaten. He had been beaten before; but this of the Roman lictors was probably the most severe of His flagellations.

Believer in Jesus, can you gaze upon Him without tears, as He stands before you the mirror of agonizing love? He is at once fair as the lily of innocence, and red as the rose with the crimson of His own blood. As we feel the sure and blessed healing which His stripes have wrought in us, do not our hearts melt at once with love and grief? If ever we have loved our Lord Jesus, surely we must feel that affection glowing now within our bosoms.

> See how the patient Jesus stands,
>> Insulted in His lowest case!
> Sinners have bound the Almighty's hands,
>> And spit in their Creator's face.
> With thorns His temples gor'd and gash'd
>> Send streams of blood from every part;
> His back's with knotted scourges lash'd
>> But sharper sources tear His heart.

THE CROWN OF THORNS *by Mrs. Charles E. Cowman*

"Instead of the thorn shall come up the fir tree, and instead of the brier shall come up the myrtle tree: and it shall be to the Lord for a name, for an everlasting sign that shall not be cut off."   ISAIAH 55:13

*A*n old legend relates that long ago some monks had found a crown of thorns which the Saviour wore on the day He was crucified. During Passion Week it was laid on the altar of the Chapel and the people looked upon the sacred crown with great reverence, awed as they saw the cruel thorns bearing still their stains of blood.

Very early on Easter morning, one of the monks entered the Chapel to remove the relic which would be so out of harmony with the glad thoughts of the day. When he opened the door he found the whole place filled with wondrous perfume. He could not understand it. As he went up to the altar, the early sunlight, coming in through the eastern window, showed him the crown still resting there, but it had become a crown of roses, every rose pouring out its marvelous fragrance.

The beautiful legend is a parable of what Christ does with earth's sorrows for all who love and trust Him. Out of pain comes blessing. The crown of thorns must be worn by the Master's own, but the thorns burst into sweet flowers as the light of heaven's morning touches them.

A CRY OF FAITH *by George MacDonald*

"About the ninth hour Jesus cried with a loud voice, saying. . . 'My God, my God, why hast thou forsaken me?'"

MATTHEW 27:46

*T*he divine horror of that moment is unfathomable by human soul. And yet He would believe. Yet He would hold fast. God was His God yet. *My God*—and in the cry came forth the Victory, and all was over soon. Of the peace that followed that cry, the peace of a perfect soul, victorious for God and His brethren, He Himself alone can ever know the breadth and length, and depth and height.

I do not think it was our Lord's deepest trial when in the garden He prayed that the cup might pass from Him, and prayed yet again that the will of the Father might be done. For that will was then present with Him. He was living and acting in that will. But now the foreseen horror has come. He is drinking the dread cup, and the Will has vanished from His eyes. Were that Will visible in His suffering, His will could bow with tearful gladness under the shelter of its grandeur. But now His will is left alone to drink the cup of The Will in torture. In the sickness of this agony, the Will of Jesus arises perfect at last; and of itself, unsupported now, declares for God in defiance of pain, of death, of apathy, of self, of negation, of the blackness within and around it; calls aloud upon the vanished God.

This is the Faith of the Son of God. God withdrew, as it were, that the perfect Will of the Son might arise and go forth to find the Will of the Father.

Is it possible that even then He thought of the lost sheep who could not believe that God was their Father; and for them, too, in all their loss and blindness and unlove, cried, saying the word they might say, knowing for them that God means Father and more, and knowing now, as He had never known till now, what a fearful thing it is to be without God and without hope? I dare not answer the question I put.

THE BLOOD OF CHRIST *by Charles H. Spurgeon*

". . .The precious blood of Christ."   1 PETER 1:19

*S*tanding at the foot of the cross, we see hands, and feet, and side, all distilling crimson streams of precious blood. It is "precious" because of its redeeming and atoning efficacy. By it the sins of Christ's people are atoned for; they are redeemed from under the law; they are reconciled to God, made one with Him. Christ's blood is also "precious" in its cleansing power; it "cleanseth from all sin." "Though your sins be as scarlet, they shall be as white as snow." Through Jesus' blood there is no spot left upon any believer, nor wrinkle nor any such thing remains. The blood of Christ is likewise "precious" in its preserving power. We are safe from the destroying angel under the sprinkled blood. Remember it is God's seeing the blood which is the true reason for our being spared. Here is comfort for us when the eye of faith is dim, for God's eye is still the same. The blood of Christ is "precious" also in its sanctifying influence. The same blood which justifies by taking away sins, does in its afteraction, quicken the new nature and lead it onward to subdue sin and to follow out the commands of God. There is no motive for holiness so great as that which streams from the veins of Jesus. And "precious," unspeakably precious, is this blood, because it has an overcoming power. It is written, "they overcame through the blood of the Lamb." How could they do otherwise? He who fights with the precious blood of Jesus fights with a weapon which cannot know defeat. The blood of Jesus! Sin dies at its presence; death ceases to be death; heaven's gates are opened. The blood of Jesus! We shall march on, conquering and to conquer, so long as we can trust its power!

APRIL 20TH

HE LOVED US TO DEATH *by Charles Dickens*

"But God commendeth his love toward us, in that, while we were yet sinners, Christ died for us."   ROMANS 5:8

*B*earing his Cross, upon his shoulder, like the commonest and most wicked criminal, our blessed Saviour, Jesus Christ, surrounded by the persecuting crowd, went out of Jerusalem to a place called in the Hebrew language, Golgotha; that is, the place of a skull. And being come to a hill called Mount Calvary, they hammered cruel nails through His hands and feet and nailed Him to the Cross, between two other crosses on each of which, a common thief was nailed in agony. Over His head, they fastened this writing "Jesus of Nazareth, the King of the Jews"—in three languages; in Hebrew, in Greek, and in Latin.

At about the sixth hour, a deep and terrible darkness came over all the land, and lasted until the ninth hour, when Jesus cried out, with a loud voice, "My God, My God, why hast thou forsaken me?" The soldiers, hearing him, dipped a sponge in some vinegar, that was standing there, and fastening it to a long reed, put it up to His Mouth. When He had received it, He said "It is finished!"—And crying "Father! Into thy hands I commend my Spirit!"—died.

112

SEEKING THE SEEKER *by Charles Dickens*

"...Why seek ye the living among the dead? He is not here, but is risen."   LUKE 24:5, 6

*M*ary Magdalene saw the stone rolled away, and waiting to see no more, ran to Peter and John who were coming towards the place, and said, "They have taken away the Lord and we know not where they have laid Him!" They immediately ran to the Tomb, but John, being the faster of the two, outran the other, and got there first. He stooped down, and looked in, and saw the linen clothes in which the body had been wrapped, lying there; but he did not go in. When Peter came up, he went in, and saw the linen clothes lying in one place, and a napkin that had been bound about the head, in another. John also went in, then, and saw the same things. Then they went home, to tell the rest.

But Mary Magdalene remained outside the sepulchre, weeping. After a little time, she stooped down, and looked in, and saw two angels, clothed in white, sitting where the body of Christ had lain. These said to her, "Woman, why weepest thou?" She answered, "Because they have taken away my Lord, and I know not where they have laid Him." As she gave this answer, she turned round, and saw Jesus standing behind her, but did not then know Him. "Woman," said He, "why weepest thou? what seekest thou?" She, supposing Him to be the gardener, replied, "Sir! If thou hast borne my Lord hence, tell me where thou hast laid Him, and I will take Him away." Jesus pronounced her name, "Mary." Then she knew Him, and, starting, exclaimed "Master!" "Touch me not," said Christ; "for I am not yet ascended to my Father; but go to my disciples, and say unto them, I ascend unto my Father, and your Father; and to my God, and to your God!"

BELIEVING IS SEEING! *by Charles Dickens*

"Now faith is the substance of things hoped for, the evidence of things not seen."　　　　　HEBREWS 11:1

*W*hen the rest said to Thomas, "we have seen the Lord!" he answered, "Except I shall see in his hands the print of the nails, and thrust my hand into his side, I will not believe!" At that moment, though the doors were all shut, Jesus again appeared, standing among them, and said, "Peace be unto you!" Then He said to Thomas, "Reach hither thy finger, and behold my hands; and reach hither thy hand, and thrust it into my side; and be not faithless, but believing." And Thomas answered, and said to him, "My Lord and my God!" Then said Jesus, "Thomas, because thou hast seen me, thou hast believed. Blessed are they that have not seen me, and yet have believed."

BEHOLD THE PURCHASE *by Captain E. G. Garré*

"Forasmuch as ye know that ye were not redeemed with corruptible things, as silver and gold. . .But with the precious blood of Christ. . ."　　　1 PETER 1:18, 19

*S*urely Calvary represents a fearful price. But your soul and mine, and the millions thus far redeemed and the millions which may yet be redeemed, a wrecked earth restored back to Eden perfection, the kingdoms of this world wrestled from the grasp of the usurper and delivered over to the reign of their rightful King! —when we shall see all this shall we not gladly say, "Behold the purchase?"

APRIL 24TH

KING OF GLORY *by T. C. Horton & Charles E. Hurlburt*

"Who is this King of glory? The LORD of hosts, he is the King of glory."   PSALM 24:10

*J*ehovah Jesus, the glorious King! Not merely a king, but glorious, excelling all others in mighty truth and power, grace and love. We almost forget for a time His absolute sovereignty as we bow in humble worship before His matchless glory, and cry again and again, "Thy Kingdom come," Oh Glorious King. Amen.

APRIL 25TH

THE CRUCIFIED ONE *by Andrew Murray*

"I am crucified with Christ: nevertheless I live; yet not I, but Christ liveth in me."   GALATIANS 2:20

"*J* am crucified with Christ." Thus the apostle expresses his assurance of his fellowship with Christ in His sufferings and death, and his full participation in all the power and the blessing of that death. And so really did he mean what he said, and know that he was now indeed dead, that he adds: "It is no longer I that live, but Christ that liveth in me." How blessed

115

must be the experience of such a union with the Lord Jesus! To be able to look upon His death as mine, just as really as it was His—upon His perfect obedience to God, His victory over sin, and complete deliverance from its power, as mine; and to realize that the power of that death does by faith work daily with a divine energy in mortifying the flesh, and renewing the whole life into the perfect conformity to the resurrection life of Jesus! Abiding in Jesus, the Crucified One, is the secret of the growth of that new life which is ever begotten of the death of nature.

APRIL 26TH

TAKE MY LIFE AND LET IT BE *by Ken Abraham*

"The blood of Jesus. . .cleanseth us from all sin."
1 JOHN 1:7

A musician whose words are worth reviewing was the remarkable nineteenth-century songwriter, Frances Ridley Havergal. Some of her classic hymns include "Take My Life and Let it Be" and "Like a River Glorious." Miss Havergal often acknowledged that the keys to her success were surrender and cleansing. On surrender, she said, "I saw it as a flash of electric light, and what you see you can never unsee. There must be full surrender before there can be full blessedness. God admits you by one into the other. . . . So I just yielded myself to Him and utterly trusted Him to keep me."

Later she wrote of her own experience, "The wonderful and glorious blessing, which so many Christians are testifying to have found, was suddenly, marvelously, sent to me last winter; and life is now what I never imagined life on earth could be. . ." Furthermore, Frances Havergal saw clearly that the cleansing blood of Jesus did a complete, purifying work in her heart. Basing her convictions upon the Scripture verse "the blood of Jesus. . .cleanses us from all sin" (1 John 1:7), Miss Havergal became convinced that not only did the blood of Jesus cleanse past sins, but believers could depend upon Christ's blood for continual cleansing.

She wrote to a friend,

> *Have we not been limiting the cleansing power of the precious blood when applied by the Holy Spirit, and also the keeping power of our God? Have we not been limiting 1 John 1:7, by practically making it refer only to "the remission of sins that are past," instead of taking the grand simplicity of "cleanseth us from all sin"?*
>
> *"All" is all; and as we may trust Him to cleanse from the stain of past sins, so we may trust Him to cleanse from all present defilement. . . .*

APRIL 27TH

THE HOPE OF GLORY *by Andrew Murray*

". . .Christ in you, the hope of glory."   COLOSSIANS 1:27

And if the thought will sometimes come: Surely this is too high for us; can it be really true? Only remember that the greatness of the privilege is justified by the greatness of the object He has in view. Christ was the revelation of the Father on earth. He could not be this if there were not the most perfect unity, the most complete communication of all the Father had to the Son. He could be it because the Father loved Him, and He abode in that love. Believers are the revelation of Christ

117

on earth. They cannot be this unless there be perfect unity, so that the world can know that He loves them and has sent them. But they can be it if Christ loves them with the infinite love that gives itself and all it has, and if they abide in that love.

GREATER WORKS! *by Andrew Murray*

"Verily, verily, I say unto you, He that believeth on me, the works that I do shall he do also; and greater works than these shall he do. . ." JOHN 14:12

*B*eliever in Jesus! you are called, you are appointed, to do the works of Jesus, and even greater works, because He has gone to the Father to receive the power to do them in and through you.

"Whatsoever ye shall ask in my Name, that will I do." Give yourself, and live, to do the works of Christ, and you will learn to pray so as to obtain wonderful answers to prayer. Give yourself, and live, to pray, and you will learn to do the works He did, and greater works. With disciples full of faith in Himself, and bold in prayer to ask great things, Christ can conquer the world.

THE PARALYSIS OF ANALYSIS *by Brother Andrew*

"Those things, which ye have both learned, and received, and heard, and seen in me, do: and the God of peace shall be with you."   PHILIPPIANS 4:9

As we spend time in Scripture and in prayer, it's important not to get sidetracked in trying to determine whether we've received an official call from God or whether we have a clear indication that we are doing God's will. It's too easy to get so caught up in the paralysis of analysis that we fail to act.

Most of us often have the idea that God must have a special calling on our lives. If we have no such calling from God, then we have not been selected by him for special service, and we can only live out our lives as drones in the kingdom, one monotonous and unimportant day at a time. But we need to understand that that is our idea, not God's.

We must never make our dreams for success or accomplishment as God's purpose for us. God's end, his purpose for us, is the process. Oswald Chambers put it so well when he said, "God's training is for now, not presently. His purpose is for this minute, not for something in the future. What men call training and preparation, God calls the end. . . If we realized that obedience is the end, then each moment is precious."

A man once approached the great preacher Charles Spurgeon with a question. "There's a Bible verse I read that's bothering me because I can't understand it," he said.

"You should be happy to have such a problem," Spurgeon replied. "It's all those Bible verses I do understand that bother me!"

God has given us in Scripture a full revelation of his nature and his character. And he has given us an unmistakably

119

clear mandate to share him and his Word with those who have not heard. If we focus on obeying him on a daily basis—wherever we are—he will lead us where he wants us to go, and to the people he wants us to reach.

THE CALLING *by Brother Andrew*

"Then saith he unto his disciples, 'The harvest truly is plenteous, but the labourers are few; Pray ye therefore the Lord of the harvest, that he will send forth labourers into his harvest.' " MATTHEW 9:37, 38

*T*he real calling of God is not to a certain place or career, but to everyday obedience. Then, as we follow his everyday call, he opens doors to where he wants us to go, and closes doors to where he does not want us to go. That way, faithfulness to God's calling is within our reach every day.

On the other hand, if we agonize over whether we have received a special call, we waste valuable time and energy and, in effect, limit the work of God in our lives. When people ask me whether they should go into full-time ministry in the traditional sense, I almost always discourage them. I tell them to follow Jesus with their whole lives and pursue full-time ministry only as a last resort.

How do we prepare to respond to that call? Part of the preparation is God's doing, and part of it must be ours. God's preparation of us began long before we decided to accept his call. The fact is, God has been using all of the events and experiences of our lives to prepare us for the kind of service he's calling us to now. Whether our past was happy or sad, godly or sordid, God is building on that experience to make us into effective servants for him.

It may take an entire lifetime of preparation for one minute of supreme service. In the case of John the Baptist, God used his whole life to prepare him for the moment when he saw the lone figure of Jesus approaching in the desert. He stopped baptizing and teaching, pointed his finger, and said, "Look, the Lamb of God, who takes away the sin of the world!" (John 1:29). What an electrifying moment in history, the first time Jesus was introduced to the world as the Lamb of God.

Lord, make me the proper tool in your hand. Cause me to grow in my relationship with you so that when opportunities arise to reap your harvest, I will be completely prepared.

MAY

SPRING IS COME *by William A. Quale*

"Bless the LORD, O my soul. O LORD my God, thou art very great; thou art clothed with honour and majesty."

PSALM 104:1

"*H*e watereth the hills from his chambers: the earth is satisfied with the fruit of thy works. He causeth the grass to grow for the cattle, and herb for the service of man: that he may bring forth food out of the earth." (Psalm 104:13, 14).

May! The wild crab blossoms! That is enough joy for any month. That wealth of aroma drenches the air. The nests are a-building. The Birds are like God's prophets giving the needed message for the heart; "Be up and doing"; but, for all, what a time to be at leisure and go gadding with the swallow whither we will; to lie on the earth and hear things grow, and see the grass spear press toward the sun; to see the flowers swing censers full of incense as a temple lamp, to hear the laughing feet of Spring stepping lightly among her blossoms, and hear her fingers toying with the fruit trees' blossoms and hear her carol till the lark stays his limpid note to hearken. To feel the touch of the moist lips of the dew upon your face, and lie out at night till dawn, careless of slumber. Have you used the blooming apple tree as a tent and slept under its curtain all the night through? Life is starlit in May. All things wear wings in May. Every lip has its song in May.

WINGS OF EAGLES *by Hannah Whitall Smith*

". . .They shall mount up with wings as eagles. . ."
                                                    ISAIAH 40:31

I say "spread our wings and mount up," because not the largest wings ever known can lift a bird one inch upward unless they are used. We must use our wings, or they avail us nothing.

It is not worth while to cry out, "Oh that I had wings and then I would flee," for we have the wings already, and what is needed is not more wings, but only that we should use those we have. The power to surrender and trust exists in every human soul, and only needs to be brought into exercise. With these two wings we can "flee" to God at any moment; but, in order really to reach Him, we must actively use them. We must not merely want to use them, but we must do it definitely and actively. We shall not "mount up" very high if we only surrender and trust in theory, or in our especially religious moments. We must do it definitely and practically about each detail of daily life as it comes to us. We must meet our disappointments, our thwartings, our persecutions, our malicious enemies, our provoking friends, our trials and temptations of every sort, with an active and experimental attitude of surrender and trust. We must spread our wings and "mount up" to the "heavenly places in Christ" above them all, where they will lose their power to harm or distress us. For from these high places we shall see things through the eye of Christ, and all earth will be glorified in the heavenly vision.

> The dove hath neither claw nor sting,
>   Nor weapon for the fight,

She owes her safety to the wing,
  Her victory to flight.
The bridegroom opens His arms of love,
  And in them folds the panting dove.

MY GUARDIAN *by St. Augustine*

"He shall cover thee with his feathers, and under his wings shalt thou trust."   PSALM 91:4

*T*hese are Thy servants, my brethren, whom Thou willest to be Thy sons; my masters, whom Thou commandest me to serve, if I would live with Thee, of Thee. But this Thy Word were little, did it only command by speaking and not go before in performing. This then I do in deed and word, this I do under Thy wings; in over great peril, were not my soul subdued unto Thee under Thy wings, and my infirmity known unto Thee. I am a little one, but my Father ever liveth, and my Guardian is sufficient for me. For He is the same who begat me, and defends me: and Thou Thyself art all my good; Thou, Almighty, Who art with me, yea, before I am with Thee. To such then whom Thou commandest me to serve will I discover, not what I have been, but what I now am and what I yet am. But neither do I judge myself. Thus therefore I would be heard.

A THRONE OF GRACE *by William Harding/John Bunyan*

"Let us therefore come boldly unto the throne of grace, that we may obtain mercy. . ."　　　　HEBREWS 4:16

*G*od has prepared a Mercy-seat, a Throne of grace to sit on; that you may come to Him, and that He may hear you and receive you. "I will commune with you," saith the Lord, "from above the mercy-seat" (Ex. 25:22). "Sinner, when you come to Me, you will find Me upon the mercy-seat. There I bring My pardons; there I hear and receive your petitions, and accept them to My favour."

God has also prepared a golden altar for you to offer your prayers and tears upon. It is called a "golden" altar to show what worth it is in God's account: for this golden altar is Jesus Christ; this altar sanctifies your gift, and makes your sacrifice acceptable. This altar, then, makes your groans, golden groans; your tears, golden tears; and your prayers, golden in the eyes of God. (Rev. 8:3; Matt. 23:19; Heb. 10:10; I Pet. 2:5).

God has strewn all along the way, from the gate of hell, where you were, to the gate of heaven, where you are going, flowers out of His own garden. Behold how the promises, invitations, calls, and encouragements, like lilies, lie around you! Be careful that you do not tread them under foot, sinner. With promises, did God say? Yes, God has mixed all those promises with His own name and His Son's name; which is also the name of mercy, goodness, compassion, love, pity, grace, forgiveness, pardon for the coming sinner to be encouraged! . . . Well, all these things are the good hand of your God upon you, to constrain, to provoke, and to make you willing and able to come, that you might in the end be saved.

"I AM" IS THE SAME *by Hannah Whitall Smith*

". . .He that hath seen me hath seen the Father; . . ."
JOHN 14:9

It is unthinkable to suppose that when God told Moses His name was "I am," He could have meant to say, "I am a stern Lawgiver," or "I am a hard Taskmaster," or "I am a God who is wrapped up in my own glory, and am indifferent to the sorrows or the fears of my people." If we should try to fill in the blank of His "I am" with such things as these, all the Christians the world over would be horrified. But do not the doubts and fears of some of these very Christians say exactly these things in secret every day of their lives?

May God grant that what we shall learn in our consideration of the names of God may make all such doubts and fears impossible to us from this time forth and forevermore.

> Jesus is God! Oh, could I now
>   But compass land and sea,
> To teach and tell this single truth,
>   How happy I should be!
> Oh, had I but an angel's voice,
>   I would proclaim so loud
> Jesus, the good, the beautiful,
>   Is the image of our God!

TRANSFORMED *by Brother Lawrence*

". . .Be ye transformed by the renewing of your mind. . . "
ROMANS 12:2

*A*s for my set hours of prayer, they are only a continuation of the same exercise. Sometimes I consider myself there as a stone before a carver, whereof he is to make a statue; presenting myself thus before God, I desire Him to form His perfect image in my soul, and make me entirely like Himself.

At other times, when I apply myself to prayer, I feel all my spirit and all my soul lift itself up without any care or effort of mine, and it continues as it were suspended and firmly fixed in God, as in its center and place of rest.

MAY 7TH

REFLECTIONS *by Hannah Hurnard*

"But the fruit of the Spirit is love, joy, peace, longsuffering, gentleness, goodness, faith."
GALATIANS 5:22

*G*oodness is such a lovely thing!
'Tis Love's own bridal dress
The wedding garment from our King
Is spotless righteousness;
And those who keep "The Royal Law,"
Shine lily white without a flaw.

O, happy, holy ones! each day
Their cup filled to the brim,

Love's table spread for them, they may
　　As God's guests, feast with him.
Their happy faces shine with bliss,
　　With joy from him and one with his.

Goodness is perfect harmony,
　　The flawless form of grace!
The golden mirror where we see
　　Reflections of love's face.
Goodness is wrong changed and put right,
　　'Tis darkness swallowed up in light.

MAY 8TH

THE JOY OF THE LOVER *by John Henry Jowett*

*"Be kindly affectioned one to another with brotherly love;
in honour perferring one another."*　　　ROMANS 12:10

*L*ove finds her joy in seeing others crowned. Envy darkens when she sees the garland given to another.

Jealousy has no festival except when she is "Queen of the May." But love thrills to another's exaltation. She feels the glow of another's triumph. When another basks in favour her own "time of singing of birds is come"!

And all this is because love has wonderful chords which vibrate to the secret things in the souls of others. Indeed, the gift of love is just the gift of delicate correspondence, the power of exquisite fellow-feeling, the ability to "rejoice with them that do rejoice, and to weep with them that weep." When, therefore, the soul of another is exultant, and the wedding-bells are ringing, love's kindred bells ring a merry peal. When the soul of another is depressed, and a funeral dirge is wailing, love's kindred chords wail in sad communion. So love can enter another's state as though it were her own.

Our Master spake condemingly of those who have lost this exquisite gift. They have lost their power of response. "We have piped with you, and ye have not danced; we have mourned with you, and ye have not lamented." They lived in selfish and loveless isolation. They have lost all power of tender communion.

THE SUNLIGHT OF HOPE
by Bernard Ruffin about Fanny Crosby

"For thou art my hope, O Lord GOD: thou art my trust from my youth."   PSALM 71:5

*A*t the age of eight Fanny Crosby was able to compose her first attempt at verse:

> Oh, what a happy child I am,
>   Although I cannot see!
> I am resolved that in this world
>   Contented I will be!

> How many blessings I enjoy
>   That other people don't!
> So weep or sigh because I'm blind,
>   I cannot—nor I won't.

"Blindness cannot keep the sunlight of hope from the trusting soul," Fanny wrote in later life. "One of the earliest resolves that I formed in my young and joyous heart was to leave all care to yesterday, and to believe that the morning would bring forth its own peculiar joy."

Fanny reiterated what she had said all her life long about her blindness:

"I believe that the greatest blessing the Creator ever bestowed on me was when He permitted my external vision to be closed. He consecrated me for the work which He created me. I have never known what it was to see, and therefore I cannot realize my personal loss. But I have had the most remarkable dreams, I have seen the prettiest eyes, the most beautiful faces, the most remarkable landscapes. The loss of sight has been no loss to me."

MAY 10TH

A PLACE THAT LASTS *by Gigi Graham Tchividjian*

"Peace I leave with you, my peace I give unto you: not as the world giveth, give I unto you. Let not your heart be troubled, neither let it be afraid." JOHN 14:27

*S*udden changes often remind me of my inner self. My emotions often resemble those weather vanes you see on the rooftops of barns—changing directions with the slightest breeze.

There are times when clouds of negativism hang over me; their constant dripping cause dreariness of soul and spirit.

There are also serene sunny days. Golden days that are free and clear of storms. Days that shine bright and steady with joy and fun and laughter.

I used to be upset, even ashamed of these changing emotions. I thought that a deeply spiritual person should not

130

and would not have these fluctuations of mood. We usually think that women are more prone to emotional currents than men, but when I began to look in Scripture for evidence of mood swings, I found many of the male writers subject to emotional ups and downs. David is so real and honest about his feelings. One minute he is down and defeated, the next laughing and extolling his Lord. The apostles Peter and Paul, Isaiah, and even the Lord Jesus Himself (remember that He was touched in every way as we are) all share with us their emotions.

I also began to notice how my spiritual life was affected by the emotional changes in my life. I discovered that when the storm clouds hang low over me and the fog rolls in thick around me and the constant drizzle of discouragement dismays me, that my spiritual life tends to blossom.

I do love sunshine, but as an old (Middle Eastern) proverb says, "All sunshine makes a desert."

So, He gives me enough sunshine to keep me healthy and happy and enough clouds and rain to keep me nourished and fertile and totally dependent upon Him.

MAY 11TH

THE BIG DIFFERENCE *by R. T. Kendall*

"God was with him."   ACTS 7:9

*T*here was something at work in Joseph's life that was wonderful and positive, a gift that God gave him. One of the keys to understanding Joseph is provided by Stephen in Acts 7:9— "God was with him." If God is with us there is no impediment, no personality difficulty, no problem about class background that can stand in the way of him making us a

131

mighty instrument for our day. God was with Joseph and he had a gift, a gift that would shape his own life and also the life of Israel. God gave him dreams. Now that may not sound very impressive. Whoever would have thought that a gift like that could mean so much? And God has given to you something that nobody else can do. Because God made you different.

It is sometimes said of a particular person, "When God made so and so he threw the mold away." But wait. He threw the mold away when he made us! We are all different from anybody else. To affirm the gift that God has given us is a way of glorifying our Creator. Subsequent events in Joseph's life would reveal that this gift, this dreaming which apparently included an ability to interpret dreams, saved his own life and the lives of his family.

MAY 12TH

WINNING LIFE'S TOUGHEST BATTLES
by Tim Hansel

"Tell me; that I may turn to the right hand, or to the left."
GENESIS 24:49

*I*n *Winning Life's Toughest Battles*, Dr. Julias Segal writes poignantly of the importance of taking action, no matter how small, in times of great stress and difficulty. The more difficult the trouble, he says, the more important it is to take some small step—to act, and, hence, reduce your feelings of hopelessness and powerlessness.

Persons traumatized by crisis often feel cut off not only from their past, but from their future as well. They become disoriented and feel lost. When one is mired in such a crisis, Segal insists that the smallest action can be the key to survival.

Segal relates story after story of people who took charge of their lives even in the most dire circumstances. Some were hostages. Some were POWs. Some endured unbelievable trauma. But the common denominator among them was their courage to act. No matter how small the action, it gave them a sense of victory.

Patti Blumenthal does exceptional work with kids from the probation department. These kids have no shortage of problems and difficulties. One day when she was telling me about her work, she kept using some initials that were unfamiliar to me. After the third or fourth time, my curiosity got the best of me.

"All right, Patti," I said, "what's this NTS?"

With great delight she explained, "Oh, that's the Next Tiny Step. These kids can't take big steps, but they can take tiny ones."

This concept has had a profound impact on my life. It has been of inestimable value, especially during times of difficulty. It has helped me realize that I can always initiate some change, no matter how small. God doesn't ask us to take big steps. . .just the next tiny step.

MAY 13TH

GOD'S ARMY *by Corrie ten Boom*

"As the Father has sent me, even so I send you."

JOHN 20:21 RSV

There is no army where only officers fight. Everyone who is in the army of God must fight, even the soldier in the lowest rank. When we obey and act on the promises, we stand on victory ground, because the ability of our Master is available to us.

133

God give us men touched with fire from above.
God give us men with a Calvary love.
God give us men who are filled with Your power.
God give us men for this day and this hour,
Men who are fearless when seeking the lost,
Men who will follow whatever the cost.
Where are the men we need?
Where are the men?
When will they heed thy call,
When, Saviour, when?
Raise up a host burning with holy fire,
Men filled with Thee and with flaming desire.
Men who will serve Thee without doubt, without fear.
God give us men who will now volunteer.

LESLEY DEWELL

MAY 14TH

THE CAPTAIN OF OUR SALVATION
by T. C. Horton & Charles E. Hurlburt

*"For it became him. . .to make the captain of their salvation
perfect through suffering."*   HEBREWS 2:10

*W*e cannot but bow our heads as we read this verse and
meditate upon the Captain of our salvation and His perfection. He was God and He was Man, we have learned. As Man
He must be manifest in the life. He is the Son of God, the
Captain (or "Author") of salvation. We are the sons of God.
The mode and method of perfection is manifested by our
Leader. He was tempted; so are we. He suffered; so must we.
He was persecuted; so must we be. He paid the price; so
must we. The climax for Him and for us is glory. Let us bow

our heads and hearts to our Leader today and obey His orders. He will be with us in every trial and suffering. Amen.

May 15TH

REASONABLE SERVICE *by Captain E. G. Garré*

"I beseech you therefore, brethren, by the mercies of God, that ye present your bodies a living sacrifice, holy, acceptable unto God, which is your reasonable service."

ROMANS 12:1

*H*yde once told me that one had to give himself if he wanted to serve God and help men, that it was not enough to give our time and our talents, that our 'life' must be given. This was true, he said, both in praying and in preaching. Alas! how few of us give of our life; when we think that our life is touched, we feel it is time to draw back. How often we have heard it said, "You will kill yourself if you work as you do; take it easy." But Hyde used to say, "Give your life for God and men." Let that vital energy, that living power within, be poured out for men.

HINDRANCES TO PRAYER *by Wesley L. Duewel*

"But if our gospel be hid, it is hid to them that are lost: In whom the god of this world hath blinded the minds of them which believe not, lest the light of the glorious gospel of Christ, who is the image of God, should shine unto them."

2 CORINTHIANS 4:3, 4

*P*rayer is the weapon God ordained by which to resist Satan. We are told to pray without ceasing and not simply that God may be persuaded to do us good.

Take an illustration: A letter is coming to us from a far country in the time of war. It belongs to us, and has been duly posted, but it has to pass through the enemy's lines before we can get it. Naturally we do all in our power to insure the arrival of what is already ours, although we have not yet got it in our hands. So, when God gives the assurance our prayers are heard, our part is to pray it through the enemy's country— the heavenlies—in order that it may be manifested on earth. It is at this point where so many Christians in their prayer-life fail. They do not persevere until the answer is prayed through, not understanding the great need to do so. Thus Satan triumphs in stopping answers to prayer because of ignorance of his wiles. It has been well said that "the secret of success in prayer is in being able to hold on for the last half-hour."

OBEDIENCE AND PURITY *by Captain E. G. Garré*

"If a man therefore purge himself from these, he shall be a vessel unto honour, sanctified, and meet for the master's use, and prepared unto every good work." 2 TIMOTHY 2:21

*G*od wants those who are willing to bear the burden of the souls of these millions without God, to go with Jesus into Gethsemane. He wants us to do this. It is a blessed experience to feel that in some measure we can enter into the fellowship of Christ's sufferings. It brings us into a precious nearness to the Son of God. And not only this, but it is God's appointed way of bringing the lost sheep back to the fold. He is saying, "Who will go for us, and whom shall I send?" Are you who read these words willing to be intercessors? If we are willing to put ourselves into God's hands, then God is willing to use us. But there are two conditions: obedience and purity. Obedience in everything, even in the least, surrendering up our wills and taking the will of God. And the next step is purity. God wants pure vessels for his service, clean channels through which to pour forth His grace. He wants purity in the very centre of the soul, and unless God can have a pure vessel, purified by the fire of the Holy Spirit, He cannot use that vessel. He is asking you now if you will let Him cleanse away part of your very life. God must have a vessel He can use.

MIGHTY PREVAILING PRAYER *by Wesley L. Duewel*

"For we wrestle not against flesh and blood, but against principalities, against powers, against the rulers of the darkness of this world, against spiritual wickedness in high places."   EPHESIANS 6:12

Let it never be forgotten: the prayer warrior who moves heaven will just as assuredly move hell. Prayer is twofold; it cuts both ways, upwards and downwards. No matter how humble the child of God may be in intellectual attainments, he has power in prayer to move heavenly forces in opposition to the spirit forces of hell. Often is it remarked: "Things are worse than they were when we began to pray!" Of course they are! Your enemy, encamped against you, is watchful and alert—you take the aggressive, and he is roused to fury! Prayer at the very beginning moves the opposing forces of the powers of darkness.

From Ephesians 6:12 it is very clear that a great war is being waged in the heavenlies against the saints of God. The air is teeming with spirits to whom God has given the ordering of things on our earth. As Charles Wesley has it:

> Angels our march oppose
>   Who still in strength excel,
> Our secret sworn eternal foes,
>   Countless, invisible;
> From thrones of glory driven,
>   By flaming vengeance hurled,
> They throng the air and darken heaven,
>   And rule this lower world.

ALL: OR NOTHING AT ALL *by Andrew Murray*

". . .Yield yourselves unto God, as those that are alive from the dead, and your members as instruments of righteousness unto God."   ROMANS 6:13

*T*he cause of the weakness of your Christian life is that you want to work it out partly, and to let God help you. And that cannot be. You must come to be utterly helpless, to let God work, and God will work gloriously. It is this that we need if we are indeed to be workers for God. I could go through Scripture, and prove to you how Moses, when he led Israel out of Egypt; how Joshua, when he brought them into the land of Canaan; how all God's servants in the Old Testament counted upon the omnipotence of God doing impossibilities. And this God lives today, and this God is the God of every child of His. And yet we are some of us wanting God to give us a little help while we do our best, instead of coming to understand what God wants, and to say: I can do nothing, God must and will do all. Have you said: In worship, in work, in sanctification, in obedience to God, I can do nothing of myself, and so my place is to worship the omnipotent God, and to believe that He will work in me every moment. Oh, may God teach us this!

STAND STILL *by Charles H. Spurgeon*

"Stand still, and see the salvation of the LORD."

EXODUS 14:13

These words contain God's command to the believer when he is reduced to great straits and brought into extraordinary difficulties. He cannot retreat; he cannot go forward; he is shut up on the right hand and on the left; what is he now to do? The Master's word to him is, "Stand still." It will be well for him if at such times he listens only to his Master's word, for other and evil advisers come with their suggestion. Despair whispers, "Lie down and die; give it all up." But God would have us put on a cheerful courage, and even in our worst ties, rejoice in His love and faithfulness. Cowardice says, "Retreat; go back to the worldling's way of action; you cannot play the Christian's part, it is too difficult. Relinquish your principles." But, however much Satan may argue this course upon you, you cannot follow it if you are a child of God. His divine fiat has bid thee go from strength to strength, and so thou shalt, and neither death nor hell shall turn thee from thy course. What, if for a while thou art called to stand still, yet this is but to renew the strength for some greater advance in due time. Precipitancy cries, "Do something. Stir yourself; to stand still and wait, is sheer idleness." We must be doing something at once—we must do it so we think—instead of loosing to the Lord, who will not only do something but will do everything. Presumption boasts, "If the sea be before you, march into it and expect a miracle." But Faith listens neither to Presumption, nor to Despair, nor to Cowardice, nor to Precipitancy, but it hears God say, "Stand still," and immoveable as a rock it stands.

FROM DISILLUSIONED TO DIS-ILLUSIONED
by Ken Abraham

"And that from a child thou hast known the holy scriptures, which are able to make thee wise unto salvation through faith which is in Christ Jesus."   2 TIMOTHY 3:15

*T*he world desperately needs more disillusioned Christians. The church lacks vision and power because we have so few disillusioned Christians. Disillusioned, that is, in the truest sense of the word. Confused? Let me explain.

The dictionary defines an illusion as "the state or fact of being intellectually deceived or misled; a misleading image presented to the vision; perception of something objectively existing in such a way as to cause misinterpretation of its actual nature." Considering the potential dangers of illusions, the great devotional writer Oswald Chambers implores that we be disillusioned Christians.

Rather than using the commonly held meaning of disillusionment, Chambers defines disillusion as being devoid of false illusions. We need to be stripped of misleading images and divested of all pretense. In "The Discipline of Disillusionment," Chambers writes:

"Dis-illusionment means that there are no more false judgments in life. disillusionment may leave us cynical and unkindly severe in our judgment of others, but the disillusionment which comes from God brings us to the place where we see men and women as they really are, and yet there is no cynicism, we have no stinging, bitter things to say."

Although many of Chambers's writings lean toward being deep and mystical, the man was a realist and, when rightly understood, his spiritual insights are eminently practical. He constantly urged others to get their heads out of the clouds and live by faith in the fact of God's Word, not in the fantasy world of illusions.

OBEDIENCE *compiled by Mary W. Tileston*

"Obey my voice, and I will be your God, and ye shall be my people: and walk ye in all the ways that I have commanded you, that it may be well unto you." JEREMIAH 7:23

> And oft, when in my heart was heard
>   Thy timely mandate, I deferred
> The task in smoother walks to stray;
>   But thee I now would serve more strictly,
>   if I may.

W. WORDSWORTH

*P*ray Him to give you what Scripture calls "an honest and good heart," or "a perfect heart"; and, without waiting, begin at once to obey Him with the best heart you have. Any obedience is better than none. You have to seek his face; obedience is the only way of seeing Him. All your duties are obediences. To do what He bids is to obey Him, and to obey Him is to approach Him. Every act of obedience is an approach—an approach to Him who is not far off, though He seems so, but close behind this visible screen of things which hides Him from us.

J. H. NEWMAN

As soon as we lay ourselves entirely at His feet, we have enough light given us to guide our own steps; as the foot-soldier, who hears nothing of the councils that determine the course of the great battle he is in, hears plainly enough the word of command which he must himself obey.

DO YOU SERVE WITH GLADNESS?
by Charles H. Spurgeon

"Serve the Lord with gladness."   PSALM 100:2

*T*he Lord looketh at the heart, and if He seeth that we serve Him from force, and not because we love Him, He will reject our offering. Service coupled with cheerfulness is heart-service, and therefore true. Do you serve the Lord with gladness?

Delight in divine service is a token of acceptance. Those who serve God with a sad countenance, because they do what is unpleasant to them, are not serving Him at all; they bring the form of homage, but the life is absent. Our God requires no slaves to grace His throne; He is the Lord of the empire of love, and would have His servants dressed in the livery of joy. The angels of God serve Him with songs, not with groans; a murmur or a sigh would be a mutiny in their ranks. That obedience which is not voluntary is disobedience. Service coupled with cheerfulness is heart-service, and therefore true. Take away joyful willingness from the Christian, and you have removed the rest of his sincerity. Cheerfulness is the support of our strength; in the joy of the Lord are we strong. It acts as the remover of difficulties. It is to our service what oil is to the wheels of a railway carriage. Without oil the axle soon grows hot, and accidents occur; and if there be not a holy cheerfulness to oil our wheels, our spirits will be clogged with weariness. The man who is cheerful in his service of God, proves that obedience is his element; he can sing,

> Make me to walk in Thy commands,
> 'Tis a delightful road.

Reader, let us put this question—do you serve the Lord with gladness? Let us show to the people of the world, who think our religion to be slavery, that it is to us a delight and a joy! Let our gladness proclaim that we serve a good Master.

MAY 24TH

WE'RE IN FOR A FIGHT *by Ken Abraham*

"Put on the whole armour of God, that ye may be able to stand against the wiles of the devil."　　　EPHESIANS 6:11

To be a Christian means that we are involved in a war, a spiritual war between God's people and the forces of Satan. As is the case in any war, we are affected whether we want to be or not.

We are at war with evil, a personal evil, a supernatural evil, spearheaded by Satan himself. The devil is not some funny-looking cartoon character with horns sticking out of his head, dressed in red leotards, and carrying a pitchfork. No, the devil is real, and he is your enemy. He has sent his demonic messengers into the world to stand against you and do all they can to keep you from being the person God wants you to be.

The war is raging in cities and towns all across the land. Furthermore, the battle is not restricted to what we might be tempted to refer to as "the devil's playgrounds"—bars, adult bookstores, and sorcery shops. The war has moved inside the doors of your church, school, and home.

Sadly, Satan is winning many victories. The devil and demonic cohorts are ripping apart friends and family relationships; they are splitting churches wide-open, sapping the life-blood out of many believers, and sucking some of your friends and family members right down into hell.

What are we going to do about it? It's time to stand up and fight back! In the name of Jesus, by the power of His Holy Spirit working in us, and by the blood of the Lamb, it's time for each of us to tell the devil where to get off. God is calling us out of our complacency to become warriors for Christ. He wants us to learn how to put on the full armor of God, to learn how to overcome the Evil One, and to challenge the demonic powers that have captured so many of the world systems, our churches, our schools, our friends, and our family members.

MAY 25TH

EQUIPPED TO WIN *by Kay Arthur*

"Put on the whole armour of God. . ."   EPHESIANS 6:11

*M*y daddy used to tell me that the best defense is a good offense! Beloved, God never intended for the Christian to constantly live on the defensive. The hymn writer so aptly put what our stance is to be, "Onward Christian soldiers marching as to war with the cross of Jesus going on before." We are to storm the gates of hell and demand that Satan's captives be set free. Ours is the victory; we are the ones who are more than conquerors. But it is a victory which must be claimed, must be pronounced, must be taken! God's Word says that the gates of hell cannot prevail, cannot stand, against the church; they must give way!

When you read of the Christian's warfare with the enemy in Ephesians 6, God clearly tells you that you are to put on the full armor of God. As you read this description of the Christian's armor, you soon realize that it only covers the front of the soldier! It allows for full protection as long as you don't turn your back! God never sounds retreat, nor do you ever have to wave the flag of surrender. Why? Because the soldier of Christ has the ultimate of weapons. It is the sword of the Spirit which is the Word of God. Thus, we come to the reason Satan would keep us from God's Word. The Word of God is the Christian's only offensive weapon. It is all he needs— nothing more! With it, the Christian is the victor, more than a conqueror; without it, all he can do is defend himself.

The shield of faith is that by which you ward off Satan's attack upon you, but the Sword, the Word of God, is for conquering, for defeating the foe! It is the same weapon that is used by Christ at the battle of Armageddon. "And from His mouth comes a sharp sword. . ." (Revelation 19:15 NAS).

When you begin to war in prayer, from your mouth must come His sharp sword. Are you prepared? Are you on the offensive or the defensive?

EXERCISING LOVE *by Brother Lawrence*

"But we all, with open face beholding as in a glass the glory of the Lord, are changed into the same image from glory to glory, even as by the Spirit of the Lord."

2 CORINTHIANS 3:18

*I*n the beginning of the spiritual life we ought to be faithful in doing our duty and denying ourselves; but after that, unspeakable pleasures follow. In difficulties we need only have recourse to Jesus Christ, and beg His grace; with that everything became easy.

Many do not advance in the Christian progress because they stick in penances and particular exercises, while they neglect the love of God, which is the end. This appeared plainly by their works, and was the reason why we see so little solid virtue.

There needed neither art nor science for going to God, but only a heart resolutely determined to apply itself to nothing but Him, or for His sake, and to love Him only.

THE SHOUT OF FAITH *by Hannah Whitall Smith*

". . .And it came to pass, when. . .the people shouted with a great shout, that the wall fell down flat."   JOSHUA 6:20

*T*he walls may look as high and as immovable as ever; and prudence may say it is not safe to shout until the victory is actually won. But the faith that can shout in the midst of the sorest stress of temptation, "Jesus saves me; He saves me now!" such a faith will be sure to win a glorious and a speedy victory. Many of God's children have tried this plan, and have found it to work far beyond even their expectations. Temptations have come in upon them like a flood; temptations to irritability, or to wicked thoughts, or to bitterness of spirit, or to a thousand other things, and they have seen their danger; and their fears and their feelings have declared that there was no hope of escape. But their faith has laid hold of this grand fact that Christ has conquered; and they have fixed their gaze on the unseen power of God's salvation, and have given their shout of victory, "The Lord saves! He saves me now! I am more than conqueror through Him that loves me!" And the result is always a glorious victory.

MAY 28TH

THE MOST DELICATE MISSION ON EARTH
by Oswald Chambers

". . .The friend of the bridegroom. . ."   JOHN 3:29

*G*oodness and purity ought never to attract attention to themselves, they ought simply to be magnets to draw to Jesus Christ. If my holiness is not drawing towards Him, it is not holiness of the right order, but an influence that will awaken inordinate affection and lead souls away into side-eddies. A beautiful saint may be a hindrance if he does not present Jesus Christ but only what Christ has done for him. He will leave the impression—"What a fine character that man is!" That is not being a true friend of the Bridegroom; I am increasing all the time, He is not.

148

In order to maintain this friendship and loyalty to the Bridegroom, we have to be more careful of our moral and vital relationship to Him than of any other thing, even of obedience. Sometimes there is nothing to obey, the only thing to do is to maintain a vital connection with Jesus Christ, to see that nothing interferes with that. Only occasionally do we have to obey. When a crisis arises we have to find out what God's will is, but the greater part of the life is not conscious obedience but the maintenance of this relationship—the friend of the Bridegroom. Christian work may be a means of evading the soul's concentration on Jesus Christ. Instead of being friends of the Bridegroom, we may become amateur providences, and may work against Him whilst we use His weapons.

MAY 29TH

PERSONAL HOLINESS *by J. I. Packer*

"And that ye put on the new man, which after God is created in righteousness and true holiness." EPHESIANS 4:24

*C*hristians are called to oppose the world. But how, in this case, can that be done? Credible opposition to secular ideologies can be shown by speaking and writing, but credible opposition to unholiness can only be shown by holy living (see Ephesians 5:3–14). Ecumenical goals for the church are defined nowadays in terms of the quest for social, racial, and economic justice, but it would be far healthier if our first aim was agreed to be personal and relational holiness in every believer's life. Much as the modern West needs the impact of Christian truth, it needs the impact of Christian holiness even more, both to demonstrate that godliness is the true humanness and to keep community life from rotting to destruction.

The pursuit of holiness is thus no mere private hobby, nor merely a path for a select few, but a vital element in Christian mission strategy today. The world's greatest need is the personal holiness of Christian people.

ACCEPTANCE WITH JOY *by Hannah Hurnard*

"For this God is our God for ever and ever: he will be our guide even unto death."　　　　　　　PSALM 48:14

"*M*y Lord, I will tell you what I learned along the paths that lead to the High Places," said Much-Afraid to the Shepherd. "Every circumstance in life no matter how crooked and distorted and ugly it is, if it is reacted to in love and forgiveness and obedience to (God's) will can be transformed.

"Therefore I begin to think, My Lord, you purposely allow us to be brought into contact with the bad and evil things that you want changed. Perhaps that is the very reason why we are here in this world, where sin and sorrow and suffering and evil abound, so that we may let you teach us so to react to them, that out of them we can create lovely qualities to live forever. That is the only really satisfactory way of dealing with evil, not simply binding it so that it cannot work harm, but whenever possible overcoming it with good."

The Shepherd answered Much-Afraid, "As long as you are willing to be called Acceptance-with-Joy and Bearing-in-Love, you can never again become crippled and you will be able to go wherever I lead you!"

IMPOSSIBLE VICTORIES *by Alan Redpath*

"The priests that bare the ark of the covenant of the LORD stood firm on dry ground in the midst of Jordan, and all the Israelites passed over on dry ground, until all the people were passed clean over Jordan." JOSHUA 3:17

The passage of Jordan means facing the impossibility, following the dying, rising, ascending Jesus into the place of all power. Get a clear view of Him who can deal with the impossibility of your life before you have reached it. For in the name of the Lord Jesus I declare this truth, that, however subtle, however strong it may be, there is no attack of Satan on the child of God but first has struck the heart of the Lord. He overcame it at the Cross, and He bids us, His children, to get a clear view of Him, to face again the impossibility that we have faced so often, then look up into His face and say, "Now, Lord Jesus, I believe that although I cannot, you can." In that moment the roar of Jordan will be silent, its violence be checked, and we will go through on dry land.

The path of the child of God from the wilderness to Canaan is by way of facing the impossible and looking up to a Risen Christ and getting hold of Him.

JUNE

THE ROSE MONTH *by William A. Quale*

"Then we which are alive and remain shall be caught up together. . .to meet the Lord in the air: and so shall we ever be with the Lord. Wherefore comfort one another with these words."   1 THESSALONIANS 4:17, 18

*J*une for the wild rose blooming! It is the sunrise pink the wild rose bush has had the genius to paint its blossoms with. O day in June when the wild rose blooms and the wind strays indolent as drowsy thoughts and the blue sky has its upleap of wonder, and the bird nesting in the rose thickets tosses on a spragly bit of rose branch and sings its madrigal in pure joy of life and nest and rose in bloom and love—when the rose thickets bloom and June days laugh out loud, heaven is nearer than the white clouds sailing fleet across the sky. Such days are raptures. They come but never go. They live through all the stress and fret of winter tempests. June day, bloom day, day of the wild rose flower and leaf, day of sky and singing stream.

DISBUDDING *by Mrs. Charles E. Cowman*

"Every branch in me that. . .beareth fruit, he purgeth it, that it may bring forth more fruit."   JOHN 15:2

*J*t takes a thousand buds to make one American Beauty rose, consequently nine hundred and ninety-nine of them must be suppressed. Think of this, dear one, when billows of trouble overwhelm you, and God seems to have hidden His face, He has in view the height to which He intends to carry the culture of your soul. He has in mind a work which your loftiest ambition has never even thought of. He wants some heroes and leaders for his work,—men and women that can stand pruning and transplanting,—and He may want you. Then think of the American Beauty and bloom out for God.

Disbudding consists in removing the buds before they have time to grow into young branches. It is a species of pruning which has for its object not only the training but also economy with regard to the resources of a tree, in order that there may be a greater supply of nourishment for the development of those buds which are allowed to remain.

If the roots are capable of absorbing a given quantity of nutritive matter for the supply of all the buds upon a stem, and if a number of those buds be removed, it must be evident that those which remain will be able to draw a greater supply of sap and grow more vigorously than they otherwise would have done. This fact has furnished the idea of DISBUDDING. It has been proved that a judicious thinning of the buds after they have been unfolded in spring is a great utility.

THE THREE GARDENS *by John Henry Jowett*

"In the midst of the street of it, and on either side of the river, was there the tree of life, which bare twelve manner of fruits, and yielded her fruit every month: and the leaves of the tree were for the healing of the nations." REVELATION 22:2

*T*he Bible opens with a garden. It closes with a garden. The first is the Paradise that was lost. The last is Paradise regained. And between the two there is a third garden, the garden of Gethsemane. And it is through the unspeakable bitterness and desolation of Gethsemane that we find again the glorious garden through which flows "the river of water of life." Without Gethsemane no New Jerusalem! Without its mysterious and unfathomable night no blessed sunrise of eternal hope! "We were reconciled to God by the death of His Son."

We are always in dire peril of regarding our redemption lightly. We hold it cheaply. Privileges easily come to be esteemed as rights. And even grace itself can lose the strength of heavenly favour and can be received and used as our due. "Gethsemane can I forget?" Yes I can; and in the forgetfulness I lose the sacred awe of my redemption, and I miss the real glory of "Paradise regained." "Ye are not your own; ye are bought with a price." That is the remembrance that keeps the spirit lowly, and that fills the heart with love for Him "whose I am," and whom I ought to serve.

IF ANY MAN THIRST *by Charles H. Spurgeon*

"In the last day, that great day of the feast, Jesus stood and cried, saying, 'If any man thirst, let him come unto me, and drink.'" JOHN 7:37

*A*dmirable indeed is the longsuffering of the Saviour in bearing with some of us year after year, notwithstanding our provocations, rebellions, and resistance of His Holy Spirit. Wonder of wonders that we are still in the land of mercy!

Provision is made most plenteously; all is provided that man can need to quench his soul's thirst. To his conscience the atonement brings peace; to his understanding the gospel brings the richest instruction; to his heart the person of Jesus is the noblest object of affection; to the whole man the truth as it is in Jesus supplies the purest nutriment. Thirst is terrible, but Jesus can remove it. Though the soul were utterly famished, Jesus can restore it.

Proclamation is made most freely that every thirsty one is welcome. It is not goodness in the creature which brings him the invitation; the Lord Jesus sends it freely, and without respect of persons.

The sinner must come to Jesus, not to works, ordinances, or doctrines, but to a personal Redeemer, who His own self bare our sins in His own body on the tree.

No waiting or preparation is so much as hinted at. A fool, a thief, a harlot can drink; and so sinfulness of character is no bar to the invitation to believe in Jesus. Blistered, leprous, filthy lips may touch the stream of divine love; they cannot pollute it, but shall themselves be purified. Jesus is the fount of hope. Dear reader, hear the dear Redeemer's loving voice as He cries to each of us.

"IF ANY MAN THIRST, LET HIM COME UNTO ME, AND DRINK."

HIDDEN WELLS *by James Stalker*

"But whosoever drinketh of the water that I shall give him shall never thirst; but the water that I shall give him shall be in him a well of water springing up into everlasting life."

JOHN 4:14

*T*he preaching of Jesus shows how deeply He had drunk into the essence of natural beauty and revelled in the changing aspects of the seasons. It was when wandering as a lad in these fields that He gathered the images of beauty which He poured out in His parables and addresses. It was on that hill that He acquired the habit of His after-life of retreating to the mountain-tops to spend the night in solitary prayer. The doctrines of His preaching were not thought out at the spur of the moment. They were poured out in a living stream when the occasion came but the water had been gathered into the hidden well for many years before. In the fields and on the mountain-side he had thought them out during the years of happy and undisturbed meditation and prayer.

IMPOVERISHED MINISTRY OF JESUS
by Oswald Chambers

"From whence then hast thou that living water?"

JOHN 4:11

*"T*he well is deep"—and a great deal deeper than the Samaritan woman knew! Think of the depths of human nature,

of human life, think of the depths of the "wells" in you. Have you been impoverishing the ministry of Jesus so that He cannot do anything? Suppose there is a well of fathomless trouble inside your heart, and Jesus comes and says— "Let not your heart be troubled"; and you shrug your shoulders and say, "But, Lord, the well is deep; You cannot draw up quietness and comfort out of it." No, He will bring them down from above. Jesus does not bring anything up from the wells of human nature. We limit the Holy One of Israel by remembering what we have allowed Him to do for us in the past, and by saying, "Of course I cannot expect God to do this thing." The thing that taxes Almightiness is the very thing which we as disciples of Jesus ought to believe He will do. We impoverish His ministry the moment we forget He is Almighty; the impoverishment is in us, not in Him. We will come to Jesus as Comforter or as Sympathizer, but we will not come to Him as Almighty.

The reason some of us are such poor specimens of Christianity is because we have no Almighty Christ. We have Christian attributes and experiences, but there is no abandonment to Jesus Christ. When we get into difficult circumstances, we impoverish His ministry by saying— "Of course He cannot do anything," and we struggle down to the deeps and try to get the water for ourselves. Beware of the satisfaction of sinking back and saying— "It can't be done"; you know it can be done if you look to Jesus. The well of your incompleteness is deep, but make the effort and look away to Him.

THE TEST OF VICTORY *by John Henry Jowett*

"David behaved himself wisely in all his ways; and the LORD was with him."   1 SAMUEL 18:14

*T*he hour of victory is a more severe moral test than the hour of defeat. Many a man can brave the perils of adversity who succumbs to the seductions of prosperity. He can stand the cold better than the heat! He is enriched by failure, but "spoilt by success." To test the real quality of a man, let us regard him just when he has slain Goliath! "David behaved himself wisely!"

He was not "eaten up with pride. . ." He went among his friends as though no Goliath had ever crossed his way. He was not forever recounting the triumph, and fishing for the compliments of his audience. He behaved wisely. So many of us tarnish our victories by the manner in which we display "soiled goods."

And in this hour of triumph David made a noble friend. In his noonday he found Jonathan, and their hearts were knit to each other in deep and intimate love. It is beautiful when our victories are so nobly borne that they introduce us into higher fellowships, and the friends of heaven become our friends.

PERFECTED STRENGTH *by Alan Redpath*

"My grace is sufficient for thee; for my strength is made perfect in weakness." 2 CORINTHIANS 12:9

*M*ost of us, God forgive us, are too big for God to use. We are too full of our own schemes and of our own way of doing things. God has to humble us and break us and empty us. So low, indeed, must God make us that we need every word of encouragement from heaven to enable us to take on the job and dare to go forward in the will of God. The world speaks about the survival of the fittest, but God gives power to the faint and He gives might to those who have no strength. He perfects His strength in weakness; He uses the things that are not to bring to nought the things that are. If Paul had been as eloquent as he confessed himself to be contemptible in speech, he could never have become the great apostle.

MONUMENTAL INSIGNIFICANCE *by Charles W. Colson*

"Humble yourselves therefore under the mighty hand of God, that he may exalt you in due time." 1 PETER 5:6

*H*istory is full of examples of God using for His greatest work those who seem most insignificant in man's eyes. There was the obscure Christian in Damascus who baptized Paul, the great propagator of the faith. Ananias was unknown before and never heard of again.

Charles Haddon Spurgeon, the great scholar and preacher, whose writings are treasured today, was converted by the testimony of a simple working man whom Spurgeon heard when he stepped into a small church to escape a raging storm.

Dr. Abraham Kuyper, Dutch scholar and theologian, had just finished an erudite sermon when a peasant woman, her head wrapped in a shawl, approached him. "Dr. Kuyper, that was an excellent sermon, but you need to be born again," she said softly. He soon was and thereafter kept a picture of a peasant woman on his desk as a constant reminder.

A butcher in England, Henry Varley, who also was a lay preacher, told Evangelist Dwight Moody, "The world has yet to see what God will do with a man fully consecrated to Him." Moody, who had been led to Christ by Edward Kimball, an obscure salesman in a shoe store, prayed that he might be that man. His ministry then exploded on two continents. Monuments are built to Moody's honor while the names of Kimball and Varley are found only in footnotes.

I like Richard Halverson's statement that "the strong need the weak so they can be close to God's strength." He so often uses people whose names may never appear in the New York Times but I'm convinced are printed in bold letters in the "Book of Life."

JUNE 10 TH

HUMILITY *by D. L. Moody*

"Wherefore let him that thinketh he standeth take heed lest he fall." 1 CORINTHIANS 10:12

*S*ome years ago I saw what is called a sensitive plant. I happened to breathe on it, and suddenly it drooped its head;

I touched it, and it withered away. Humility is as sensitive as that; it cannot safely be brought out on exhibition. A man who is flattering himself that he is humble and is walking close to the Master, is self-deceived. It consists not in thinking meanly of ourselves, but in not thinking of ourselves at all. Moses wist not that his face shone. If humility speaks of itself, it is gone.

BE STRONG AND OF GOOD COURAGE *by R. T. Kendall*

"So are my ways higher than your ways."   ISAIAH 55:9

Joseph wanted his gift to be recognized. He had said to the butler, "Don't forget me; don't forget me." His brothers had made fun of his gift. But the day came when his gift was affirmed by the Pharaoh. It came at an unexpected time in an unexpected place by an unexpected person. But it came God's way.

I have a gift that I am so afraid won't be recognized. If I go about exalting myself—pulling strings and doing anything like that, I am going to find that it will elude me. Success will always be outside my grasp. But once we get right with God and are willing for God to use us as He wills, "Eye hath not seen, nor ear heard, neither have entered into the heart of man" what God will do.

Humiliation today, exaltation tomorrow. Pharaoh said to Joseph, "I've set you over the land of Egypt." Pharaoh took off his ring from his hand and put it on Joseph's hand and "arrayed him in vestures of fine linen, and put a gold chain about his neck; and he made him to ride in the second chariot which he had; and they cried before him, Bow the knee."

Pharaoh said to Joseph, "I am Pharaoh, and without thee shall no man lift up his hand or foot in all the land of Egypt" (Gen. 41:42–44).

What is the humiliation that is required? Two things: First, be open, for you don't know the way God wants to do it. Second, affirm Him. Don't question His judgment. His ways are higher than our ways (Isa. 55:9). You may ask: what will my exaltation be? I don't know. There was no way to calculate what God would do through Joseph. But I can tell you this: no cross, no crown.

JUNE 12TH

BATHED IN HUMILITY *by Charles Dickens*

"Humble yourselves therefore under the mighty hand of God, that he may exalt you in due time."   1 PETER 5:6

*J*esus continued to heal the sick, and to do good, and went and lodged at Bethany; a place that was very near the City of Jerusalem, but not within the walls.

One night, at that place, He rose from Supper at which He was seated with His Disciples, and taking a cloth and a basin of water, washed their feet. Simon Peter, one of the Disciples, would have prevented Him from washing his feet; but our Saviour told him that He did this, in order that they, remembering it, might be always kind and gentle to one another, and might know no pride or ill-will among themselves.

CHILDLIKENESS *by George MacDonald*

"Whosoever therefore shall humble himself as this little child, the same is greatest in the kingdom of heaven."

MATTHEW 18:4

*T*he disciples had been disputing who should be the greatest, and the Lord wanted to show them that such a dispute had nothing whatever to do with the way things went in His kingdom. Therefore, as a specimen of His subjects, He took a child and set him before them. It was not to show the scope but the nature of the kingdom.

The child was employed as a manifestation, utterance, and sign of the truth that lay in his childhood, in order that the eyes as well as the ears should be channels to the heart. It was essential—not that the child should be beautiful but —that the child should be childlike.

He told them they could not enter the kingdom save by becoming little children—by humbling themselves. For the idea of ruling was excluded where childlikeness was the one essential quality. It was to be no more who should rule, but who should serve; no more who should look down upon his fellows from the conquered heights of authority—even of sacred authority, but who should look up honoring humanity, and ministering to it, so that humanity itself might at length be persuaded of its own honor as a temple of the living God. It was to impress this lesson upon them that He showed them the child; therefore, I repeat, the lesson lay in the childhood of the child.

CORRECTION TO PERFECTION *by R. T. Kendall*

"[God chastens us] for our profit, that we might be partakers of his holiness." HEBREWS 12:10

*W*hen God chastens us, He is not getting even with us for our sin. There is hardly a pastor in the world who hasn't come across someone who, having experienced some tragedy, calamity, or adversity, has hastily concluded, "I know why this has happened to me. God is angry for something I once did." The Bible says that God "hath not dealt with us after our sins; nor rewarded us according to our iniquities. . . As far as the east is from the west, so far hath he removed our transgressions from us" (Ps. 103:10, 12).

It does not follow that God will not sometimes chasten a disobedient Christian. That is obviously true (see 2 Sam. 12: 1–23). But the chastening isn't God getting even; it is preparing that person for something better, more valuable and worthwhile. God chastens us "for our profit, that we might be partakers of his holiness" (Heb. 12:10). Often God chastens the very one who, as far as anybody could tell, didn't apparently need it or deserve it. Job "was perfect and upright" (Job 1:1). God put him through a trial that was extreme, but not because Job had sinned. "For whom the Lord loveth he chasteneth, and scourgeth every son whom he receiveth" (Heb. 12:6). You don't have to do anything wrong for God to decide to chasten you. The promise is already there. You can be living the most godly kind of Christian life and quite suddenly be tapped on the shoulder by God saying, "I have got a little trial for you."

It is through much tribulation that we enter the kingdom of God (Acts 14:22).

PERSEVERING PRAYER *by Charles H. Spurgeon*

"And he went a little farther, and fell on his face, and prayed." MATTHEW 26:39

*T*here are several instructive features in our Saviour's prayer in His hour of trial. It was lonely prayer. He withdrew even from His three favoured disciples. Believer, be much in solitary prayer, especially in times of trial. Family prayer, social prayer, prayer in the Church, will not suffice; these are very precious, but the best beaten spice will smoke in your censer in your private devotions, where no ear hears but God's.

It was humble prayer. Luke says He knelt, but another evangelist says He "fell on His face." Where, then, must be thy place, thou humble servant of the great Master? What dust and ashes should cover thy head! Humility gives us good foot-hold in prayer. There is no hope of prevalence with God unless we abase ourselves that He may exalt us in due time.

It was filial prayer. "Abba, Father." You will find it a stronghold in the day of trial to plead your adoption. You have no rights as a subject, you have forfeited them by your treason; but nothing can forfeit a child's right to a father's protection. Be not afraid to say, "My Father, hear my cry."

Observe that it was persevering prayer. He prayed three times. Cease not until you prevail. Be as the importunate widow, whose continual coming earned what her first supplication could not win. Continue in prayer, and watch in the same with thanksgiving.

Lastly, it was the prayer of resignation. "Nevertheless, not as I will, but as thou wilt." Yield, and God yields. Let it be as God wills, and God will determine for the best. Be thou content to leave thy prayer in His hands, who knows when to give, and how to give, and what to give, and what to withhold. So pleading earnestly, importunately, yet with humility and resignation, thou shalt surely prevail.

ASSUMING A PROMISE *by Ken Abraham*

". . .What he had promised, he was able also to perform."
ROMANS 4:21

*A*braham assumed he was walking in the center of God's will for his life. But by taking things into his own hands, Abraham was soon to learn one of the most difficult lessons a child of God can learn. God let him wander in the wilderness of his own mistakes for the next thirteen years! Abraham was eighty-six years old at the conception of Ishmael, and the Bible does not mention that God spoke to him again until he was ninety-nine (Genesis 17:1).

For thirteen years, it seemed to Abraham that the heavens were brass. Worse still, during that entire time, Abraham probably thought he was in the will of God! How painful it must have been for him to discover that he had been so deluded.

God was teaching Abraham an important lesson: When a child of God takes things into his or her own hands and attempts to manipulate people, relationships or situations, God will allow him to do it. He may not even say a word. Then He will allow His child to struggle through the darkness and foolishness he or she has created.

Thankfully, God's grace is greater than our foolishness and He is able to clean up the messes we make. If you have learned the lesson God has been trying to teach you through delays and detours, you will probably be more than ready to listen to him the next time He speaks. That's what happened in Abraham's life, and the next word he received from God was the promise that within a year their long awaited son would be born. . .and God kept His promise.

He will keep His promises to you.

JUNE 17TH

CHARIOTS OF SALVATION *by Hannah Whitall Smith*

". . .Who maketh the clouds his chariots. . ." PSALM 104:3

The Bible tells us that when God went forth for the salvation of His people, then He "did ride upon His horses and chariots of salvation." And it is the same now. Everything becomes a "chariot of salvation" when God rides upon it. He maketh even the "clouds his chariot," we are told, and "rideth on the wings of the wind." Therefore the clouds and storms that darken our skies and seem to shut out the shining of the sun of righteousness are really only God's chariots, into which we may mount with Him, and "ride prosperously" over all the darkness. Dear reader, have you made the clouds in your life the chariots? Are you "riding prosperously" with God on top of them all?

DRAW NIGH TO GOD *by Leonard Ravenhill*

"Draw nigh to God, and he will draw nigh to you. . ."
JAMES 4:8

Nearness presupposes a mutual confidence. In the spiritual realm nearness means love, and love is based on confidence. In its very nature, love draws towards someone, and in so doing draws away from others. Since humans are not omnipresent, they have to choose their company. We must either draw nigh to men and so draw away from God, or draw nigh to God and away from men. The choice, though not easy, is always ours. To the prayer closet, there is no conscription, but there is a constraint, a constraint of love. We may as well "settle" this once and for all—there are no short cuts to the high peaks of spirituality, and no ski lifts. One does not need to be an anchorite to live on "heaven's tableland," but there must be a practiced withdrawing. Love is an isolationist. Love has a supreme lover.

OTHER GODS *by John Henry Jowett*

"Thou shalt have no other gods before me." EXODUS 20:3

If we kept that commandment all the other commandments would be obeyed. If we secure this queenbee we are given the swarm. To put nothing "before" God! What is left in the circle of obedience? God first, always and everywhere. Nothing allowed to usurp His throne for an hour! I was once allowed to sit on an earthly throne for a few seconds, but even that is not to be allowed with the throne of God. Nothing is to share His sovereignty, even for a moment. His dominion is to be unconditional and unbroken. "Thou shalt have no other gods beside Me."

But we have many gods we set upon His throne. We put money there, and fame, and pleasure, and ease. Yes, we sometimes usurp God's throne, and we ourselves dare to sit there for days, and weeks, and years, at a time. Self is the idol, and we enthrone it, and we fall down and worship it. But no peace comes from such sovereignty, and no deep and vital joy. For the real King is not dead, and He is out and about, and our poor little monarchy is as the reign of the midge on a summer's night. Our real kingship is in the acknowledgment of the King of kings. When we worship Him, and Him only, He will ask us to sit on His throne.

JUNE 20TH

KNOWING HIM *by Malcolm Smith*

"My flesh and my heart faileth: but God is the strength of my heart, and my portion forever."　　　PSALM 73:26

The uninhibited worship of God involved every physical and emotional sense. The vast choirs and orchestras moved the soul Godward, and there were moments when time and space seemed to be swallowed up by eternity. But the thrill of God's presence cannot be confused with the experience of knowing Him in covenant relationship. God ordained the choirs and the music, but not as a substitute for knowing Him. . .they were meant to be an expression of a relationship with Him.

169

Praise is not a heavenly drug to deaden the pain of life. It is because we know God that, in the midst of the hurts of life, we can praise Him. Our relationship with God is primarily a faith response, which is often contrary to appearances and feelings. Our life is founded upon Who God is, not upon how we may feel about Him today.

JUNE 21ST

HIS LOVING-KINDNESS *by Charles H. Spurgeon*

"With lovingkindness have I drawn thee."   JEREMIAH 31:3

The thunders of the laws and the terrors of judgment are all used to bring us to Christ; but the final victory is effected by loving-kindness. The prodigal set out to his father's house from a sense of need; but his father saw him a great way off, and ran to meet him; so that the last steps he took towards his father's house were with the kiss still warm upon his cheek, and the welcome still musical in his ears.

> Law and terrors do but harden
>   All the while they work alone;
> But a sense of blood-bought pardon
>   Will dissolve a heart of stone.

The Master came one night to the door, and knocked with the iron hand of the law; the door shook and trembled upon its hinges; but the man piled every piece of furniture which he could find against the door, for he said, "I will not admit the man." The Master turned away, but by-and-by He came back, and with His own soft hand, using most that part where the nail had penetrated, He knocked again—oh, so softly and tenderly. This time the door did not shake, but, strange to say, it opened, and there upon his knees the once unwilling host was found rejoicing to receive his guest. "Come in, come in; thou hast so knocked that my bowels are moved for thee. I could not think of thy pierced hand leaving its blood-mark on my door, and of thy going away houseless, 'Thy head filled with dew, and thy locks with the drops of the night.' I yield, I yield, Thy love has won my heart." So in every case; loving-kindness wins the day. What Moses with the tablets of stone could never do Christ does with His pierced hand.

JUNE 22ND

THE KINGDOM OF GOD *by Henry Drummond*

"Behold, the kingdom of God is within you."   LUKE 17:21

*T*ens of thousands of persons who are familiar with religious truths have not noticed yet that Christ never founded a Society at all. The reason is partly that people have read texts instead of reading their Bible, partly that they have studied Theology instead of studying Christianity and partly because of the noiselessness and invisibility of the Kingdom of God itself. Nothing truer was ever said of this Kingdom than "It cometh without observation." Its first discovery, therefore, comes to the Christian with all the force of a revelation. The sense of belonging to such a Society transforms life. It is the difference between being a solitary knight tilting single-handed, and often defeated, at whatever enemy one chances to meet on one's little acres of life, and the feel of belonging to a mighty army marching throughout all time to a certain victory. This note of universality given to even the humblest

171

work we do, this sense of comradeship, this link with history, this thought of a definite campaign, this promise of success, is the possession of every obscurest unit in the Kingdom of God.

LOVE NEVER FAILS *by Jill Briscoe*

"Love never fails."   1 CORINTHIANS 13:8 NIV

*L*ove cannot keep quiet. It has to tell of its love! The King of Hearts in Proverbs 31 praised his wife. He loved his Queen so thoroughly, he delighted to tell her so, and He delights to tell us so.

Our heavenly King of Hearts is tender and sweet and precious. He knows how to make us feel like a million dollars when people tell us we're not worth a penny. He's written us a very long and beautiful love letter. It's called the Bible. What's more, we don't have to earn anything for His favor. We don't have to charm Him, or pretend we are something we're not, so He will like us. We don't have to compete with other women for His attention, either. All we have to do is be still and know that He is God. Just be still enough—long enough—to be loved by His everlasting love. The love of God is shed abroad in a Queen of Hearts' heart by the Holy Spirit, which is given unto us. "I love you; I love you; I love you"; the Spirit of the king whispers—and this when others are shouting, "I hate you! I hate you! I hate you!"

A MAN IN DISTRESS *by Charles Dickens*

"Hear me when I call, O God of my righteousness: thou hast enlarged me when I was in distress; have mercy upon me, and hear my prayer." PSALM 4:1

"*T*here was once a Man", he told them, "who had two sons: and the younger of them said one day, 'Father, give me my share of your riches now, and let me do with it what I please?' The father granting his request, he travelled away with his money into a distant country, and soon spent it in riotous living.

"When he had spent all, there came a time, through all that country, of great public distress and famine, when there was no bread, and when the corn, and the grass, and all the things that grow in the ground were all dried up and blighted. The Prodigal Son fell into such distress and hunger, that he hired himself out as a servant to feed swine in the fields. And he would have been glad to eat, even the poor coarse husks that the swine were fed with, but his Master gave him none. In this distress, he said to himself, 'How many of my father's servants have bread enough, and to spare, while I perish with hunger! I will arise and go to my father, and will say unto him, 'Father! I have sinned against Heaven, and before thee, and am no more worthy to be called Thy Son!'

"And so he travelled back again, in great pain and sorrow and difficulty, to his father's house. When he was yet a great way off, his father saw him, and knew him in the midst of all his rags and misery, and ran towards him, and wept, and fell upon his neck, and kissed him. And he told his servants to clothe this poor repentant son in the best robes, and to make a great feast to celebrate his return. Which was done and they began to be merry."

CARING AND SHARING *by Hannah Hurnard*

"Beloved, let us love one another: for love is of God; and every one that loveth is born of God, and knoweth God."
1 JOHN 4:7

*L*ove can never rest until real peace, which is perfect harmony with the law of love, is brought to the hearts of all men everywhere. This is the impelling incentive and motive for all witness and all the ministry of love in which you are being trained. For love must share with others or die. It must give to others all that it receives or it cannot remain love. Love can only live in your heart as it propagates itself by sharing.

THE PEACEMAKER *by Charles Dickens*

"Now the LORD of peace himself give you peace always by all means. . . ."
2 THESSALONIANS 3:16

*J*esus Christ went down to the waterside, to go in a boat, to a more retired place. And in the boat, He fell asleep, while His Disciples were sitting on the deck. While He was still sleeping a violent storm arose, so that the waves washed over the boat and the howling wind so rocked and shook it, that they thought it would sink. In their fright the disciples awoke Our Saviour, and said "Lord! Save us, or we are lost!" He stood up, and raising His arm, said to the rolling Sea and to the whistling wind, "Peace! Be still!"

And immediately it was calm and pleasant weather, and the boat went safely on, through the smooth waters.

MOONLESS TRUST *by Elisabeth Elliot*

"And they that know thy name will put their trust in thee: for thou, LORD, hast not forsaken them that seek thee."

PSALM 9:10

*S*ome of you are perhaps feeling that you are voyaging just now on a moonless sea. Uncertainty surrounds you. There seem to be no signs to follow. Perhaps you feel about to be engulfed by loneliness. Amy Carmichael wrote of such a feeling when. . .she had to leave Japan because of poor health. (This preceded her going to India, where she stayed for fifty-three years.) "All along, let us remember, we are not asked to understand, but simply to obey. . .We had come on board on Friday night, and just as the tender (a small boat) where were the dear friends who had come to say goodbye was moving off, and the chill of loneliness shivered through me, like a warm love-clasp came the long-loved lines—'And only Heaven is better than to walk with Christ at midnight, over moonless seas.' I couldn't feel frightened then. Praise Him for the moonless seas—all the better the opportunity for proving Him to be indeed the El Shaddai, 'the God who is Enough.' "

Let me add my own word of witness to hers and to that of the tens of thousands who have learned that He is indeed Enough. He is not all we would ask (if we were honest), but it is precisely when we do not have what we would ask for, and *only then*, that we can clearly perceive His all-sufficiency. It is when the sea is moonless that the Lord has become my Light.

175

THE PLACE OF PRIVILEGE *by Hannah Whitall Smith*

"The Lord is my rock, and my fortress, and my deliverer; my God, my strength, in whom I will trust; my buckler, and the horn of my salvation, and my high tower."

PSALM 18:2

*B*etter and sweeter than health, or friends, or money, or fame, or ease, or prosperity, is the adorable will of our God. It gilds the darkest hours with a divine halo, and sheds brightest sunshine on the gloomiest paths. He always reigns who has made it his kingdom, and nothing can go amiss to him. Surely, then, it is only a glorious privilege that is opening before you when I tell you that the first step you must take in order to enter into the life hid with Christ in God is that of entire consecration. I beg of you not to look at it as a hard and stern demand. You must do it gladly, thankfully, enthusiastically. You must go in on what I call the privilege side of consecration; and I can assure you, from the universal testimony of all who have tried it, that you will find it the happiest place you have ever entered yet.

A LIFETIME OF FRIENDSHIP
by James Dobson as told to Gloria Gaither

"And these words, . . .shall be in thine heart: And thou shalt teach them diligently unto thy children. . .when thou sittest in thine house. . .when thou walkest by the way. . .when thou liest down. . .when thou risest up."

DEUTERONOMY 6:6, 7

The very happiest days of my growing up years occurred when I was between ten and thirteen years of age. My dad and I would rise very early before the sun came up on a wintry morning. We'd put on our hunting clothes and heavy boots and drive twenty miles. After parking the car and climbing over a fence, we entered a wooded area where we would slip down to the creek bed and follow the winding stream several miles back into the forest.

Then my dad would hide me under a fallen tree which made a little room with its branches. He would find a similar shelter for himself around a bend in the creek. My dad and I were then ready to watch as the breathtaking panorama of the morning unfolded and spoke so eloquently of the God who made all things.

Most important was what occurred out there in the forest between my dad and me. The intense love and affection generated on those mornings set the tone for a lifetime of friendship. There was a closeness and a oneness that made me want to be like that man. . .that made me choose his values as my values, his dreams as my dreams, his God as my God.

James C. Dobson, Sr. was a man of many intense loves. His greatest passion was his love for Jesus Christ. His every thought and deed were influenced by his desire to serve his

177

Lord. And I can truthfully say that we were never together without my being drawn closer to God by simply being in my dad's presence.

WHEN GOD SAYS "THANK YOU" *by Jill Briscoe*

"His lord said unto him, 'Well done, thou good and faithful servant: thou hast been faithful over a few things, I will make thee ruler over many things: enter thou into the joy of thy lord.' " MATTHEW 25:21

$\mathcal{M}$ost of our lives we concentrate on the fact that we must affirm our faith in God and appreciate Him. It's quite different to think of God affirming His faith in us, and appreciating us. It's a new concept for many of us that He can be pleased with us at all! But it's a good concept! Once a human being has been on his knees and felt the hand of God upon his head in praise, he will never be the same again. There is nothing that makes you feel quite so loved, warm and complete as when God says, "Thank you." No matter if all the world rejects you—His word of affirmation is enough. We must learn to live our lives looking for that word.

JULY

THE HIRED MAN *by William Quale*

"Sing forth the honour of his name: make his praise glorious. All the earth shall worship thee, and shall sing unto thee; they shall sing to thy name." PSALM 66:2, 4

*J*uly is the farmer of the year. Stalwart, singing like a plowboy, working like an owner of a farm glad for the chance. July fairly tires a strong man out just by its tirelessness of toil. July doesn't grow fatigued; but you do, watching him. Everything leaps toward flower or fruit. Harvests yellow on plains and hill. Seen from afar the golden wheat fields with their thousand tents remind you of Heaven whose pavements are all of gold. Blackberries are ripe. Things grown in gardens are ready and make your mouth water. Then wild iris blooms in marshy places. Mourning doves drift along the fields in company, father, mother, children all out for an evening's frolic. The wheat fields are peopled with farmer folk loading the wheat for stacking or thrashing. In July, the days are hot but arduous. Things are doing when July rolls up his sleeves, but his toiling is as the toiling of the happy heart. No peevish scolding, no querulous fault-finding, only a radiant joy of having work to do and rejoicing in the doing of it.

PRAYING IS A FORM OF WORK
by Mrs. Charles E. Cowman

"Men ought always to pray, and not to faint." LUKE 18:1

*T*hat little "ought" is emphatic. It implies obligation as high as heaven. Jesus said, "Men ought always to pray," and added, "and not to faint."

I confess I do not always feel like praying—when, judging by my feelings, there is no one listening to my prayer. And then these words have stirred me to pray:

> *I ought to pray—*
> *I ought always to pray—*
> *I should not grow faint in praying.*

"Praying is a form of work. The farmer ploughs his field often when he does not feel like it, but he confidently expects a crop for his labors. Now, if prayer is a form of work, and our labor is not in vain in the Lord, should we not pray regardless of feelings? Once when I knelt for morning prayers I felt a sort of deadness in my soul, and just then the "accuser of the brethren" became busy reminding me of things that had long since been under the Blood. I cried to God for help, and the blessed Comforter reminded me that my Great High Priest was pleading my case; that I must come boldly to the throne of grace. I did, and the enemy was routed! Had I fainted instead of fighting I could not have received wages because I had not labored fervently in prayer; I could not have reaped because I had not sown."

The late Commissioner
SAMUEL LOGAN BRENGLE

THE HABIT OF WAITING *by A. B. Simpson*

"But they that wait upon the LORD shall renew their strength; they shall mount up with wings as eagles; they shall run, and not be weary; and they shall walk, and not faint."   ISAIAH 40:31

*W*ait on the Lord. How often this is said in the Bible; how little understood! It is what the old monk called the "practice of the presence of God." It is the habit of prayer. It is the continual communion that not only asks, but receives. People often ask us to pray for them and we have to say, "Why, God has answered our prayer for you; now you must take the answer. It is awaiting you, and you must take it by waiting on the Lord."

It is this that renews our strength until we "mount up with wings as eagles, run and are not weary, walk and are not faint." Our hearts are too limited to take in His fullness at a single breath. We must live in the atmosphere of His presence till we absorb His very life. This is the secret of spiritual depth and rest, of power and fullness, of love and prayer, of hope and holy usefulness. Wait, I say, on the Lord.

I am waiting in communion at the blessed mercy seat;
I am waiting, sweetly waiting on the Lord;
I am drinking of His fullness; I am sitting at His feet;
I am hearkening to the whispers of His Word.

JULY 4TH

ACTS OF FREEDOM *by Brother Lawrence*

"Now the Lord is that Spirit: and where the Spirit of the Lord is, there is liberty."   2 Corinthians 3:17

*W*hen we are faithful to keep ourselves in His holy presence, and set Him always before us, this not only hinders our offending Him and doing anything that may displease Him, at least wilfully, but it also begets in us a holy freedom, and, if I may so speak a familiarity with God, wherewith we ask, and that successfully, the graces we stand in need of. In time, by often repeating these acts, they become habitual, and the presence of God rendered as it were natural to us. Give Him thanks, if you please, with me, for His great goodness toward me, which I can never sufficiently admire, for the many favors He has done to so miserable a sinner as I am. May all things praise Him. Amen.

JULY 5TH

RELIGIOUS FREEDOM *by Charles G. Finney*

"For ye have not received the spirit of bondage again to fear; but ye have received the Spirit of adoption, whereby we cry, Abba, Father."   ROMANS 8:15

I had in fact oftentimes experienced inexpressible joys, and very deep communion with God; but all this had fallen so into the shade, under my enlarged experience, that frequently I would tell the Lord that I had never before had any

182

conception of the wonderful things revealed in his blessed Gospel, and the wonderful grace there is in Christ Jesus.

As the great excitement of that season subsided, and my mind became more calm, I saw more clearly the different steps of my Christian experience, and came to recognize the connection of things, as all wrought by God from beginning to end. I can come to God with more calmness, because with more perfect confidence He enables me now to rest in Him, and let everything sink into His perfect will.

I have felt since then a religious freedom, a religious buoyancy and delight in God, and in His word, a steadiness of faith, a Christian liberty and overflowing love, that I had only experienced, I may say, occasionally before. My bondage seemed to be at that time, entirely broken; and since then, I have had the freedom of a child with a loving parent. It seems to me that I can find God within me, in such a sense, that I can rest upon Him and be quiet, lay my heart in His hand, and nestle down in His perfect will, and have no anxiety.

JULY 6TH

GOD NEVER VIOLATES OUR FREEDOM OF CHOICE *by A. W. Tozer*

". . .And whosover will, let him take the water of life freely."
Revelation 22:17

$\mathcal{I}$t is inherent in the nature of man that his will must be free. Made in the image of God who is completely free, man must enjoy a measure of freedom. This enables him to select his companions for this world and the next; it enables him to yield his soul to whom he will, to give allegiance to God or the devil.

And God respects this freedom. God once saw everything that He had made, and behold, it was very good. To find fault with the smallest thing God has made is to find fault with its Maker. It is a false humility that would lament that God wrought but imperfectly when He made man in His own image. When accepted, there is nothing in human nature to apologize for. This was confirmed forever when the Eternal Son became permanently incarnated in human flesh!

So highly does God regard His handiwork that He will not for any reason violate it. He will take nine steps toward us but He will not take the tenth. He will incline us to repent, but He cannot do our repenting for us. It is of the essence of repentance that it can only be done by the one who committed the act to be repented of. God can wait on the sinning man, He can withhold judgment, He can exercise long-suffering to the point where He appears lax in His judicial administration—but He cannot force a man to repent. To do this would be to violate the man's freedom and void the gift of God originally bestowed upon him. The believer knows he is free to choose —and with that knowledge he chooses forever the blessed will of God!

JULY 7TH

LIVING WITH YOUR DREAMS *by Ken Abraham*

"Delight thyself also in the LORD; and he shall give thee the desires of thine heart." PSALM 37:4

I can almost hear you saying, "Oh, yeah? If that's so, then what's the problem?"

In his book, *Living With Your Dreams,* Dr. David Seamands explains:

Our dreams, aspirations, and visions are often God-given

and are one of His ways of communicating with us. Through them He wants to develop and use our uniqueness and gifts to accomplish His purposes.

But those dreams can become mixed with our own pride, selfishness, immaturity and sin, and need to be purified, tested, matured, refined, and sometimes even refashioned.

Furthermore, in this fallen, imperfect world these dreams are often interrupted, broken, shattered, and unfulfilled. This can happen through the sins and choices of others, events and circumstances over which we have no control, our own sins and wrong choices, or by a combination of these factors.

When this happens God does not want us to abandon those dreams, but will lovingly work with us to refine our unrealistic dreams, to restore our broken dreams, to realize our delayed dreams, and to redesign our shattered dreams so both His purposes and our dreams can be fulfilled.

JULY 8TH

REVISITING OLD ALTARS *by John Henry Jowett*

"I will make there an altar unto God, who answered me in the day of my distress . . ."   GENESIS 35:3

*J*t is a blessed thing to revisit our early altars. It is good to return to the haunts of early vision. Places and things have their sanctifying influences, and can recall us to lost experiences. I know a man to whom the scent of a white, wild rose is always a call to prayer. I know another to whom Grasmere is always the window of holy vision. Sometimes a particular pew in a particular church can throw the heavens open, and we see the Son of God. The old Sunday-school has sometimes taken an old man back to his childhood and back to his God.

So I do not wonder that God led Jacob back to Bethel, and that in the old place of blessing he reconsecrated himself to the Lord.

It is a revelation of the loving-kindness of God that we have all these helps to the recovery of past experiences. Let us use them with reverence. And in our early days let us make them. Let us build altars of communion which in later life we shall love to revisit. Let us make our early home "the house of God and the gate of heaven." Let us multiply deeds of service which will make countless places fragrant for all our after years.

JULY 9TH

BUILDING MONUMENTS AGAINST FORGETFULNESS *by Jack Hayford*

". . .Ye shall pass over this Jordan, to go in to possess the land, . . .remember the word which Moses the servant of the LORD commanded you, saying, 'The LORD your God hath given you rest, and hath given you this land.' "

JOSHUA 1:11, 13

Joshua placed a monument in the river—a pillar that would require all who passed that way to acknowledge, "They really did pass through Jordan!"

The evidence was there. This was no random pile of boulders stacked by the flood. The stonework was large and arranged to rise above the waters at any season, eloquently declaring, "The waters are never too deep. God can take you through!" It brings to mind a promise we all can receive as surely as those in that ancient day:

"When you pass through the waters, I will be with you;

186

And through the rivers, they shall not overflow you. When you walk through the fire, you shall not be burned, nor shall the flame scorch you" (Isaiah 43:2).

The pillars in Jordan and at Gilgal picture a beginning discipline to frame tomorrow, to close in our focus on the practical disciplines that will bring our tomorrows into our todays.

1. Build your own monuments against forgetfulness!
2. Build them for yourself, and build them for your children.
3. Build them for any others God lets you tell.

Building monuments can be done in the simplest ways, even including monuments erected just for your own remembering.

JULY 10TH

GOD WANTS IN ON OUR VACATION *by Jack Hayford*

"The law of truth was in his mouth, and iniquity was not found in his lips: he walked with me in peace and equity..."
MALACHI 2:6

*S*everal years ago, we were provided a week at a beach house for our family's vacation use. It was during those days on the Pacific shore that I arose one morning with a sense of emptiness. That "sense" became an unforgettable occasion of God's reminding me how much I need an intimate, daily walk with Him.

The days "away" had become so relaxed and filled with loving and fulfilling family activity, I had neglected my private devotions. The feeling of "emptiness" struck me about the third day. At first I was puzzled, wondering why such a lovely time suddenly was seeming so hollow with all the enjoyment the family was experiencing. That's when I suddenly realized, "God wants in on our vacation!"

At dinner, that evening, we joined in a happy time of prayer and songful worship. The next day I woke quite early and, sensing His instruction to do so, took a walk with Him on the beach.

There was a moving sense of His presence as I strode through the sand. I was very aware of a Companion who cares so tenderly for His own that He will allow an emptiness to come to our souls if we forget Him—however inadvertently.

Some distance down the beach, I turned away from the sea and began to retrace my path. While hiking along, my eyes fell on a rail spike, lying by the side of the track. I picked it up and took it home, thinking to myself, "I want to remember this day and its lesson—to 'nail' it in my mind unforgettably, forever."

I still have that spike. To this day it is a holy reminder of a precious vacation with our family and a tender experience with God. It's a monument—a constant reminder of His desire for an intimate walk with me and my commitment to an intimate walk with Him.

CREATIVITY AND PRAYER *by Edith Schaeffer*

"Honour and majesty are before him: strength and beauty are in his sanctuary. . . . Let the heavens rejoice, and let the earth be glad; let the sea roar, and the fulness thereof. Let the field be joyful, and all that is therein: then shall all the trees of the wood rejoice." PSALM 96:6, 11, 12

GOD THE CREATOR

You have shown by what you have made and done
    how the world has been planned from eternity.
The earth is your creation, Lord,
    yours that are true to every generation
    just when you judge,
    your strength and splendor a marvel.
Such competence yours in creating,
    such skill in setting firm the things you make,
    your goodness apparent in this world we see
You are loyal to those who trust you,
    merciful, compassionate.

*P*eople are meant to understand something of God—the Artist, the Creator of beauty to be enjoyed—meant to understand that He has communicated and does communicate through His creation, as well as through His Word.

Look around you. Are you on a farm plowing? Are you in a city with a lake or a park? Do you have a tiny garden or a large one with sprouts of tulips or vegetables piercing up from the earth? Can you see the sky when the stars come out? Have you a place where you can watch the sunset sky with a new moon appearing in the midst of fading apricot which had just been blazing?

In variety of color, texture, fragrances, shapes, and sizes of everything from the tropical fruits, flowers, birds, and trees of Jamaica to the totally different ones of Alaska, God has shown His goodness and love in providing things for people's enjoyment, as well as for their food, clothing, and raw materials for their own creativity.

JULY 12TH

THIS IS MY FATHER'S WORLD *by Kenneth W. Osbeck*

"The heavens declare the glory of God; and the firmament sheweth his handywork. Day unto day uttereth speech, and night unto night sheweth knowledge."　　PSALM 19:1, 2

*E*ven though we are constantly reminded of the violence, tragedy, and ugliness in today's world, we can still rejoice that the beauty of nature all around is ours to enjoy.

Maltbie D. Babcock revealed his great admiration for nature in his lovely hymn, "This Is My Father's World." Although he was recognized as one of the outstanding Presbyterian ministers of his generation, Dr. Babcock was also a skilled athlete who enjoyed all outdoor activity, especially his early morning walks. He would always comment, "I'm going out to see my Father's world." Since Dr. Babcock was an accomplished performer on the organ, the piano and the violin, we can see why nature seemed to him to be "the music of the spheres."

This is my Father's world,
　　And to my list'ning ears,
All nature sings, and round me rings

The music of the spheres.
This is my Father's world!
I rest me in the thought
Of rocks and trees, of skies and seas—
His hand the wonders wrought.

This is my Father's world
O let me ne'er forget
That though the wrong seems oft so strong,
God is the Ruler yet.
This is my Father's world!
The battle is not done,
Jesus who died shall be satisfied,
And earth and heav'n be one.

JULY 13TH

IN THE VALLEY, I DREAM AND PRAY
by Fanny Crosby/Bernard Ruffin

"But I have trusted in thy mercy; my heart shall rejoice in thy salvation. I will sing unto the LORD, because he hath dealt bountifully with me."   PSALM 13:5, 6

*F*anny Crosby penned the following poem:

I walked through the world with the worldly.
I craved what the world never gave,
And I said, "In the world, each ideal
That shines like a star on life's wave
Is tossed on the shores of the Real,
And sleeps like a dream in its grave. . . ."

And still did I pine for the Perfect,
   Yet still found the false with the true,
And sought, 'mid the human, for heaven,
   But caught a mere glimpse of the blue,
And I wept where the clouds of the mortal
   Veiled even that glimpse from my view.

And I toiled on, heart-tired of human,
   And I moaned, 'mid the masses of men,
Until I knelt long at an altar
   And heard a voice call me—since then
I have walked down the Valley of Silence
   That is far beyond mortal ken.

Do you ask what I found in this Valley?
   'Tis my trysting place with the Divine,
For I fell at the feet of the Holy,
   And above me a voice said, "Be mine."
And there rose from the depth of my spirit,
   The echo, "My heart shall be Thine."

She concluded:

Do you ask how I live in this Valley?
   I weep and I dream and I pray;
But my tears are so sweet as the dewdrops
   That fall from the roses in May,
And my prayer, like a perfume from censers,
   Ascendeth to God night and day.

192

MY SOUL HAS FOUND A RESTING PLACE
by Vance Havner

" . . .*My presence shall go with thee, and I will give thee rest.*"   EXODUS 33:14

*W*e can take a vacation within if not one without. You need not seek rest in the mountains or by the sea if you do not have it in your heart. You cannot get away from it all if you carry it all with you. Paul did not end his days basking in a village by the sea writing his memoirs. He was awaiting an executioner's axe but his heart was at rest. He carried a portable chapel within and there he withdrew to renew his strength. So did our Lord who had no place to lay His head. You too must find that retreat within for no earthly hideaway can give you rest without. Take your vacation all along and when your life is hid with Christ in God you learn in whatever state you are to be content, gloriously independent of time or place. As Madam Guyon put it:

> To me remains nor place nor time;
>   My country is in every clime:
> I can be calm and free from care
>   On any shore, since God is there.

GOD'S CREATION *by Edith Schaeffer*

"O LORD our Lord, how excellent is thy name in all the earth! who hast set thy glory above the heavens. . . . When I consider thy heavens, the work of thy fingers, the moon and the stars, which thou hast ordained; What is man, that thou art mindful of him?" PSALM 8:1, 3, 4

*G*od has communicated in His written Word, the Bible, and it remains fresh and gives deeper understanding as we read and reread, but as He has told us that His creation communicates His glory to us, His revelation also never comes to an end. We are to search for more understanding and appreciation of who our Redeemer is, who our Eternal God is, as we walk through woods with a friend or with children, as we ski over fresh powder snow mountains, or as we walk along a sandy beach or sit on a rock and examine a beautiful insect or a wildflower.

Just as in an art museum we are to enjoy the work of an artist and be glad that Rembrandt painted as he did or that Mary Cassatt's paintings of mothers and children delight us as they do, we are also to search for understanding of the artist. Just so, God's creation is to be enjoyed, but we are to be sensitive to the reality of what we are finding out about Him, the way we are getting to know Him.

The making of human beings with a capacity for creativity was not an accident, but a glorious creation which could bring a two-way communication, a response to what God has given so generously and lovingly to be enjoyed. The heart of man, the heart of woman, the hearts of children, had people not been blinded by selfishness and sin, would overflow with thankfulness in every form that fertile imaginations could express it! Worship and adoration of the magnificent Creator would have been spontaneous, had it not been so horribly spoiled.

I WILL SING! *by Jack Hayford*

"Sing forth the honour of his name: make his praise glorious. . . . All the earth shall worship thee, and shall sing unto thee; they shall sing to they name." PSALM 66:2, 4

*T*he word "psalm" actually means "song," originally referring to one sung to the accompaniment of a psaltery, an ancient stringed instrument. Psalm-singing was important from the very beginning of Christianity, especially to express the sheer exuberance and joy Christians experience: "Is anyone cheerful? Let him sing psalms" (James 5:13).

Part of the power of song is that it is a beautiful expression of devotion both for the solitary worshiper at private devotions, at work or in the car, and for the congregation gathered for public worship. People can make no more expressive sounds than in song. Singing releases the pent-up joy and thanksgiving we feel because of God's grace and goodness; so the psalmist sings, "To You, O my Strength, I will sing praises" (Psalm 59:17).

You say you don't have a good voice? You don't know music? Both can be developed but never without "singing anyway"! Remember, *God* likes your voice; and even if you never learn to carry a tune, use it. You carry around with you the most important instrument for singing: *your heart.* Make melody in and with it!

FAIREST LORD JESUS! *by Kenneth W. Osbeck*

"For by him were all things created, that are in heaven, and that are in earth, visible and invisible, whether they be thrones, or dominions, or principalities, or powers: all things were created by him, and for him." COLOSSIANS 1:16

Fairest Lord Jesus! Ruler of all nature!
O Thou of God and man the Son!
Thee will I cherish, Thee will I honor,
Thou my soul's glory, joy, and crown!

Fair are the meadows, Fairer still the woodlands,
Robed in the blooming garb of spring;
Jesus is fairer, Jesus is purer,
Who makes the woeful heart to sing!
Fair is the sunshine, Fairer still the moonlight,
And all the twinkling starry host:
Jesus shines brighter, Jesus shines purer,
Than all the angels heav'n can boast!

Beautiful Savior! Lord of all the nations!
Son of God and Son of Man!
Glory and honor, praise, adoration,
Now and forevermore be Thine!

*T*his lovely hymn extolling the beauty and virtues of Christ leads us to the praise and worship of our "beautiful Savior." The vivid comparisons of all the enjoyable sights of nature with Jesus, who is the very source and essence of all beauty, fill us with awe. Then we are reminded that our

Savior outshines all creations of God, including the hosts of angels.

Whatever the actual origin of the hymn may be, Christians for centuries have been blessed with this worshipful and joyful text, which focuses our view on the fair Son of God who reveals to us the glory of the Father.

JULY 18TH

THE HILLS ON WHICH I NEED TO GAZE
by Ruth Bell Graham

"I will praise thee, O LORD, with my whole heart: I will shew forth all thy marvellous works. I will be glad and rejoice in thee: I will sing praise to thy name, O thou most High."
PSALM 9:1, 2

I climbed the hill
        through yesterday:
and I am young
        and strong again;
my children climb
        these hills with me,
and all the time
        they shout and play;
their laughter fills
        the coves among
the rhododendron and the oak
        till we have struggled to
the ridge top
        where the chestnuts grew.
Breathless, tired, and content
        we let the mountain

breeze blow through
    our busy minds
and through our hair
    refresh our bodies hot and spent
and drink
    from some cool mountain spring,
the view refreshing everything—
    Infinity, with hill between,
silent, hazy, wild-serene.
    Then. . .
when I return to now
    I pray,
"Thank You, God,
    for yesterday."

JULY 19TH

FAMILY LIFE *by Edith Schaeffer*

*"Lo, children are an heritage of the LORD: and the fruit of
the womb is his reward."*   PSALM 127:3

*F*amily life is a lost art in many places today. People may
live in the same house, apartment, cottage, condominium, boat,
or cabin, but they have no pattern for a growing life togther.
A home, a family, should provide an appreciative audience
for encouragement in drawing, painting, sculpting, smoking
meat, cooking, gardening, playing instruments, and com-
posing original music!

Family life is not necessarily sweetness and light all the
time in order to be good family life. Where originality and
creativity are being stimulated, very frequently you have

198

conflict of ideas and so freedom of choice needs to be understood. Two people cannot play the piano with two totally different kinds of music at the same time! Two people cannot clash with their drums and flutes or violins and horns playing wildly differing music in the same small living room with the family trying to listen with enjoyment. The meaning of freedom and compassion, of my rights and another person's rights in other areas of life, can be discussed better in the midst of a vivid musical illustration! Music as a part of family life can be used to point out what harmony sounds like and what clashing discord sounds like.

Life is too short to spend days, weeks, or months throwing away beauty. Yes—an evening is too short to lose—but "family life" is the tragic loss for those who have thrown it away.

Not only is music a help to family life and to the relationships developing between parents and children, brothers and sisters, cousins, aunts and uncles, and friends, but one generation should be handing down knowledge and love from one generation to the next.

JULY 20TH

THE FAMILY WAS DESIGNED BY GOD
by Dr. James Dobson

"Children's children are the crown of old men; and the glory of children are their fathers."　　　PROVERBS 17:6

*T*he family was designed by God Almighty to have a specific purpose and function: when it operates as intended, the emotional and physical needs of husbands, wives, and children are met in a beautiful relationship of symbiotic love. But when that function is inhibited or destroyed, then every member of the family experiences the discomfort of unmet needs. That is my message. When the family conforms to God's blueprint, then self-esteem is available for everyone—which satisfies romantic aspirations—which abolishes loneliness, isolation, and boredom—which contributes to sexual fulfillment—which binds the marriage together in fidelity—which provides security for children—which gives parents a sense of purpose—which contributes to self-esteem once more. The chain has no weak links. It reveals the beauty of God's own creation, as does the rest of his universe.

JULY 21ST

PASSION AND WONDER
by Joni Eareckson Tada as told to Gloria Gaither

"Hear, ye children, the instruction of a father, and attend to know understanding."   PROVERBS 4:1

*M*usic and art were especially sacred in our family. It was not uncommon to sit around the dinner table after dessert and sing a few old hymns. Even weekend trips in the car were a treat as we invented beautiful harmonies to help the miles pass quickly. I shall never forget sitting in the back seat of my mother's old Buick, near tears, thinking, "This is so beautiful . . .and I'm helping to make it sound this way." Sometimes I would simply stop singing just to listen. Somehow, we always knew that we were making music to the Lord.

WHAT DID MY PARENTS DO RIGHT?
by Gloria Gaither

"And ye shall teach them your children, speaking of them when thou sittest in thine house, and when thou walkest by the way, when thou liest down, and when thou risest up."
DEUTERONOMY 11:19

*W*hile teaching us to not take ourselves too seriously, my parents took us very seriously as human beings and as fellow Christians. In our home, we could ask any question without being belittled and question any answer without being condemned. But we could not say, "I can't." Failure was allowed, but we were always expected to try. I don't remember my parents ever talking down to us, but instead they included us in family decisions and important discussions. Daddy would say, "The Word promises that when two or three agree together touching any one thing, it shall be done, so let's agree together now about this need."

I don't remember my parents ever telling us to try to impress or conform to someone in the church or to do or not to do something because we were the preacher's kids. Instead, they often told us to "mind God no matter what happens," and they made it clear that if we were obedient in our commitment to God, they would stand by us even when others didn't understand us or agree. When peers in high school or college were making destructive choices, one of my greatest deterrents from wrong and encouragements toward right was my parents' trust. They believed in me and in my good judgment, and that trust was a treasure so precious that I didn't want to risk losing it.

To this day, my mother and sister are two of my dearest

friends, and there are days—especially when Bill and I have written a new song when my first impulse is to run and share it with Daddy. Somehow in God's eternal present tense, I know that Daddy is hearing the song waft its way through time and space to vibrate down the corridors of heaven. His eyes twinkle, and I hear him say, with a pleased grin, "That's good, Shug. The Lord is pleased and so am I."

JULY 23RD

REACH OUT AND TOUCH
by Gail and Gordon MacDonald

"My little children; let us not love in word, neither in tongue, but in deed and in truth."　　　1 JOHN 3:18

*C*atherine Booth, co-founder of the Salvation Army, was a remarkably sensitive person. And her discernment showed best in her relationship to William, her husband. In a letter written to him, she declares her intent that their home will always be a place sensitive to his needs and concerns:

"I am delighted; it makes me happy to hear you speak as you do about home. Yes, if you will seek home, love home, be happy at home, I will spend my energies in trying to make it a more than ordinary one; it shall, if my ability can do it, be a spot sunny and bright, pure and calm, refined and tender, a fit school in which to train immortal spirits for a holy and glorious heaven; a fit resting-place for a spirit pressed and anxious about public duties; but oh, I know it is easy to talk, I feel how liable I am to fall short; but it is well to purpose right, to aim high, to hope much; yes, we will make home to each other the brightest spot on earth, we will be tender, thoughtful, loving, and forbearing, will we not? Yes, we will."

These are the words of a woman who was reaching out to touch, who had looked within a man and found something to which she could minister.

DREAMER FOR THE KINGDOM
by Dr. Anthony Campolo as told to Gloria Gaither

"Her children arise up, and call her blessed; her husband also, and he praiseth her." PROVERBS 31:28

*S*he was a dreamer who never stopped dreaming. She was convinced that her life could count for Christ.

My mother had a way of minimizing my failures and accentuating my accomplishments. Over and over again she told me how proud she was of anything I did that had any value. I don't ever remember her saying, "You could have done better." Instead, she always made me feel that I had done more than had been expected of me. I would hear her tell her friends, "That boy of mine is really something. He doesn't have the advantages of most kids in this neighborhood, but look how well he's doing in school. Who would have guessed that my boy would be so successful?"

Every day as I left the house, the last thing she would say to me was, "Remember! You can go over the top for Jesus!" We joked about that, but the last conversation I had with her before she died ended with those exact words. My mother made me feel special. She made me feel that I could do great things. She convinced me that, with Jesus, any limitations in my background could be overcome. In her eyes, I was the greatest child who ever lived, and that faith in me was one of her greatest gifts.

GOD IS ENOUGH *by Hannah Whitall Smith*

"Train up a child in the way he should go: and when he is old, he will not depart from it." PROVERBS 22:6

The all-sufficiency of God ought to be as complete to the child of God as the all-sufficiency of a good mother is to the child of that mother. We all know the utter rest of the little child in the mother's presence and the mother's love. That its mother is there is enough to make all fears and all troubles disappear. It does not need the mother to make any promises; she herself, just as she is, without promises and without explanations, is all that the child needs.

My own experience as a child taught me this, beyond any possibility of question. My mother was the remedy for all my own ills, and, I fully believed, for the ills of the whole world, if only they could be brought to her. And when anyone expressed doubts as to her capacity to remedy everything, I remembered with what fine scorn I used to annihilate them, by saying, "Ah! But you don't know my mother."

And now, when any tempest-tossed soul fails to see that God is enough, I feel like saying, not with scorn, but with infinite pity, "Ah, dear friend, you do not know God! Did you know Him, you could not help seeing that He is the remedy for every need of your soul, and that He is an all-sufficient remedy. God is enough, even though no promise may seem to fit your case, nor an inward assurance give you confidence. The Promiser is more than His promises; and His existence is a surer ground of confidence than the most fervent inward feelings."

Oh, utter but the name of God
Down in your heart of hearts,
And see how from the soul at once
All anxious fear departs.

ASSURANCE OF FAITH *by D. L. Moody*

"The eternal God is thy refuge, and underneath are the ever-lasting arms: and he shall thrust out the enemy from before thee; and shall say, 'Destroy them.'" DEUTERONOMY 33:27

I was standing with a friend at his garden gate one evening when two little children came by. As they approached us he said to me:

"Watch the difference in these two boys."

Taking one of them in his arms he stood him on the gatepost, and stepping back a few feet he folded his arms and called to the little fellow to jump. In an instant the boy sprang toward him and was caught in his arms. Then turning to the second boy he tried the same experiment. But in the second case it was different. The child trembled and refused to move. My friend held out his arms and tried to induce the child to trust to his strength, but nothing could move him. At last my friend had to lift him down from the post and let him go.

"What makes such a difference in the two?" I asked.

My friend smiled and said, "The first is my own boy and knows me; but the other is a stranger's child whom I have never seen before."

There was all the difference. My friend was equally able to prevent both from falling, but the difference was in the boys themselves. The first had assurance in his father's ability and acted upon it, while the second, although he might have believed in the ability to save him from harm, would not put his belief into action.

So it is with us. We hesitate to trust ourselves to the loving One whose plans for us are far higher than any we have ourselves made. He, too, with outstretched arms, calls us.

JULY 27TH

FATHER PROVIDES *by Andrew Murray*

"But seek ye first the kingdom of God, and his righteousness; and all these things shall be added unto you."

MATTHEW 6:33

"Give us this day our daily bread." When first the child has yielded himself to the Father in the care of His Name, His kingdom, and His Will, he has full liberty to ask for his daily bread. A master cares for the food of his servant, a general of his soldiers, a father of his child. And will not the Father in heaven care for the child who has in prayer given himself up to His interests? We may indeed in full confidence say: "Father, I live for Thy honour and Thy work; I know Thou carest for me." Consecration to God and His will gives wonderful liberty in prayer for temporal things: the whole earthly life is given to the Father's loving care.

CROWDING OUR GOD *by John Henry Jowett*

"Only take heed to thyself, and keep thy soul diligently, lest thou forget the things which thine eyes have seen, and lest they depart from thy heart. . . ."   DEUTERONOMY 4:9

That is surely the worst affront we can put upon anybody. We may oppose a man and hinder him in his work, or we may directly injure him, or we may ignore him, and treat him as nothing. Or we may forget him! Opposition, injury, contempt, neglect, forgetfulness! Surely this is a descending scale, and the last is the worst. And yet we can forget the Lord God. We can forget all His benefits. We can easily put Him out of mind. We can live as though He were dead. "My children have forgotten Me."

What shall we do to escape this great disaster? "Take heed to thyself!" To take heed is to be at the helm and not asleep in the cabin. It is to steer and not to drift. It is to keep our eyes on the compass and our hands on the wheel. It is to know where we are going. We never deliberately forget our Lord; we carelessly drift into it. "Take heed."

"And keep thy soul diligently." Gardens run to seed, and ill weeds grow apace. The fair things are crowded out, and the weed reigns everywhere. It is ever so with my soul. If I neglect it, the flowers of holy desire and devotion will be choked by weeds of worldliness. God will be crowded out, and the garden of the soul will become a wilderness of neglect and sin.

MARKING OUR COURSE *by A. B. Simpson*

". . .He went out, not knowing whither he went."

HEBREWS 11:8

*I*n crossing the Atlantic by ship, I observed this very principle of faith. We could see no path upon the water or sign of the shore. And yet day by day the helmsman was in a path as exactly as if he had been following a great chalk line upon the sea. And when we came within 20 miles of land he knew where we were as surely as if he had seen it all 3,000 miles ahead.

How had we measured and marked our course? Day by day our captain had taken his instruments, and looking up to the sky had fixed his course by the sun. He was sailing by the heavenly lights, not the earthly lights. So faith looks up and sails on, by God's great Sun, not seeing one shoreline or earthly lighthouse or path upon the way. Often our steps seem to lead into utter uncertainty or even darkness and disaster. But He opens the way, making our midnight hours the very gates of day.

Let us go forth this day, not knowing, yet trusting.

REST IN THE LORD *compiled by Mary W. Tileston*

"The Lord shall give thee rest from thy sorrow, and from thy fear, and from the hard bondage wherein thou wast made to serve."　　　　　　　　　　　　　　　ISAIAH 14:3

Today, beneath Thy chastening eye,
　　I crave alone for peace and rest;
Submissive in Thy hand to lie,
　　And feel that it is best.

　　　　　　　　　　　　　　J. G. WHITTIER

O Lord, who are as the Shadow of a great Rock in a weary land, who beholdest Thy weak creatures weary of labour, weary of pleasure, weary of hope deferred, weary of self; in Thine abundant compassion, and unutterable tenderness, bring us, I pray Thee, unto Thy rest. Amen.

　　　　　　　　　　　　　　CHRISTINA G. ROSSETTI

Grant to me above all things that can be desired, to rest in Thee, and in Thee to have my heart at peace. Thou art the true peace of the heart, Thou its only rest; out of Thee all things are hard and restless. In this very peace, that is, in Thee, the One Chiefest Eternal Good, I will sleep and rest. Amen.

　　　　　　　　　　　　　　THOMAS Á KEMPIS

Thou hast made us for Thyself, O Lord; and our heart is restless until it rests in Thee.

　　　　　　　　　　　　　　ST. AUGUSTINE

THE FIXED HELM *by A. B. Simpson*

"Thou wilt keep him in perfect peace, whose mind is stayed on thee: because he trusteth in thee."   ISAIAH 26:3

In the old creation, the week began with work and ended with Sabbath rest. The resurrection week begins with the first day—first rest, then labor.

So we must first cease from our own works as God did from His, and enter into His rest. And then, with rested hearts, we will work His works with effectual power.

But why labor to enter into rest? See that sailing craft—how restfully it glides over the waters, its canvas swelling with the wind and borne without an effort! And yet, look at that man at the helm. See how firmly he holds the rudder, bearing against the wind, and holding her steady to her position. Let him for a moment relax his steady hold and the vessel will fall listlessly along the wind. The sails will flap, the waves will toss the craft at their will, and all rest and power will have gone. It is the fixed helm that brings the steadying power of the wind. And so we read, "Thou wilt keep him in perfect peace, whose mind is stayed on thee: because he trusteth in thee" (Isaiah 26:3). The steady will and stayed heart are ours. The keeping is the Lord's. So let us labor to enter and abide in His rest.

AUGUST

CHIMES OF PRAISE *by William A. Quale*

*"Let every thing that hath breath praise the LORD. Praise ye
the LORD."*   PSALM 150:6

O what a heyday of music the insects make in August! I
revel in it. The crickets chirp. The tree toad sets his instrument going. The wild bees hum drowsily enough to put you
to sleep. The tame bees go into the clover blossoms and drink
them dry at a single gulp. Then a score of voices chime coming from what insects I cannot tell but full of all that blessed
gladness which God has so kindly put into the heart of every
living thing. I listen and praise. Such a happy world, so full
of song. In August, birds have grown tired singing or are
grown too fat to sing, and in any case sing but little. Then the
insects tune up. At night, the tree toads set up a storm of min-
strels. At noon and night and the day through, you shall hear
the strident locust which in the Spring you seldom hear, save
at evening. How the locust's voice—with its blur of sound—
delights my ear. I go and stand near a branch or a hedge to
wait till he tunes up again and fairly stumbles in his tune so
full of life. So is the August heat squeezing this music out of
him as honey from the comb.

DAILY LIFE OF PRAISE AND PRAYER
by Kenneth W. Osbeck

"I will bless the LORD at all times: his praise shall continually be in my mouth. . .I sought the LORD, and he heard me, and delivered me from all my fears." PSALM 34:1, 4

*E*ven a casual visit to a bookstore will impress a viewer with the many "how to" or self-improvement books that are available today. How to be happy, be healthy, be successful, be a good parent . . .and the list goes on.

But what are the "how-to's" for an effective spiritual life? Are there daily practices that Christians should pursue?

First and foremost, there needs to be an appreciative awareness of God's amazing grace in our lives.

Secondly, let me suggest these key words that also need to be a vital part of every believer's daily experience: Praise —Prayer—Love:

A daily life of praise, thanksgiving, and the adoration of God.

A daily life of prayer, fellowship, and a communion with God.

A daily life of love, a delight in the personal assurance of God's love and a desire to share His love with others.

Two basic resource books are available to help us in this spiritual well-being: the Bible, and the church hymnal. Regular study of the Bible, God's infallible rule of faith and practice, is an absolute essential for Christian living. Nothing ever replaces our daily need for His trustworthy Word. The church hymnal, a most important heritage of the Christian church, is one of the finest collections of man's thoughts and feelings about God.

Allow God to speak directly to you through the Scriptures. Then respond to Him with your own expressions of praise, prayer, and love. Carry a musical truth with you throughout each day. And as you do, you will become increasingly aware of God's amazing grace and His power that enables you to live an effective and victorious Christian life.

AUGUST 3RD

BLESS THE LORD *by Samuel Bagster*

"Because thy lovingkindness is better than life, my lips shall praise thee. Thus will I bless thee. . ."   PSALM 63:3, 4

*B*less the LORD, O my soul: and all that is within me, bless his holy name. Bless the LORD, O my soul, and forget not all his benefits. I will bless the LORD at all times: his praise shall continually be in my mouth. Every day will I bless thee; and I will praise thy name for ever and ever.

Because thy lovingkindness is better than life, my lips shall praise thee. Thus will I bless thee while I live: I will lift up my hands in thy name. My soul shall be satisfied as with marrow and fatness; and my mouth shall praise thee with joyful lips.

My soul doth magnify the LORD, and my spirit hath rejoiced in God my Saviour.

Thou art worthy, O LORD, to receive glory and honour and power: for thou hast created all things, and for thy pleasure they are and were created.

SINGING FOR HOLINESS *by Donald Grey Barnhouse*

"What time I am afraid, I will trust in thee. In God I will praise his word, in God I have put my trust; I will not fear. . ."

PSALM 56:3, 4

*R*obert Murray M'Cheyne, the great Scottish preacher, was a very gifted man in many ways. He had no inconsiderable knowledge of music and his voice was frequently heard in praise to God.

In his diary, which is one of the outstanding documents of its kind in Christian literature, we see the growth of this great soul as he so earnestly sought after God's own holiness. He wrote, "Is it the desire of my heart to be made altogether holy? Is there any sin I wish to retain? Is sin a grief to me, the sudden risings and overcoming thereof especially? Lord, Thou knowest all things. Thou knowest that I hate all sin and desire to be made altogether like Thee. . .Felt much deadness, and much grief that I cannot grieve for this deadness. Towards evening revived. Got a calm spirit through Psalmody and prayer."

Here is the experience of a heavy heart singing its way to peace. Of M'Cheyne it could be said that when he was spiritually cold he sang the praises of God until his heart was warm.

Christ, in the midst of His people, was always praising the Father. It is said in the Old Testament and quoted in the New that our Lord is the one who leads the singing of His saints. "I will declare the name unto my brethren, in the midst of the church will I sing praise unto thee" (Psalm 22:22; Hebrews 2:12).

If you are despondent or discouraged, speak now to the

Lord who dwells within your heart. Say to Him that you know you have been redeemed, and acknowledge His presence and His character as being more than worthy of praise. Ask Him to kindle the song. Have it on your lips even if you do not feel it in your heart. Ask Him to give you a realization of the truth of your singing, for then praise will go to your heart as you yield your song of praise to the Lord.

SING UNTO THE LORD A NEW SONG
by Samuel Bagster

"And he hath put a new song in my mouth, even praise unto our God: many shall see it, and fear, and shall trust in the Lord."   PSALM 40:3

*S*ing aloud unto God our strength; make a joyful noise unto the God of Jacob. Take a psalm, and bring hither the timbre, the pleasant harp with the psaltery. He hath put a new song in my mouth, even praise unto our God: many shall see it, and fear, and shall trust in the LORD.

Be strong and of a good courage; be not afraid, neither be thou dismayed: for the LORD thy God is with thee whithersoever thou goest. The joy of the LORD is your strength. Paul. . . thanked God, and took courage.

Knowing the time, that now it is high time to awake out of sleep: for now is our salvation nearer than when we believed. The night is far spent, the day is at hand: let us therefore cast off the works of darkness, and let us put on the armour of light. Let us walk honestly, as in the day; not in rioting and drunkenness, not in chambering and wantoness, not in strife and envying. But put ye on the LORD

Jesus Christ, and make not provision for the flesh, to fulfil the lusts thereof.

DOXOLOGY *by Kenneth W. Osbeck*

"I will praise thee, O Lord my God, with all my heart: and I will glorify thy name for evermore." PSALM 86:12

$\mathcal{T}$ he lines of the Doxology have been the most frequently sung words of any known song for more than 300 years. Even today nearly every English-speaking Protestant congregation unites at least once each Sunday in this noble overture of praise. It has been said that the "Doxology" has done more to teach the doctrine of the Trinity than all the theology books ever written.

Instead of being merely a perfunctory hymn that is sung each week, the "Doxology" should be regarded by Christians as an offering or sacrifice of praise to God for all of His blessings in the past week (Hebrews 13–15). True worship always involves an offering. In the Old Testament period, Levitical priests offered blood sacrifices to God on behalf of their people. In this New Testament era, God wants our sacrifice of praise. Other sacrifices desired by God of New Testament believer-priests include: Our bodies (Romans 12:1); the service of our faith (Philippians 2:17); our material gifts (Philippians 4:18); our good works and communication (Hebrews 13:16).

It has been said that a Christian's theology must become his doxology. As a believer, are you offering to God the sacrifices that He desires? Give Him your praise even now as you sing the "Doxology":

Praise God, from whom all blessings flow;
Praise Him, all creatures here below;
Praise Him above, ye heavenly host;
Praise Father, Son, and Holy Ghost!

Amen.

I PRAISE THEE, O GOD *by Susanna Wesley/Edith Dean*

"He taught me also, and said unto me, Let thine heart retain my words: keep my commandments, and live. Get wisdom, get understanding: forget it not; neither decline from the words of my mouth." PROVERBS 4:4, 5

I praise Thee, O God, for illuminating my mind and for enabling me to prove demonstratively that Thy wisdom is as infinite as Thy power. Help me to use these discoveries to praise and love and obey Thee, and may I be exceedingly careful that my affections keep pace with my knowledge.

As I am more rationally persuaded that thou art infinitely wise, so may I learn by this knowledge to practice a more hearty and universal subjection to Thee, more cheerfully to bow before the order of thy providence, to submit my reason so far to my faith as not to doubt those points of faith which are mysterious to me through the weakness of my understanding.

May I adore the mystery I cannot comprehend. Help me to be not too curious in prying into those secret things that are known only to Thee, O God, nor too rash in censuring what I do not understand. May I not perplex myself about those methods of providence that seem to me involved and intricate, but resolve them into Thine infinite wisdom, who knowest the spirits of all flesh and dost best understand how to govern those souls Thou hast created.

We are of yesterday and know nothing. But Thy boundless mind comprehends, at one view, all things, past, present, and future, and as Thou dost see all things, Thou dost best understand what is good and proper for each individual and for me, with relation to both worlds. So deal with me, O my God. Amen.

AUGUST 8TH

MUSIC IS A UNIVERSAL LANGUAGE *by Dan Dick*

"Take a psalm, and bring hither the timbrel, the pleasant harp with the psaltery."   PSALM 81:2

*B*eth was different when she was singing. Somehow the pressures of the world disappeared when the music filled her head and heart. Her whole life felt somehow lighter, brighter, when she lifted her voice in praise through song. Music was the best expression of who she was and what she believed. Music made God real to Beth.

Music is a universal language. Every culture has its music, and it is revered as one of the finest arts. Music brings people together and can move us closer to God. God loves music and the spirit from which music springs. The quality is not nearly as important as the intention of the heart. Sing out to God, and He will bless you richly.

Music touches my heart in a special way, Lord. Speak to me through the beauty of music. Touch me day by day. Amen.

SOUTHERN EXPOSURE *by Donald Grey Barnhouse*

"And at midnight Paul and Silas prayed, and sang praises unto God: and the prisoners heard them. And suddenly there was a great earthquake, so that the foundations of the prison were shaken: and immediately all the doors were opened, and every one's bands were loosed."   ACTS 16:25, 26

*J*n the book of Ezekiel there is a wonderful prophecy of the Kingdom age and the glories of that time. There is a description of the temple of God and its surroundings. In the midst of the description there is a beautiful phrase about the apartments of the singers: "Without the inner gate were the chambers of the singers. . .and their prospect was toward the south" (Ezekiel 40:44). Southern exposure! Their life was the life of song, and their chambers were filled with the sunshine of God. When they looked out their windows they could see the landscape, drenched with beauty, and praised God.

In prison Paul and Silas "prayed, and sang praises unto God: and the prisoners heard them" (Acts 16:25). There was southern exposure at midnight; there was a jail filled with the sunshine of God's blessings. Their backs were lacerated with the scourge and they were in circumstances that called for weeping, as far as the world is concerned. They were not even facing toward the frigid north; they were in the darkness of the world's midnight. But the darkness and light are both alike to our God (Psalm 139:12). Happy are the men who learn this truth and bring the sunlight of God into the chambers of their dwelling, always looking out over the southern prospect which God has given them.

THE DAY STAR *by T. C. Horton & Charles E. Hurlburt*

"We have also a more sure word of prophecy; whereunto ye do well that ye take heed. . .until. . .the day star arise in your hearts."   2 PETER 1:19

*I*n the Gospel of John, we read: "In Him was life and the life was the Light of men." We have the sure Word of God. It is a lamp to our feet and a light unto our path. Our hearts are darkened by the evil nature within us, but when Jesus comes into our hearts He illumines the Word of God and shines with all the effulgence of His glory. Perpetual day is for those who walk in His light. Every day is a good day and the eternal glory awaits us.

Blessed Lord, our Light, shine in our hearts and lives this day and may we reflect Thy glory. Amen.

PRAISE HIM! PRAISE HIM! *by Kenneth W. Osbeck*

"While I live will I praise the LORD: will sing praises unto my God while I have any being."   PSALM 146:2

*P*raise is our Lord's most righteous due. It is not an option whether we will offer praise—it is one of God's commands. Scriptures clearly teach that we are to offer a sacrifice of praise to God continually (Hebrews 13:15, 16). Our daily sacrifice of praise should include joyful songs for who Christ is—"our blessed redeemer." Then we need to praise God for all of His daily blessings, which are beyond number. We should offer praise even for the trials of life for they are often blessings in disguise. Finally, our sacrifice should include praise for His leading in ways yet to be experienced.

"Praise Him! Praise Him!" is another of the many favorite gospel hymns written by Fanny Crosby, blind American poetess. In all she wrote between 8,000 and 9,000 gospel hymn texts and supplied our hymnals with more beloved hymns that are still sung today than any other writer.

"Praise Him! Praise Him!" first appeared in a Sunday school hymnal, *Bright Jewels,* which was published in 1869. The song was originally titled "Praise, Give Thanks." And still today, these words evoke praise from each believing heart:

Praise Him! praise Him! Jesus, our
blessed Redeemer! Sing, O Earth,
His wonderful love proclaim!
Hail Him! hail Him! highest archangels in glory;
Strength and honor give to His holy name!
Like a shepherd, Jesus will guard His children.
In His arms He carries them all day long;
Praise Him! praise Him! tell of His
excellent greatness; praise Him!
praise Him! ever in joyful song!

Go forth with a renewed awareness of Christ's presence in your life.

A THANKFUL HEART *by A. W. Tozer*

"Giving thanks always for all things unto God and the Father in the name of our Lord Jesus Christ." EPHESIANS 5:20

Let me recommend the cultivation of the habit of thankfulness as an effective cure for the cynical, sour habits of fault-finding among Christian believers.

Thanksgiving has great curative power. The heart that is constantly overflowing with gratitude will be safe from those attacks of resentfulness and gloom that bother so many religious persons. A thankful heart cannot be cynical!

Please be aware that I am not recommending any of the "applied psychology" nostrums so popular in liberal circles. We who have been introduced to God through the miracle of the new birth realize that there is good scriptural authority for the cultivation of gratitude as a cure for spiritual sourness. Further, experience teaches us that it works!

We should never take any blessing for granted, but accept everything as a gift from the Father of Lights. We should write on a tablet, one by one, the things for which we are grateful to God and to our fellow men.

Personally, I have gotten great help from the practice of talking over with God the many kindnesses I have received. I like to begin with thanking Him for His thoughts of me back to creation; for giving His Son to die for me when I was still a sinner; for giving the Bible and His blessed Spirit who inwardly gives us understanding of it. I thank Him for my parents, teachers, statesmen, patriots.

I am grateful to God for all of these and more—and I shall not let God forget that I am!

THE LORD HEARS MY VOICE *by Samuel Bagster*

"Be careful for nothing; but in every thing by prayer and supplication with thanksgiving let your requests be made known unto God." PHILIPPIANS 4:6

"*I* love the LORD, because He hath heard my voice and my supplications. Because He hath inclined His ear unto me, therefore will I call upon Him as long as I live" (Psalm 116:1, 2).

"When ye pray, use not vain repetitions, as the heathen do: for they think that they shall be heard for their much speaking. The Spirit. . .helpeth our infirmities: for we know not what we should pray for as we ought: but the Spirit itself maketh intercession for us with groanings which cannot be uttered" (Matthew 6:7, Romans 8:26).

"I will therefore that men pray every where, lifting up holy hands, without wrath and doubting. Praying always with all prayer and supplication in the Spirit, and watching thereunto with all perseverance and supplication for all saints" (1 Timothy 2:8, Ephesians 6:18).

"If two of you shall agree on earth as touching any thing that they shall ask, it shall be done for them of my Father which is in heaven" (Matthew 18:19).

CHRIST JESUS: THE END *by Brother Lawrence*

"For in him we live, and move, and have our being. . ."
                                                    ACTS 17:28

*I*t is however, necessary to put our whole trust in God, laying aside all other cares, and even some particular forms of devotion, though very good in themselves, yet such as one often engages is unreasonable, because these devotions are only a means to attain the end. So when by this exercise of the presence of God we are with Him who is our end, it is then useless to return to the means; but we may continue with Him our commerce of love, preserving in his holy presence, by an act of praise, of adoration, or of desire.

LORD AND SAVIOR JESUS CHRIST
by T. C. Horton & Charles E. Hurlburt

"But grow in grace, and in the knowledge of our Lord and Saviour Jesus Christ."   2 PETER 3:18

"*G*row in grace!" Thank God, it is possible and it is our bounden duty so to do. "And in the knowledge of—!" Here we pause and face a most remarkable exhortation. The vastness of the suggestion of growing in the "knowledge of the Lord, the Saviour, Jesus and Christ" sets before us a task which will last throughout eternity. Growing into Him—this marvellous One whom we do not know, thank God—is a part of eternal life. How shall we obey this command? Study His Word. It is the Lamp and Light. Search this Word. It is a mine of treasures. Submit to the commandments of the Word. Then will we be wise indeed.

Our Lord and Saviour, Jesus Christ, bowing in Thy glorious presence, we submit to Thee. Help us to know and love Thee more and more as the days go by. Amen.

YOU WILL FIND CHRIST EVERYWHERE IN THE BIBLE *by A. W. Tozer*

" . . .To us there is but one God, the Father, of whom are all things, and we in him; and one Lord Jesus Christ, by whom are all things. . ."   1 CORINTHIANS 8:6

I do not mind telling you that I have always found Jesus Christ beckoning to me throughout the Scriptures. I am convinced that it was God's design that we should find the divine Creator, Redeemer and Lord whenever we search the Scriptures.

The Son of God is described by almost every fair and worthy name in the creation. He is called the Sun of Righteousness with healing in His wings. He is called the Star that shone on Jacob. He is described as coming forth with His bride, clear as the moon. His Presence is likened unto the rain coming down upon the earth, bringing beauty and fruitfulness. He is pictured as the great sea and as the towering rock. He is likened to the strong cedars. A figure is used of Him as of a great eagle, going literally over the earth.

Where the person of Jesus Christ does not stand out tall and beautiful and commanding, as a pine tree against the sky, you will find Him behind the lattice, but stretching forth His hand. If He does not appear as the sun shining in His strength, He may be discerned in the reviving by the promised gentle rains.

Our Lord Jesus Christ was that One divinely commissioned to set forth the mystery and majesty and the wonder and the glory of the Godhead throughout the universe. It is more than an accident that both the Old and New Testaments comb heaven and earth for figures of speech or simile to set forth the wonder and glory of God!

AUGUST 17TH

TIME WITH GOD *by Andrew Murray*

"For this shall every one that is godly pray unto thee in a time when thou mayest be found. . ."   PSALM 32:6

O my God ! I do believe in Thee. I believe in Thee as the Father, Infinite in Thy Love and Power. And as the Son, my Redeemer and my Life. And as the Holy Spirit, Comforter and Guide and Strength. Three-in-One God, I have faith in Thee. I know and am sure that all that Thou art Thou art to me, that all Thou hast promised Thou wilt perform.

Lord Jesus, increase this faith! Teach me to take time, and wait and worship in the Holy Presence until my faith takes in all there is in my God for me. Let it see Him as the Fountain of all Life, working with Almighty Strength to accomplish His will in the world and in me. Let it see Him in His Love longing to meet and fulfil my desires. Let it so take possession of my heart and life that through faith God alone may dwell there. Lord Jesus, help me! With my whole heart would I believe in God. Let faith in God each moment fill me.

THE MAN CHRIST JESUS
by T. C. Horton & Charles E. Hurlburt

"For there is one God and one mediator between God and man, the man Christ Jesus."　　　1 TIMOTHY 2:5

*W*e have considered Christ as Mediator and now we have the emphasis upon Christ, our Mediator, as the Man Christ Jesus. In these days when He is being demeaned by so many who are robbing Him of His Deity, we should rejoice in the privilege offered us of magnifying Him as both man and God. "Great is the mystery of Godliness—God manifest in the flesh." No picture in the Bible is so marvelously thrilling, so calculated to convince and convert, as that of God dying for men. Hold Him in your thoughts and see Him today—arms outstretched above a blood-stained body, saying, "Come unto Me. I will give you rest."

Oh, Thou crucified, risen God-Man, we adore Thee. Guide us today in our worship and work for Thee. Amen.

JESUS CHRIST: OUR CHIEF JOY AND DELIGHT
by A. W. Tozer

"Be glad in the LORD, and rejoice, ye righteous: and shout for joy, all ye that are upright in heart."　　　PSALM 32:11

I must agree with the psalmist, even in our modern day, that the joy of the Lord is still the strength of His people. I

227

do believe that the sad world around us is attracted to spiritual sunshine—the genuine thing, that is!

Some churches train their greeters and ushers to smile, showing as many teeth as possible. But I can sense that kind of display—and when I am greeted by a man who is smiling because he has been trained to smile, I know I am shaking the flipper of a trained seal!

But when the warmth and delight and joy of the Holy Spirit are in a congregation and the folks are just spontaneously joyful and unable to hide the happy grin, the result is a wonderful influence upon others. Conversely, the reason we have to search for so many things to cheer us up is the fact that we are not really joyful and contentedly happy within!

I admit that we live in a gloomy world and that international affairs, nuclear rumors and threats, earthquakes and riots cause people to shake their heads in despair and say, "What's the use?"

But we are Christians and Christians have every right to be the happiest people in the world! We do not have to look to other sources—for we look to the Word of God and discover how we can know the faithful God above and draw from His resources.

Why should the children of the King hang their heads and tote their own burdens, missing the mark about Christian victory? All this time the Holy Spirit has been wanting to make Jesus Christ our chief joy and delight!

THE JOY OF JESUS *by Leonard Ravenhill*

"These things have I spoken unto you, that my joy might remain in you, and that your joy might be full."

JOHN 15:11

*J*oy! What a scarce commodity this is. There are many who say that they are abiding in Christ. There are few who show that they are abounding in Him. Joy! How elusive. How indescribably blessed is the believer who has his soul filled with it.

Isaiah had predicted, "With joy shall ye draw waters from the wells of salvation." Our blessed Lord in His high priestly prayer requested from His Father for His disciples, "That they might have my joy fulfilled in themselves." He prayed this for every soul that should ever believe on Him. ". . .for them also which shall believe on me through their word" (John 17:20).

Joy is not created by possessions, or by positions, but by a Person—Him! Let me add, however, that joy is not an inflexible, unvariable thing. It is not a deposit placed in the soul after salvation without any chance of deterioration. It can stand all pressures Satan or circumstances bring against it; but, and ponder this well, the sun of joy in the soul can be eclipsed by our own disobedience.

Joy requires at least two conditions: submission and service. "If ye abide" —submission—means staying put when it might seem smart to quit. It means believing God when it appears far wiser to believe everybody else. It means defying one's feelings and fears and saying triumphantly, "Thy will be done!"

Joy comes through service. Most Christians are activists;

they get caught up in some kind of church work. But not all of it is good. Not all of it is essential. Even missionaries find themselves tangled in lesser things than winning the lost. Unprayerful souls soon get diverted from the supreme task He appointed for them.

THE WAY TO ENJOY PEACE AND JOY
by Leonard Ravenhill

"Looking unto Jesus the author and finisher of our faith; who for the joy that was set before him endured the cross, despising the shame, and is set down at the right hand of the throne of God." HEBREWS 12:2

The way to enjoy indestructible peace and joy is to determine:
1. To do whatever God commands, however difficult.
2. To endure whatever God appoints, however severe.
3. To obtain whatever God promises, however seemingly unattainable.
4. To die daily, however costly the crucifixion.
5. To love my "enemies," however misunderstood in this.
6. To pray without ceasing, and in everything give thanks.

This will give one a healthy soul and a conscience void of offense before God and man. Otherwise we may cry with Joel: "Joy is withered away from the sons of men. . .Is not the meat cut off before our eyes, yea, joy and gladness from the house of our God?" (Joel 1:12, 16).

Joy is not in having possessions. Treasures in the material sense can be comforting one minute and killing the next. Investments, the best of them, can fail. Houses and lands are subject to change and decay. They all are exposed to taxation and other burdens. They all may pass in one nuclear blast—then what?

Positions. These are certainly insecure. The top flight executive may be eliminated in a merger of companies. The skilled doctor may be eclipsed by the appointment of some brilliant and maybe brash young rookie. A throne can topple in a night. A dictator lives in constant fear of assassination.

But joy is a Person—Him! Joy is maintained by abiding in Him, by believing in Him, by obeying Him.

AUGUST 22ND

THE SPIRIT'S WITNESS *by J. I. Packer*

"We also joy in God through our Lord Jesus Christ."
ROMANS 5:11

*T*o know that God is your Father and that He loves you, His adopted child, no less than He loves His only begotten Son and to know that enjoyment of God's love and glory for all eternity are pledged to you brings inward delight that is sometimes overwhelming; and this also is the Spirit's doing. For the "joy in the Holy Spirit," in terms of which Paul defines the kingdom of God in Romans 14:17, is the "rejoicing in God" spoken of in Romans 5:2, 11 and it is the Spirit's witness to God's love for us that calls forth this joy.

SPIRITUAL DISCERNMENT *by Oswald Chambers*

"Finally, brethren, whatsoever things are true, whatsoever things are honest, whatsoever things are just, whatsoever things are pure, whatsoever things are lovely, whatsoever things are of a good report; if there be any virtue, and if there be any praise, think on these things." PHILIPPIANS 4:8

*B*e careful for nothing; but in every thing by prayer and supplication with thanksgiving let your requests be made known unto God (Phil. 4:6).

Genuine saints will discern whatsoever things are true, just, pure, lovely, and of good report. True holiness discerns virtuous and praiseworthy people and deeds, and delights in these.

The discerning of spirits is one of the gifts of the Spirit (*see* 1 Cor. 12:10). Real discernment does not consist of the vague impressions of a lively imagination. Discernment works by the Word of God. The Holy Spirit glorified Jesus; and the Spirit-filled, sanctified saint intuitively discerns any person, teaching, or doctrine that does not glorify Him as Lord.

A sanctified person immediately recognizes spiritual error because the Holy Spirit will bring to remembrance all that Jesus taught. The Holy Spirit will lead one into all truth and will help every "sheep of the Lord" to detect a stranger's voice.

Spiritual discernment is keenly sensitive to the glory of God. A spiritually discerning saint walks in the light and with the Light who is Jesus Christ. *I desire to know truth. Grant to me, Lord, wisdom to discern the truth.*

UNSUNG BUT SINGING *by A. W. Tozer*

"Speaking to yourselves in psalms and hymns and spiritual songs, singing and making melody in your heart to the Lord."
EPHESIANS 5:19

*T*o value the esteem of mankind and for Christ's sake to renounce it is a form of crucifixion suffered by true Christians since the days of the apostles. It cannot be denied that the way of the cross is unpopular and that it brings a measure of reproach upon those who take it.

The learned historians tell of councils and persecutions and religious wars, but in the midst of all the mummery were a few who saw the Eternal City in full view and managed almost to walk on earth as if they had already gone to heaven. These were the joyous ones who got little recognition from the world of institutionalized religion, and might have gone altogether unnoticed except for their singing.

Unsung but singing: this is the short and simple story of many today whose names are not known beyond the small circle of their own company. Their gifts are not many nor great, but their song is sweet and clear!

John Milton lost his sight and mourned that loss in the third book of his *Paradise Lost*. But in spite of his affliction he refused to be desolate. If he could not see, he could still think and he could still pray. Like the nightingale he could sing in the darkness

> . . .as the wakeful bird
> Sings darkling, and, in shadiest covert hid,
> Tunes her nocturnal.

We are never sure where a true Christian may be found
—and the busy world may actually not even know he is
there—except that they hear him singing!

GIVE HAPPINESS TO OTHERS
compiled by Mary W. Tileston

*"Finally, be ye all of one mind, having compassion one for
another; love as brethren, be pitiful, be courteous."*

1 PETER 3:8

Make us of one heart and mind;
    Courteous, pitiful, and kind;
Lowly, meek, in thought and word,
    Altogether like our Lord.

CHARLES WESLEY

A little thought will show you how vastly your own happiness depends on the way other people bear themselves toward you. The looks and tones at your breakfast-table, the conduct of your fellow-workers or employers, the faithful or unreliable men you deal with, what people say to you on the street, the way you cook and do your work, the letters you get, the friends or foes you meet,—these things make up very much of the pleasure or misery of your day. Turn the idea around, and remember that just so much are you adding to the pleasure or the misery of other people's days. And this is the half of the matter which you can control. Whether any particular day shall bring to you more of happiness or of suffering is largely beyond your power to determine. Whether each day of your life shall give happiness or suffering rests with yourself.

GEORGE S. MERRIAM

GIVING IS LIVING *by Hannah Hurnard*

"By this shall all men know that ye are my disciples, if ye have love one to another."　　　　　JOHN 13:35

There is one law by which we live,
　　"Love loves to give and give and give!"
And on this "royal law," so named,
　　The universe itself is framed.
No lasting joy is anywhere
　　Saved in the hearts of those who share.
Life yields a thousandfold and more
　　To those who practice love's great law.
That love is far too weak and small
　　Which will love some but not love all.
If love to one it will decline,
　　'Tis human love and not divine.
Love cannot be content to rest
　　Till the beloved is fully blest.
Love leaps to succor all who fall,
　　And finds his joy in giving all.

WE MUST RUN AGROUND *by Elisabeth Elliot*

"For we know that. . .we have a building of God, an house made not with hands, eternal in the heavens."

2 CORINTHIANS 5:1

*H*ave you ever put heart and soul into something, prayed over it, worked at it with a good heart because you believed it to be what God wanted, and finally seen it "run aground"?

The story of Paul's voyage as a prisoner across the Adriatic Sea tells how an angel stood beside him and told him not to be afraid (in spite of winds of hurricane force), for God would spare his life and the lives of all with him on board ship. Paul cheered his guards and fellow passengers with that word, but added, "Nevertheless, we must run aground on some island" (Acts 27:26, NIV).

It would seem that the God who promises to spare all hands might have "done the job right," saved the ship as well, and spared them the ignominy of having to make it to land on the flotsam and jetsam that was left. The fact is He did not, nor does He always spare us.

Heaven is not *here*, it's *There*. If we were given all we wanted here, our hearts would settle for this world rather than the next. God is forever luring us up and away from this one, wooing us to Himself and His still invisible Kingdom, where we will certainly find what we so keenly long for.

"Running aground," then, is not the end of the world. But it helps to make the world a bit less appealing. It may even be God's answer to "Lead us not into temptation"— the temptation complacently to settle for visible things.

PRECIOUS BUT PERSONAL *by A. B. Simpson*

"Ye have the poor with you always; . . .but me ye have not always." MARK 14:7

"Lovest thou me?" the Master asks of each disciple. He expects our first and highest love for Himself, personally, and He has a right to it. More than all our service, more than all our work to build up a cause, He desires our personal devotion to Him. Mary's gift was precious because it was personal. "Ye have the poor with you always; . . .but me ye have not always" (Mark 14:7).

We must beware of danger which defeats His purpose—our being more occupied with the work of Christ than with Christ Himself.

We need the love of Christ in order to fit us for His work. Nothing else will give it its true aim and center; nothing else will sustain us amid its pressures.

When Jesus was about to send Simon to take care of His flock, He did not ask Him, "Lovest thou my sheep and my lambs?" He asked, "Lovest thou me?" Mere love for people will not enable us to be true to them; but love for Christ will give us a reflected love for others that will enable us to touch them for Him and to bless them as our direct touch never could.

WOULD YOU RECOGNIZE JESUS?
by Catherine Booth/Edith Dean

"And the King shall answer and say unto them, Verily I say unto you, Inasmuch as ye have done it unto one of the least of these my brethren, ye have done it unto me."

MATTHEW 25:40

*T*here are thousands talking about His second coming who will neither see nor receive Him in the person of His humble and persecuted followers. No. They are looking for Him in the clouds! What a sensation there would be if He were to come again in a carpenter's coat. How many would recognize Him then, I wonder? I am afraid it would be the old story, "Crucify Him!" . . .Oh for grace always to see Him where He is to be seen, for verily, flesh and blood doth not reveal this unto us! Well, bless the Lord, I keep seeing Him risen again in the forms of drunkards and ruffians of all descriptions.

FAITH: LOVE'S RESPONSE
by Hannah Hurnard

"So then faith cometh by hearing, and hearing by the word of God."

ROMANS 10:17

*F*aith is response to love's dear call,
    Of love's dear face the sight;
To do love's bidding now is all
    That gives the heart delight.

To love thy voice and to reply,
    "Lord, here am I."

As blows the wind through summer trees,
    And all the leaves are stirred,
O Spirit move as thou dost please,
    My heart yields at thy word.
Faith hears thee calling from beyond
    And doth respond.

"What thou dost will—that I desire,
    Through me let it be done,
Thy will and mine in love's own fire
    Are welded into one."
"Lord, I believe!" Nay, rather say,
    "Lord, I obey."

AUGUST 31ST

QUIET THOUGHTS AND GODLY MEDITATIONS
compiled by Mary W. Tileston

*"The hand of our God is upon all them for good that seek
him."*   EZRA 8:22

Thou layest Thy hand on the fluttering heart,
    And sayest, "Be still!"
The silence and shadow are only a part
    Of Thy sweet will;
Thy presence is with me, and where thou art
    I fear no ill.

                                        F. R. HAVERGAL

$\mathcal{B}$e still and cool in thy own mind and spirit from thy own thoughts, and then thou wilt feel the principle of God, to turn my mind to the Lord God, from whom life comes; whereby thou mayest receive His strength, and power to allay all blustering storms and tempests. That is what works up into patience, into innocency, into soberness, into stillness, into stayedness, into quietness, up to God with His power. . . . Therefore be still awhile, stayed in the principle of God in thee, that it may raise thy mind up to God, and stay it upon God; and thou will find strength from Him, and find Him to be a God at hand, a present help in the time of trouble and need.

GEORGE FOX

SEPTEMBER

CLUSTERS OF GRAPES *by William A. Quale*

"I am the true vine. . . Every branch in me that beareth not fruit he taketh away: and every branch that beareth fruit, he purgeth it, that it may bring forth more fruit."

JOHN 15:1, 2

*S*eptember is the grape month. What other praise needs to be sung for September? One look at the vineyard suffices to put a body in love with the month that holds such clusters in her hand. What can be more artistic than a grape cluster shadowed by grape leaves? The color, the grape shape, the frost wherewith God has seen fit to cloud the purple of His grape cluster, the way clusters hang with indolence luxuriously graceful as a Venetian gondolier, the mild fragrance which gives to every vineyard its own atmosphere. The bees know where to come and seek this wine ready for their lips. The sky half Summer and half Fall. In September the sweat of growth is ended. The rush toward fruitage has given way to the quiet smile as at evening after work is done.

ABIDING IN CHRIST *by R. A. Torrey*

"Abide in me, and I in you. As the branch cannot bear fruit of itself, except it abide in the vine; no more can ye, except ye abide in me."   JOHN 15:4

*W*hat is it to abide in Christ?

Some explanations are so mystical or so profound that many children of God think they mean practically nothing at all. But, what Jesus meant was really very simple.

He had been comparing Himself to a vine, His disciples to the branches in the vine. Some branches continued in the vine —in living union—so that the sap or life of the vine constantly flowed into the branches. Their buds, leaves, blossoms, and fruit were not really theirs, but the buds, leaves, blossoms, and fruit of the vine. Other branches were completely severed from the vine, or the flow of the sap or life of the vine was in some way hindered. For us to abide in Christ is to bear the same relationship to Him that the first sort of branches bear to the vine. We must simply and constantly look to Christ to think His thoughts in us, to form His purposes in us, to feel His emotions and affections in us. When we do this, our prayers will obtain that which we seek from God.

This must necessarily be so, for our desires will not be our own desires but Christ's. Our prayers will not in reality be our own prayers, but Christ praying in us.

To abide in Christ, one must already be in Christ through the acceptance of Christ as an atoning Savior from the guilt of sin. He must be acknowledged as a risen Savior from the power of sin and a Lord and Master over all the believer's life. Being in Christ, all that we have to do to abide (or continue) in Christ is simply to renounce our self-life. We must utterly renounce every thought, purpose, desire, and affection of our own and continually look to Jesus Christ for His thoughts, purposes, affections, and desires in us.

CHRIST'S WORDS IN US *by R. A. Torrey*

"If ye abide in me, and my words abide in you, ye shall ask what ye will, and it shall be done unto you."   JOHN 15:7

*I*f we are to receive from God all we ask from Him, Christ's words must abide in us. We must study His words and let them sink into our thoughts and heart. We must keep them in our memory, obey them constantly in our life, and let them shape and mold our daily life and our every act.

This is really the method of abiding in Christ. It is through His words that Jesus imparts Himself to us. The words He speaks unto us, they are spirit and they are life (John 6:63). It is vain to expect power in prayer unless we meditate upon the words of Christ and let them sink deep and find a permanent abode in our hearts. There are many who wonder why they are so powerless in prayer. The very simple explanation of it all is found in their neglect of the words of Christ. They have not hidden His words in their hearts; His words do not abide in them. It is not by moments of mystical meditation and rapturous experiences that we learn to abide in Christ. It is by feeding upon His Word, his written Word in the Bible, and looking to the Spirit to implant these words in our heart—to make them a living thing in our heart. If we thus let the words of Christ abide in us, they will stir us up to prayer.

The Word of God is the instrument through which the Holy Spirit works. It is the sword of the Spirit in more senses than one. The person who wants to know the work of the Holy Spirit in any direction must feed upon the Word. The person who desires to pray in the Spirit must meditate on the Word, so that the Holy Spirit may have something through which He can work. The Holy Spirit words His prayers in us through the Word. If we seek to feed the fire of our prayers with the fuel of God's Word, all our difficulties in prayer will disappear.

SEPTEMBER 4TH

OUR PRAYER-UNION *by Andrew Murray*

"I am the vine, ye are the branches: He that abideth in me, and I in him, the same bringeth forth much fruit: for without me ye can do nothing."   JOHN 15:5

*T*he union between the Vine and the branch is in very deed a prayer-union. The highest conformity to Christ, the most blessed participation in the glory of His heavenly life, is that we take part in His work of intercession: He and we live ever to pray. In the experience of our union with Him, praying without ceasing becomes a possibility, a reality, the holiest and most blessed part of our holy and blessed fellowship with God. We have our abode within the veil, in the presence of the Father. What the Father says, we do; what the Son says, the Father does. Praying without ceasing is the earthly manifestation of heaven come down to us, the foretaste of the life where they rest not day or night in the song of worship and adoration.

MY SHARE IN THE MIRACLE *by John Henry Jowett*

"His mother saith unto the servants, 'Whatsoever he saith unto you, do it.' "   JOHN 2:5

*O*ur Lord always demands our best. He will not work with our second-best. His gracious "extra" is given when our own resources are exhausted. We must do our best before our Master will do His miracle. We must "fill the water-pots with water"! We must bring "the five loaves and two fishes"! We must "let down the net"! We must be willing "to be made whole," and we must make the effort to rise! Yes, the Lord will have my best.

Our Lord transforms our best into His better. He changes water into wine. He turns the handful of seed into a harvest. Our aspirations become inspirations. Our willings become magnetic with the mystic power of grace. Our bread becomes sacramental, and He Himself reveals to us at the feast. Our ordinary converse becomes a Divine fellowship, and "our hearts burn within us" as He talks to us by the way.

And our Lord ever keeps His best wine until the last. "Greater things than these shall ye do!" "I will see you again," and there shall be grander transformations still! "The best is yet to be." "Dreams cannot picture a word so fair." "Eye hath not seen, nor ear heard, neither hath it entered into the heart of man to conceive the things which God hath prepared for them that love Him."

THE SECRET TO SPIRITUAL SUCCESS
by Ken Abraham

"The life which I now live in the flesh I live by the faith of the Son of God, who loved me, and gave himself for me. . . ."

GALATIANS 2:20

*H*udson Taylor had discovered the secret to spiritual success; It was resting in the knowledge that Christ was in him and he was "in Christ." With overflowing joy, he gushed concerning the peace he had found:

"The sweetest part, if one may speak of one part being sweeter than another, is the rest which full identification with Christ brings. I am no longer anxious about anything, as I realize this; for He, I know, is able to carry out His will, and His will is mine. It makes no matter where He places me, or how. That is rather for Him to consider than for me; for in the easiest position He must give me His grace, and in the most difficult His grace is sufficient. . . .

And since Christ has thus dwelt in my heart by faith, how happy I have been!. . .I am no better than before. In a sense, I did not wish to be, nor am I striving to be. But I am dead and buried with Christ—and risen too! And now Christ lives in me, and "the life that I now live in the flesh I live by the faith of the Son of God, who loved me and gave himself for me. . ." (Galatians 2:20).

In concluding his letter, Hudson Taylor, always concerned for the spiritual welfare of others, exhorted his sister to find the secret of Christ's fullness for herself. Allow his words to encourage you, as well:

"May God give you to lay hold on these blessed truths . . .do not let us consider Him as far off, when God has made us one with Him, members of His very body. Nor should we look upon this experience, these truths, as for a few. They are the birthright of every child of God, and no one can dispense with them without dishonoring our Lord. The only power for deliverance from sin or for true service is Christ."

NEVER TOO LATE *by Charles Dickens*

"For the kindgom of heaven is like unto a man that is an householder, which went out early in the morning to hire labourers into his vineyard."　　　　　　MATTHEW 20:1

*A*nd he told them another story, and said, "There was a certain Farmer once, who had a Vineyard, and he went out early in the morning, and agreed with some labourers to work there all day, for a Penny. And bye and bye, when it was later, he went out again and engaged some more labourers on the same terms; and bye and bye went out again; and so on, several times, until the afternoon. When the day was over, and they all came to be paid, those who had worked since morning complained that those who had not begun to work until late in the day had the same money as themselves, and they said it was not fair. But the Master, said, 'Friend, I agreed with you for a Penny; and is it less money to you, because I give the same money to another man?' "

Our Saviour meant to teach them by this, that people who have done good all their lives long, will go to Heaven. But that people who have been wicked, because of their being miserable, or not having parents and friends to take care of them when young, and who are truly sorry for it, however late in their lives, and pray God to forgive them, will be forgiven and will go to Heaven too.

THE TRADESMAN *by James Stalker*

". . .It is good and comely for one. . .to enjoy the good of all his labour. . .for it is his portion."   ECCLESIASTES 5:18

*T*hat He worked as a carpenter in Joseph's shop there can be no doubt. Who could know better than His own townsmen, who asked, in their astonishment at His preaching, "Is not this the carpenter?" It would be difficult to exhaust the significance of the fact that God chose for His Son, when He dwelt among men, out of all the possible positions in which He might have placed Him, the lot of a working man. It stamped men's common toils with everlasting honor. It acquainted Jesus with the feelings of the multitude, and helped Him to know what was in man. It was afterwards said that He knew this so well that He needed not that any man should teach Him.

DAY BY DAY *by Andrew Murray*

". . .And the people shall go out and gather a certain rate every day. . ."   EXODUS 16:4

*T*he day's portion in its day: Such was the rule for God's giving and man's working in the ingathering of the manna. It is still the law in all the dealings of God's grace with His children. A clear insight into the beauty and application of this arrangement is a wonderful help in understanding how one, who feels himself utterly weak, can have the confidence and the perseverance to hold on brightly through all the years of his earthly course. A doctor was once asked by a patient who had met with a serious accident: "Doctor, how long shall I have to lie here?" The answer, "Only a day at a time," taught the patient a precious lesson. It was the same lesson God had recorded for His people of all ages long before: The day's portion in its day.

SEPTEMBER 10TH

THE REST OF GOD *by D. L. Moody*

"Come unto me, all ye that labour and are heavy laden, and I will give you rest."　　　　　　　　　　MATTHEW 11:28

A lady in Wales told me this little story: An English friend of hers, a mother, had a child that was sick. At first they considered there was no danger, until one day the doctor came in and said that the symptoms were very unfavorable. He took the mother out of the room, and told her that the child could not live. It came like a thunderbolt. After the doctor had gone the mother went into the room where the child lay and began to talk to the child, and tried to divert its mind.

"Darling, do you know you will soon hear the music of heaven? You will hear a sweeter song than you have ever heard on earth. You will hear them sing the song of Moses and the Lamb. You are very fond of music. Won't it be sweet, darling?"

And the little tired, sick child turned its head away, and said, "Oh, mamma, I am so tired and so sick that I think it would make me worse to hear all that music."

"Well," the mother said, "you will soon see Jesus. You

will see the seraphim and cherubim and the streets all paved with gold"; and she went on picturing heaven as it is described in Revelation.

The little tired child again turned its head away, and said, "Oh, mamma, I am so tired that I think it would make me worse to see all those beautiful things!"

At last the mother took the child up in her arms, and pressed her to her loving heart. And the little sick one whispered:

"Oh, mamma, that is what I want. If Jesus will only take me in His arms and let me rest!"

Dear friend, are you not tired and weary of sin? Are you not weary of the turmoil of life? You can find rest on the bosom of the Son of God.

SEPTEMBER 11TH

THE COLLEGE OF CONTENT
by Charles H. Spurgeon

"I have learned, in whatsoever state I am, therewith to be content."   PHILIPPIANS 4:11

*T*hese words show us that contentment is not a natural propensity of man. "Ill weeds grow apace." Covetousness, discontent, and murmuring are as natural to man as thorns are to the soil. We need not sow thistles and brambles; they come up naturally enough, because they are indigenous to earth; and so, we need not teach men to complain; they complain fast enough without any education. But the precious things of the earth must be cultivated. If we would have wheat, we must plough and sow; if we want flowers, there must be the garden, and all the gardener's care. Now, contentment is one of the flowers of heaven, and if we would have it, it must be cultivated; it will not grow in us by nature. Paul says, "I have learned. . .to be content"; as much as to say, he did not know how at one time. It cost him some pains to attain to the mystery of that great truth. No doubt he sometimes thought he had learned, and then broke down. And when at last he had strained unto it, and could say, "I have learned in whatsoever state I am, therewith to be content," he was an old, grey-headed man, upon the borders of the grave—a poor prisoner shut up in Nero's dungeon at Rome. We might well be willing to endure Paul's infirmities, and share the cold dungeon with him, if we too might by any means attain unto his good degree. Do not indulge the notion that you can be contented without learning, or learn with discipline. It is not a power that may be exercised naturally, but a science to be acquired gradually. We know this from experience. Brother, hush that murmur, natural though it be, and continue a diligent pupil in the College of Content.

SEPTEMBER 12TH

MUCH SERVICE, MUCH COMMUNION
by Charles H. Spurgeon

"Martha was cumbered about much serving." LUKE 10:40

*H*er fault was not that she served: the condition of a servant well becomes every Christian. "I serve," should be the motto of all the princes of the royal family of heaven. Nor was it her fault that she had "much serving." We cannot do too much. Let us do all that we possibly can; let head and heart and hands be engaged in the Master's service. It was no fault of hers that she was busy preparing a feast for the Master. Happy Martha, to have an opportunity of entertaining so

251

blessed a guest; and happy, too, to have the spirit to throw her whole soul so heartily into the engagement. Her fault was that she grew "cumbered with much serving," so that she forgot Him, and only remembered the service. She allowed service to override communion, and so presented one duty stained with the blood of another. We ought to be Martha and Mary in one; We should do much service, and have much communion at the same time. For this we need great grace. It is easier to serve than to commune. Joshua never grew weary in fighting with the Amalekites; but Moses, on the top of the mountain in prayer needed two helpers to sustain his hands.

SAINTS & SEMI-SAINTS *by Philip Yancey*

"For we are his workmanship, created in Christ Jesus unto good works."   EPHESIANS 2:10

*T*he biblical characters Ezra and Nehemiah, exact contemporaries, faced the same leadership challenge. Each sought to revive dispirited refugees in Jerusalem by persuading them to rebuild city walls and clean up their morals. But what different tactics the two men used. . .one pulls out his own hair in grief; another pulls out other people's hair in anger. . . Ezra and Nehemiah got me thinking about the different approaches people take in living out their Christian faith. If Ezra was a saint, Nehemiah was a semi-saint.

A saint (as I am using the term) is a radical. . .semi-saints may play a less glamorous role, but can anyone doubt that an organization like Bread for the World accomplishes as much on behalf of the poor and hungry as does, say, Mother Teresa?

Ezra and Nehemiah, telling the same story from two points of view, make clear that neither approach is entirely effective on its own. Nehemiah, the obsessive, management-oriented bureaucrat, completed in fifty-two days a mission that Ezra had failed to accomplish in a dozen years: he got a wall built around Jerusalem to provide security for the residents inside.

On the other hand, once the construction project was completed, Nehemiah turned to Ezra to lead the religious celebration... Working in tandem, the two leaders—Nehemiah with his no-nonsense pragmatism and Ezra with his unimpeachable integrity—directed a spiritual revival such as had not been seen in a thousand years. In that revival, both saints and semi-saints played a part.

SEPTEMBER 14TH

AMAZING GRACE *by Charles H. Spurgeon*

"My grace is sufficient for thee. . . ." 2 CORINTHIANS 12:9

If none of God's saints were poor and tired, we should not know half so well the consolations of divine grace. When we find the wanderer who has not where to lay his head, who yet can say, "Still I will trust in the Lord"; when we see the pauper starving on bread and water, who still glories in Jesus; when we see the bereaved widow overwhelmed in affliction, and yet having faith in Christ, oh! what honour it reflects on the gospel. Saints bear up under every discouragement, believing that all things work together for their good, and that out of apparent evils a real blessing shall ultimately spring— that their God will either work a deliverance for them speedily, or most assuredly support them in the trouble, as long as

He is pleased to keep them in it. This patience of the saints proves the power of divine grace. There is a lighthouse out at sea; it is a calm night—I cannot tell whether the edifice is firm; the tempest must rage about it, and then I shall know whether it will stand. So with the Spirit's work: if it were not on many occasions surrounded with tempestuous waters, we should not know that it was true and strong; if the winds did not blow upon it, we should not know how firm and secure it was. The Master-works of God are those men who stand in the midst of difficulties, steadfast, unmovable—

Calm 'mid the bewildering cry,
    Confident of victory.

If then, yours be a much-tried path, rejoice in it, because you will the better show forth the all-sufficient grace of God. As for His failing you, never dream of it—hate the thought. The God who has been sufficient until now should be trusted to the end.

SEPTEMBER 15TH

HELP WANTED! *by Captain E. G. Garré*

*The harvest truly is plenteous, but, the labourers are few. . .
Pray. . ."*   MATTHEW 9:37, 38

A hundred million people in India today have not heard of Jesus Christ, and as things are now have not the remotest chance to hear about Him. There are other millions in Africa and other countries in the same condition. Why is it so? Because prayer closets are deserted, family altars are broken down, and pulpit prayers are formal and dead!

254

Bible schools and seminaries can never supply the workers needed. My own sainted mother prayed as a young girl that the doors of the heathen countries might be opened. Afterwards, as the mother of ten children (eight of whom grew to manhood and womanhood), she prayed for labourers to enter these open doors, and God sent one of her sons to India and two of her daughters to China.

Grandmother Lois and mother Eunice prayed, and when the Great Apostle Paul to the Gentiles was about to take his departure he could lay his hands on their son Timothy and commission him to "Preach the Word!"

John Hyde was an answer to prayer, and when in other years he prayed in India, God raised up scores of native workers in answer to his prayers. The Great Head of the Church has provided one method for securing labourers. He said:

"Look on the fields. . .they are white. . .the labourers are few. . .PRAY!"

SEPTEMBER 16TH

THE SACRIFICE OF GIVING *by Charles Dickens*

"God loveth a cheerful giver."   2 CORINTHIANS 9:7

s he was teaching, Jesus sat near the Public Treasury, where people as they passed along the street, were accustomed to drop money into the box for the poor; and many rich persons, passing while Jesus sat there, had put in a great deal of money. At last there came a poor Widow who dropped in two mites, each half a farthing in value, and then went quietly away. Jesus, seeing her do this as he rose to leave the place, called his disciples about him, and said to

255

them that that poor widow had been more truly charitable than all the rest who had given money that day; for the others were rich and would never miss what they had given, but she was very poor, and had given those two mites which might have bought her bread to eat.

Let us never forget what the poor widow did, when we think we are charitable.

SEPTEMBER 17TH

DO GOODERS *by Charles Dickens*

"Let your light so shine before men, that they may see your good works, and glorify your Father which is in heaven."
MATTHEW 5:16

*R*emember!—It is Christianity to do good always — even to those who do evil to us. It is Christianity to love our neighbour as ourself, and to do to all men as we would have them do to us. It is Christianity to be gentle, merciful, and forgiving, and to keep those qualities quiet in our own hearts, and never make a boast of them, or of our prayers or of our love of God, but always to show that we love Him by humbly trying to do right in everything. If we do this, and remember the life and lessons of Our Lord Jesus Christ, and try to act up to them, we may confidently hope that God will forgive us our sins and mistakes, and enable us to live and die in Peace.

GOD PROVIDES FOR OUR TOMORROW
compiled by Mary W. Tileston

"Take no thought for your life, what ye shall eat, or what ye shall drink, nor yet for your body, what ye shall put on."
                                             MATTHEW 6:25

*I*t has been well said that no man ever sank under the burden of the day. It is when tomorrow's burden is added to the burden of today that the weight is more than a man can bear. Never load yourselves so, my friends. If you find yourselves so loaded, at least remember this: it is your own doing, not God's. He begs you to leave the future to Him, and mind the present.

                                             GEORGE MACDONALD

SEPTEMBER 19TH

POLISHED AND PREPARED *by R. T. Kendall*

"The Lord will perfect that which concerneth me."
                                             PSALM 138:8

*T*he fact that we have a gift from God doesn't guarantee that we will have the wisdom or common sense to use it. Joseph told the dream, and it didn't take any "dream expert" to give the interpretation. Joseph's brothers got the message like a flash. They said, "Shalt thou indeed reign over us? or shalt thou indeed have dominion over us?" Flaunting a gift springs from a desire to be admired. But the result is always the opposite: it makes people positively dislike us.

Joseph just wasn't ready to be used of God. Many of us may think we are right and ready because the gift is in operation. But God knows better. God had a plan for Joseph and for his people. Do we have a gift? Have we abused it? My counsel is to be sure that we have given ourselves completely to God. We may say, "If I give myself to God, my gift will never be known." I promise you, the only way our gift can be of value is for it to be sanctified and in the hands of our Creator and our Redeemer. When we give our lives utterly to God, even the silly mistakes we have made will turn out for good. This is that wonderful truth found in Romans 8:28, "All things work together for good. . ." The most stupid things we have done turn out right. God does that!

What Joseph needed was preparation. Polishing. "We must through much tribulation enter into the kingdom of God" (Acts 14:22). "But the God of all grace, who hath called us unto his eternal glory by Christ Jesus, after that ye have suffered a while, make you perfect, stablish, strengthen, settle you" (1 Pet. 5:10). "The Lord will perfect that which concerneth me" (Ps. 138:8).

SEPTEMBER 20TH

BRICKS AND BOOKS *by Ken Abraham*

"And we know that all things work together for good to them that love God, to them who are the called according to his purpose."   ROMANS 8:28

*O*ne of my spiritual heroes is Samuel Logan Brengle, the brilliant but humble Salvation Army Commissioner whose books on holiness have been a source of spiritual blessing to millions of readers. One night in Boston, a drunken thug hurled a brick at Brengle as he stood in the doorway of the Salvation Army building. The man was barely ten feet away so the brick blasted full force into Brengle's head, smashing it into the doorpost.

For weeks, the preacher who had laid his life on the line to help the poor and needy lay in limbo between life and death at the hands of one to whom he had come to minister. As a result of the blow, Brengle was incapacitated for more than eighteen months. For the rest of his life, he experienced recurring bouts of depression and intense headaches that his doctors attributed to the blow from the brick.

During his recuperation, Brengle kept busy by writing articles for *The War Cry,* a Salvationist magazine. Later, those articles were collected into a short but powerful book, *Helps to Holiness.* The book was an instant success. The little volume was distributed around the world and translated into dozens of languages. It continues to be an encouraging guide for many Christians searching for a deeper walk with Christ.

Whenever people complimented Brengle or thanked him for the blessing that his book had been to them, Brengle would smile and say, "Well, if there had been no little brick, there would have been no little book!"

SEPTEMBER 21ST

TROUBLE OR TRIUMPH *by Kay Arthur*

"Call upon me in the day of trouble: I will deliver thee, and thou shalt glorify me." PSALM 50:15

*W*hen you are in trouble or in need, where do you run for help? What is your first instinct? Do you run to man or to God? When you are hurting or confused, when you don't know what to do, whose counsel do you seek first? Isn't it usually the counsel of another human being rather than the counsel found in waiting upon God in prayer? Why is it? Why do we run to man before we run to God? Why do we boast in chariots or horses rather than in the name of our Lord? Is it because we can see chariots and horses? In Old Testament days, chariots and horses were two means of protection and/or escape. Today our chariots and horses come with different labels, shapes, and forms; even so, they are still visible means of help, escape, or protection. Yet are these really a source of safety? No. "The horse is prepared against the day of battle: but safety is of the Lord" (Proverbs 21:31).

What is the problem? Why do so many Christians run to the arm of flesh rather than the arms of our all-sufficient God? I think, Beloved, it is because most of us do not really know our God. Why is it that many collapse in the day of trouble and testing? Why is it that Christians are immobilized rather than taking an aggressive stand in the face of fear? It is because Christians, for the most part, cannot boast in the name of their God.

What do I mean when I say "boast in the name of our God"? To boast in means to have confidence in, to trust in His name. Therefore, to boast in God's name means to have confidence in His name. In biblical times, a name represented a person's character. God's name represents His character, His attributes, His nature. To know His name is to know Him. To boast in His name is to have confidence in who He is!

LOOK UP! *by F. B. Meyer*

"And when these things begin to come to pass, then look up, and lift up your heads; for your redemption draweth nigh."
LUKE 21:28

*E*ach great crisis in the past has helped to advance the glorious reign of Christ. Was the fall of Babylon a crisis? It gave mankind a universal speech—the language spoken by Alexander and his soldiers—the delicate, subtle Greek in which the New Testament was written. Was the fall of Rome a crisis? It opened the way to the rise of the northern nations, which have ever been the home of Liberty and the Gospel. Was the fall of Feudalism, in the French Revolution, a crisis? It made the splendid achievements of the nineteenth century possible. And we may look without dismay on events that cast a shadow on our hearts. They also shall serve the cause of the Gospel. In ways we cannot tell, they shall prepare for the triumph of our King. Through the throes of the present travail the new heavens and earth shall be born. The agony is not as the expiring groan of the dying gladiator, but as the sigh of the mother bringing forth her first-born. These things, said our Lord, must needs be; and they are the beginning of travail (Matt. 24:8, R.V.). And amid all Jesus rides in triumph to His destined glory and the crown of all the earth.

FAITHFUL SERVANTS *by A. B. Simpson*

"I know him. . .that [he] shall keep the way of the Lord."
GENESIS 18:19

*G*od wants people whom He can depend upon. He could say of Abraham, *I know him, . . .that the Lord may bring upon Abraham that which he hath spoken of him.* God can be depended upon. He wants us to be just as decided, just as reliable and just as stable. This is what faith means. God is looking for men on whom He can put the weight of all His love and power and faithful promises. When God finds such a soul there is nothing He will not do for him. God's engines are strong enough to pull any weight we attach to them. Unfortunately, the cable which we fasten to the engine is often too weak to hold the weight of our prayer; therefore, God is drilling us, disciplining us and training us that we may achieve stability and certainty in the life of faith. Let us learn our lessons and let us stand fast.

God has His best things for the few
    Who dare to stand the test;
God has His second choice for those
    Who will not have His best.

Give me, O Lord, Thy highest choice,
    Let others take the rest.
Their good things have no charm for me,
    For I have got Thy best.

LITTLE FAITH: BIG PROMISE *by Andrew Murray*

". . .If ye have faith as a grain of mustard seed. . . nothing shall be impossible unto you."   MATTHEW 17:20

*D*isciples of Jesus! who have asked the Master to teach you to pray, come now and accept His lessons. He tells you that prayer is the path to faith, strong faith, that can cast out devils. He tells you: "If ye have faith, nothing shall be impossible unto you"; let this glorious promise encourage you to pray much. Is the prize not worth the price? Shall we not give up all to follow Jesus in the path He opens to us here; shall we not, if need be, fast? Shall we not do anything that neither the body nor the world around hinder us in our great life-work,—having intercourse with our God in prayer, that we may become men of faith, whom He can use in His work of saving the world?

RECKONING UP THINGS *by John Henry Jowett*

"So teach us to number our days, that we may apply our hearts unto wisdom."   PSALM 90:12

*N*umbering things is one of the healthful exercises of the spiritual life. Unless we count, memory is apt to be very tricky and to snare us into strange forgetfulness. Unless we count what we have given away, we are very apt to exaggerate our bounty. We often think we have given when we have only listened to appeals; the mere audience has been mistaken for active beneficence. The remedy for all this is occasionally to count our benevolence and see how we stand in a balance-sheet which we could present to the Lord Himself.

And we must count our blessings. It is when our arithmetic fails in the task, and when counting God's blessings is like telling the number of the stars, that our souls bow low before the eternal goodness, and all murmuring dies away like cloud-spots in the dawn.

And we must also "number our days." We are wasteful with them, and we throw them away as though they are ours in endless procession. And yet there are only seven days in a week! A day is of immeasurable preciousness, for what high accomplisment may it not witness? A day in health or in sickness, spent unto God, and applied unto wisdom, will gather treasures more precious than rubies and gold.

SEPTEMBER 26TH

GOD'S BLANK CHECK BOOK
by Mrs. Charles E. Cowman

"I AM THAT I AM. . ."   EXODUS 3:14

$\mathcal{G}$ od gave Moses a blank check, and as life went forward for the next forty years, Moses kept filling in the blank with his special need. He filled in fearlessness before Pharaoh. He filled in guidance across the Red Sea. He filled in manna for the whole population. He filled in water from the rock. He filled in guidance through the wilderness. He filled in victory over Amalek. He filled in clear revelation at Sinai.

264

And so Moses, for the rest of his life, had little else to do than to go quietly alone, and taking God's blank check book, signed by God's name, I AM THAT I AM , wrote in I AM guidance; I AM bread. He presented the check and God honored it.

And whenever you come to live upon God's plan as Moses from that moment did, you may absolutely trust God. And when you come down to the end you will say, "Not one good thing hath failed of all the good things which the LORD your God spake concerning you" (Joshua 23:14).

DR. A. B. SIMPSON

SEPTEMBER 27TH

LET DOWN YOUR NET AGAIN *by Charles Dickens*

". . .Master, we have toiled all the night, and have taken nothing: nevertheless at thy word I will let down the net. And when they had this done, they inclosed a great multitude of fishes: and their net brake." LUKE 5:5, 6

*T*he first four of the Disciples were poor fishermen who were sitting in their boats by the seaside, mending their nets, when Christ passed by. He stopped, and went into Simon Peter's boat, and asked Him if he had caught many fish. Peter said "No; though they had worked all night with their nets, they had caught nothing." Christ said, "Let down the net again." They did so; and it was immediately so full of fish, that it required the strength of many men (who came and helped them) to lift it out of the water, and even then it was very hard to do. This was another of the miracles of Jesus Christ.

Jesus then said, "Come with me." And they followed Him directly. And from that time the Twelve disciples or apostles were always with Him.

ESTABLISHED IN OUR LIVES *by A. B. Simpson*

"Whereto we have already attained, let us walk by the same rule, let us mind the same thing." PHILIPPIANS 3:16

It is good to be able to receive new truth and blessing without sacrificing the truths already proved or abandoning foundations already laid.

Some persons are always laying the foundations, until, finally, they appear like a number of abandoned sites and half-constructed buildings. Nothing is ever brought to completion.

If today you are abandoning for some new truth the things that a year ago you counted most precious and believed to be divinely true, this should be sufficient evidence that a year from now you will probably abandon your present convictions for the next new light that comes to you.

God wants to continually add to us, to develop us, to enlarge us, to teach us more and more but always building on what He has already taught us and what He has established in our lives.

SEPTEMBER 29TH

LOST AND FOUND *by Charles H. Spurgeon*

"I sought him, but I found him not."

SONG OF SOLOMON 3:1

Tell me where you lost the company of Christ, and I will tell you the most likely place to find Him. Have you lost

Christ in the closet by restraining prayer? Then it is there you must seek and find Him. Did you lose Christ by sin? You will find Christ in no other way but by the giving up of the sin, and seeking by the Holy Spirit to mortify the member in which the lust doth dwell. Do you lose Christ by neglecting the Scriptures? You must find Christ in the Scriptures. It is a true proverb, "Look for a thing where you dropped it, it is there." So look for Christ where you lost Him, for He has not gone away. But it is hard work to go back for Christ. Bunyan tells us, the pilgrim found the piece of the road back to the Arbour of Ease, where he lost his roll, the hardest he had ever traveled. Twenty miles onward is easier than to go one mile back for the lost evidence.

Take care, then, when you find your Master, to cling close to Him. But how is it you have lost Him? One would have thought you would never have parted with such a precious Friend, whose presence is so sweet, whose words are so comforting, and whose company is so dear to you! How is it that you did not watch Him every moment for fear of losing sight of Him? Yet, since you have let Him go, what a mercy that you are seeking Him, even though you mournfully groan, "O that I knew where I might find Him!" Go on seeking, for it is dangerous to be without thy Lord. Without Christ you are like a sheep without its shepherd; like a tree without water at its roots; like a sere leaf in the tempest—not bound to the tree of life. With thine whole heart seek Him, and He will be found of thee; only give thyself thoroughly up to the search, and verily, thou shalt yet discover Him to thy joy and gladness.

ENDURANCE *by Mrs. Charles E. Cowman*

"He knoweth the way that I take: when he hath tried me, I shall come forth as gold."   JOB 23:10

A number of years ago I knew a woman who found God to be a very wonderful Friend. She had a rich Christian experience, but there came into her life a very great trial: her home was broken up; the crash was unspeakable; in the midst of it all it seemed that the Father forsook her.

One evening after prayer-meeting she arose and gave this testimony. We all knew how precious God was to her. Her face was pale and thin. She had suffered much. "God and I have been such wonderful friends, but He seems very far away. He seems to have withdrawn Himself from me. I seem to be left utterly alone." Then looking off in the distance, and with tears, she continued, "But if I never see His face again, I will keep looking at the spot where I saw His face last."

I have never seen nor heard of anything finer than that. That is mighty, sublime, glorious faith that keeps going on. There is a wonderful outcome to the trials in a life of victorious faith like this. This was Job's greatest triumph. "He knoweth the way that I take. The Lord gave and the Lord hath taken away. Blessed be the Name of the Lord."

DEAN DUTTON, D. D.

OCTOBER

GATHERING WITH PURPOSE *by William A. Quale*

*"Be kindly affectioned one to another with brotherly love;
in honour preferring one another."* ROMANS 12:10

$\mathcal{I}$n October the birds are grown neighborly. They are flocking so as to be gone from us. Robins in Summer cared for none of their kind save their immediate family, but when October comes the robins cluster together in rose-breasted brigades. I have counted in a group this October a hundred and twenty robins taking supper. They are grown sociable making ready for their Southward flight. It brings Autumn to my heart to think of the going of the birds; but I know when they return they will bring Springtime with them to my heart, and so I begin my tune in minors but end it in rejoicing majors.

The blackbirds always social, in October gather in black clouds which change when they go out to practice flying maneuvers for the long southward flight. Their voices click and click as if their wings needed oiling. How they fly in spirals up and out and their unnumbered voices say, "Ordered South."

269

LORD OF THE HARVEST *by Andrew Murray*

". . .The harvest truly is great, but the labourers are few:
pray ye therefore the Lord of the harvest. . .would send forth
labourers into his harvest." LUKE 10:2

O let us pray for a life so one with Christ, that His compassion may stream into us, and His Spirit be able to assure us that our prayer avails.

Such a prayer will ask and obtain a twofold blessing. There will first be the desire for the increase of men entirely given up to the service of God. It is a terrible blot upon the Church of Christ that there are times when actually men cannot be found for the service of the Master as ministers, missionaries, or teachers of God's Word. As God's children make this a matter of supplication for their own circle or Church, it will be given. The Lord Jesus is now Lord of the harvest. He has been exalted to bestow gifts—the gifts of the Spirit. His chief gifts are men filled with the Spirit. But the supply and distribution of the gifts depend on the co-operation of Head and members. It is just prayer that will lead to such co-operation; the believing suppliants will be stirred to find the men and the means for the work.

DIVERSITY, NOT UNIFORMITY *by Dr. F. F. Bruce*

"Now there are diversities of gifts, but the same Spirit. And there are differences of administrations, but the same Lord. And there are diversities of operations, but it is the same God which worketh all in all." 1 CORINTHIANS 12:4–6

*D*iversity, not uniformity, is the mark of God's handiwork. It is so in nature; it is so in grace, too, and nowhere more so than in the Christian community. Here are many men and women with the most diverse kinds of parentage, environment, temperament, and capacity. Not only so, but since they became Christians they have been endowed by God with a great variety of spiritual gifts as well. Yet because and by means of that diversity, all can co-operate for the good of the whole. Whatever kind of service is to be rendered in the church, let it be rendered heartily and faithfully by those divinely qualified, whether it be prophesying, teaching, admonishing, administering, making material gifts, sick-visiting, or performing any other kind of ministry.

To illustrate what he means, Paul uses the figure of a human body in 1 Corinthians 12:12–27. Each part of the body has its own distinctive work to do, yet in a healthy body all the parts function harmoniously and interdependently for the good of the whole body. So should it be in the church, which is the body of Christ.

THE EAGERNESS OF THE EMANCIPATED SOUL
by F. B. Meyer

"The woman then left her waterpot, and went her way into the city, and saith to the men, 'Come, see a man, which told me all things that ever I did: is not this the Christ?' "

JOHN 4:28, 29

*A*s we have seen, the woman left her waterpot! The spring had overflowed within her heart and was demanding expression. Those who are one with Christ through the Spirit find themselves filled with a love that kindles a revival in other hearts as well as in their own. It was because of the love that glowed in this wondrously transformed soul, that the Samaritans came to Christ. The love of God glowed in her heart and the spring of eternal love had begun to rise within.

In a large mining center, during the Welsh Revival, the evening meeting was commencing in the crowded chapel an hour before the advertised time. Some were praying, some giving their experience, many were singing or reciting texts of Scripture. In the midst of the excitement, Evan Roberts entered, and knelt for a time in silent prayer. His sensitive nature soon became aware that the meeting was stirred more by emotion than by the love and power of God. So he rose, silenced the hubbub, and for a whole half-hour made the great congregation remain hushed beneath the searching light of the Holy Spirit. At the end of that period, one of the best-known mine-owners of the neighborhood rose from his seat and extended his hand to another mine-owner, and the two men, professing Christians, who had been at feud for years, were reconciled. Instantly, the entire atmosphere of the meeting was changed. The keynote was Calvary, and the power was that of

Pentecost. Scores were born into the kingdom of God, and all were conscious of the overshadowing presence of the Saviour. Like one vast choir, the people sang a new song, and to those two men the blessed consciousness of God's love came at full tide. You must get right with God, if you would have springing-water.

POWER IN UNITY *by Andrew Murray*

". . .Whatsoever ye shall bind on earth shall be bound in heaven. . .For where two or three are gathered together in my name. . ." MATTHEW 18:18, 20

*B*lessed Lord! It is when we are one in love and desire that our faith has Thy presence and the Father's answer. O let the thought of Thy presence and the Father's favour draw us all nearer to each other.

Grant especially, Blessed Lord, that Thy Church may believe that it is by the power of united prayer that she can bind and loose in heaven; that Satan can be cast out; that souls can be saved; that mountains can be removed; that the kingdom can be hastened. And grant, good Lord! that in the circle with which I pray, the prayer of the Church may indeed be the power through which Thy Name and Word are glorified. Amen.

NO SINFUL WORD *compiled by Mary W. Tileston*

"I said, I will take heed to my ways, that I sin not with my tongue."   PSALM 39:1

> No sinful word, nor deed of wrong,
>   Nor thoughts that idly rove;
> But simple truth be on our tongue,
>   And in our hearts be love.

ST. AMBROSE

*L*et us all resolve,—First, to attain the grace of SILENCE; Second, to deem all FAULT-FINDING that does no good a SIN, and to resolve, when we are happy ourselves, not to poison the atmosphere for our neighbours by calling on them to remark every painful and disagreeable feature of their daily life; Third to practice the grace and virtue of PRAISE.

HARRIET B. STOWE

Surrounded by those who constantly exhibit defects of character and conduct, if we yield to a complaining and impatient spirit, we shall mar our own peace without having the satisfaction of benefiting others.

T. C. UPHAM

OCTOBER 7TH

PEACE WITH A DIFFERENCE *by Captain E. G. Garré*

*"And the multitude of them that believed were of one heart
and of one soul."*   ACTS 4:32

*H*ow much better it would be to settle our differences
by meeting together to pray, by allowing the Holy Spirit to
have His way with us. Since then I have put this matter more
than once to the test. When at committee meetings or con-
ferences disputes arose and feelings ran high, when men
began to get excited and fight for their own opinions, the
best way to meet all this was to keep quiet in a corner, praying that the Holy Spirit might come and reveal His will and
direct men's thoughts in the right path, how wonderfully He
has led us out of the mazes and brought peace and happiness
to men's minds.

OCTOBER 8TH

RIGHTEOUS ANGER, UNRIGHTEOUS ANGER
by Charles H. Spurgeon

"God said to Jonah, 'Doest thou well to be angry?. . .' "
                                                    JONAH 4:9

*A*nger is not always or necessarily sinful, but it has such
a tendency to run wild that whenever it displays itself, we
should be quick to question its character with this enquiry,
"Doest thou well to be angry?" It may be that we can answer
"YES." Very frequently anger is the madman's firebrand, but

sometimes it is Elijah's fire from heaven. We do well when we are angry with sin, because of the wrong which it commits against our good and gracious God; or with ourselves because we remain so foolish after so much divine instruction; or with others when the sole cause of anger is the evil which they do. He who is not angry at transgression becomes a partaker in it. Sin is a loathsome and hateful thing, and no renewed heart can patiently endure it. God Himself is angry with the wicked every day, and it is written in His Word, "Ye that love the Lord, hate evil."

Far more frequently it is to be feared that our anger is not commendable or even justifiable, and then we must answer, "NO." Why should we be fretful with children, passionate with servants, and wrathful with companions? Is such anger honourable to our Christian profession, or glorifying to God? Is it not the old evil heart seeking to gain dominion, and should we not resist it with all the might of our newborn nature? Many professors give way to temper as though it were useless to attempt resistance; but let the believer remember that he must be a conqueror in every point, or else he cannot be crowned. If we cannot control our tempers, what has grace done for us? We must not make natural infirmity an excuse for sin, but we must fly to the cross and pray the Lord to crucify our tempers, and renew us in gentleness and meekness after His own image.

GRUDGES *by John Henry Jowett*

"Thou shalt not avenge, nor bear any grudge against the children of thy people, but thou shalt love thy neighbour as thyself: I am the LORD." LEVITICUS 19:18

*H*ow searching is that demand upon the soul! My forgiveness of my brother is to be complete. No sulleness is to remain, no sulky temper which so easily gives birth to thunder and lightning. There is to be no painful aloofness, no assumption of a superiority which rains contempt upon the offender. When I forgive, I am not to carry any powder forward on the journey. I am to empty out all my explosives, all my ammunition of anger and revenge. I am not to "bear any grudge."

I cannot meet this demand. It is altogether beyond me. I might utter words of forgiveness, but I cannot reveal a clear, bright, blue sky without a touch of storm brewing anywhere. But the Lord of grace can do it for me. He can change my weather. He can create a new climate. He can "renew a right spirit within me," and in that holy atmosphere nothing shall live which seeks to poison and destroy. Grudges shall die "like cloud-spots in the dawn." Revenge, that was full creation of the unclean, feverish soul, shall give place to good-will, the strong genial presence which makes its home in a new heart.

PERSONALLY YOURS *by R. T. Kendall*

"Behold, thou desirest truth in the inward parts: and in the hidden part thou shalt make me to know wisdom."

PSALM 51:6

*D*o we want to be used of God? Are we quite sure that we are ready to be used of the Lord? God knows whether we are. In the case of Joseph, there was a lot of sorting out in his personality that had to be done, and I can tell you this: God can do it. God, as he prepares us to do his work, will sort out our personality defects, many of which may have been superimposed upon us. It is easy for us to say, "I am like this because my mother was this way" or "My father did this or that." It is easy to blame our parents for the way we are. We may be shy. We may be forward. We may be reserved. We may be arrogant. But we should never think that any personality trait or hang-up (or any other blemish) rules us out as God's messengers to our generation, for God can deal with us. He certainly dealt with Joseph. All the happy trimmings that accompanied Joseph's life at this time would shortly be purged by a sovereign God.

We must remember that parents have their faults too. The reason that Joseph was the favorite child was partly because he was the son of Jacob's old age. That doesn't excuse Jacob. But we must forgive our parents and then hope that our children will forgive us. Nothing is more ridiculous than being bitter against our parents all our lives. We must sort ourselves out and let God deal with us until we are responsible for being just like we are.

FIRST, MY BROTHER *by John Henry Jowett*

"Therefore if thou bring thy gift to the altar, and there rememberest that thy brother hath ought against thee; Leave there thy gift before the altar, and go thy way; first be reconciled to thy brother, and then come and offer thy gift."

MATTHEW 5:23, 24

"*F*irst be reconciled to thy brother." We are to put first things first. When we bring a gift unto the Lord he looks at the hand that brings it. If the hand is defiled the gift is rejected. "Wash you, make you clean." "First be reconciled to thy brother, and then come and offer thy gift."

All this tells us why some resplendent gifts are rejected, and why some commonplace gifts are received amid heavenly song. This is why the widow's mite goes shining through the years. The hand that offered it was hallowed and purified with sacrifice. Shall we say that in that palm there was something akin to the pierced hands of the Lord? The mite had intimate associations with the Cross.

And it also tells me why so much of our public worship is offensive to our Lord. We come to the church from a broken friendship. Some holy thing has been broken on the way. Someone's estate has been invaded, and his treasure spoiled. Someone has been wronged, and God will not touch our gift. "Leave there thy gift; first be reconciled to thy brother."

AM I CARNALLY MINDED? *by Oswald Chambers*

"Whereas there is among you envying, and strife, and divisions, are ye not carnal?. . ."　　　　1 CORINTHIANS 3:3

No natural man knows anything about carnality. The flesh lusting against the Spirit that came in at regeneration, and the Spirit lusting against the flesh, produces carnality. "Walk in the Spirit," says Paul, "and ye shall not fullfil the lusts of the flesh"; and carnality will disappear.

Are you contentious, easily troubled about trifles? "Oh, but none who is a Christian ever is!" Paul says they are, he connects these things with carnality. Is there a truth in the Bible that instantly awakens petulance in you? That is a proof that you are yet carnal. If sanctification is being worked out, there is no trace of that spirit left.

If the Spirit of God detects anything in you that is wrong, He does not ask you to put it right; He asks you to accept the light, and He will put it right. A child of the light confesses instantly and stands bared before God; a child of the darkness says—"Oh, I can explain that away." When once the light breaks and the conviction of wrong comes, be a child of the light, and confess, and God will deal with what is wrong; if you vindicate yourself, you prove yourself to be a child of the darkness.

What is the proof that carnality has gone? Never deceive yourself; when carnality is gone it is the most real thing imaginable. God will see that you have any number of opportunities to prove to yourself the marvel of His grace. The practical test is the only proof. "Why," you say, "if this had happened before, there would have been the spirit of resentment!" You will never cease to be the most amazed person on earth at what God has done for you on the inside.

MY SHEPHERD *by T. C. Horton & Charles E. Hurlburt*

"The Lord is my shepherd; I shall not want." PSALM 23:1

$\mathcal{T}$ o say, "The Lord is MY SHEPHERD," must carry with it in our understanding not merely grateful praise for the infinite grace and tenderness of the Great Shepherd who leads us by still waters and in green pastures, but confession of our own helplessness and need of a Shepherd's care. And a remembrance also of our lost, undone condition, until:

> All through the mountains, thunder-riven,
> And up from the rocky steep,
> There arose a glad cry to the gates of heaven,
> "Rejoice! I have found My sheep!"

Lord Jesus, Thou tender Shepherd, lead us forth this day in glad service for Thee. Amen.

OCTOBER 14TH

JUDGE NOT! *compiled by Mary W. Tileston*

"Why beholdest thou the mote that is in thy brother's eye, but perceivest not the beam that is in thine own eye?"
LUKE 6:41

> Judge not, the workings of his brain
> And of his heart thou canst not see;
> What looks to thy dim eyes a stain,
> In God's pure light may only be

A scar, brought from some well-worn field,
Where thou wouldst only faint and yield.

ADELAIDE A. PROCTER

*W*hen you behold an aspect for whose constant gloom and frown you cannot account, whose unvarying cloud exasperates you by its apparent causelessness, be sure that there is a canker somewhere, and a canker not the less deeply corroding because concealed.

CHARLOTTE BRONTË

While we are coldly discussing a man's career, sneering at his mistakes, blaming his rashness, and labelling his opinions—"Evangelical and narrow," or "Latitudinarian and Pantheistic," or "Anglican and supercilious"—that man, in his solitude, is perhaps shedding hot tears because his sacrifice is a hard one, because strength and patience are failing him to speak the difficult word, and do the difficult deed.

GEORGE ELIOT

OCTOBER 15TH

RESPONSE AND RESTORATION *by Malcolm Smith*

"Have mercy upon me, O God, according to thy loving-kindness: according unto the multitude of thy tender mercies blot out my transgressions."   PSALM 51:1

*O*ne of the most amazing verses in that prayer is verse 11: Do not cast me away from Thy presence, and do not take Thy Holy Spirit from me. David knew that God had not cast him off and that the Holy Spirit was still with him.

Whatever people said, he rested in the God Whose love would not let him go.

Are you wounded and lonely, ridden with true guilt? With everything people are saying about you, it may be difficult to believe, but your first step is to realize that you are loved. You need to understand that you have failed but, having done so, you need to know God says that He accepts you.

Before the grace of God can take our mistakes and turn them into our strengths, there must be a response to Him. That response is repentance and faith.

Repentance is simply changing our minds about ourselves and our actions. We see things God's way. It means that we admit to God that we are wrong and turn helplessly to Him. If we choose the path of sin, refusing to acknowledge it as sin, we cannot expect the redemption of our failures, only a compounding of despair.

OCTOBER 16TH

NO FISHING ALLOWED *by Corrie ten Boom*

"As far as the east is from the west, so far hath he removed our transgressions from us." PSALM 103:12

*G*uilt is a useful experience because it shows where things are wrong. It is dangerous when it is not there at all, just as the absence of pain when someone is ill can be dangerous.

When we belong to Jesus we are not called to carry our guilt ourselves. God has laid on Jesus the sins of the whole world. What you have to do is to tell Him everything, confess your guilt and sin and repent, and then He will cleanse you and throw all your sins into the depths of the sea. Don't forget there is a sign that reads NO FISHING ALLOWED. If somebody has suffered through your guilt, then make restitution in the power and wisdom of the Lord.

Lord, thank You that where You have carried our guilt we have not to carry it ourselves. Help us not to listen to the accuser of the brethren, the devil, anymore, but to Your Holy Spirit, who always points to the finished work on the cross.

OCTOBER 17TH

THIS MIND *by Joy Dawson*

"Let the words of my mouth, and the meditation of my heart, be acceptable in thy sight, O LORD, my strength, and my redeemer."   PSALM 19:14

*A*ll sin starts in the mind; therefore, we are only as holy as our "thought lives" are holy. "For as he thinketh in his heart, so is he. . . " (Proverbs 23:7).

I believe our thoughts sound as loudly in heaven as our words do on earth. "The thoughts of the wicked are an abomination to the Lord, the words of the pure are pleasing to him" (Proverbs 15:26). Would we want our thoughts to be written on a wall at the end of a day for anyone to see? God has done it before; He can do it again!

". . .Jesus bent down and wrote with his finger on the ground" (John 8:6, 8). By the time Jesus had finished writing, there was no one left of the woman's accusers showing that in either thought or deed, all were guilty of the same sin.

It is not sufficient to repent of sin committed with our words and actions alone. Repentance of our sinful thoughts is equally important. "Let the wicked forsake his way, and the unrighteous man his thoughts: and let him return unto the Lord, and he will have mercy upon him; and to our God, for he will abundantly pardon" (Isaiah 55:7). "Let the words of my mouth, and the meditation of my heart, be acceptable in thy sight, O Lord, my strength, and my redeemer" (Psalm 19:14).

When David was repenting of the sin of adultery, as recorded in Psalm 51:6, he said to God, "Behold, thou desirest truth in the inward parts; therefore teach me wisdom in my secret heart." The inward being and the secret heart refer to his thought life. He knew what every person knows who has committed acts of immorality, that the act with the body starts with the sin of lust in the mind. That is why David asked for wisdom in his secret heart, which means the fear of the Lord upon his thought life, because "the fear of the Lord is the beginning of wisdom" (Psalm 111:10).

OCTOBER 18TH

CHRIST, MY LAW *by Andrew Murray*

"Let this mind be in you, which was also in Christ Jesus."
PHILIPPIANS 2:5

Let us yield our hearts to God in prayer, for Him to search us and discover in us whether the life of Christ has actually been the law that we have taken for the guide of our life. I do not speak about attainment, but let us ask, Have I actually said: "Oh, how blessed it would be! Oh, this is what I covet, and what I wait upon God for! I want to live for God in the way Christ lived"? It almost sounds as if it were too high and presumptuous. But what does Christ mean when He said so often: "As I, even so you; as I loved, even so love one another; as I kept the commandments of My Father, so, if ye keep His commandments, ye shall abide in My love"? What does the Holy Spirit mean when He says, "Let this

285

mind be in you which was also in Christ Jesus, who made Himself of no reputation, but humbled Himself and became obedient unto death"? The mind of Christ must be my mind, my disposition, and my life.

SAVED TO THE UTTERMOST *by Hannah Whitall Smith*

"Now unto him that is able to keep you from falling, and to present you faultless before the presence of his glory with exceeding joy." JUDE 24

*I*n order to prevent failure, or to discover its cause, if we find we have failed, it is necessary to keep continually before us this prayer: "Search me, O God, and know my heart; try me and know my thoughts; and see if there be any wicked way in me, and lead me in the way everlasting."

Let me beg of you, however, dear Christians, do not think, because I have said all this about failure, that I believe in it. There is no necessity for it whatever. The Lord Jesus is able, according to the declaration concerning Him, to deliver us out of the hands of our enemies, that we may "serve him without fear, in holiness and righteousness before him all the days of our life." Let us then pray, every one of us, day and night, *Lord, keep us from sinning, and make us living witnesses of Thy mighty power to save to the uttermost;* and let us never be satisfied until we are so pliable in His hands, and have learned so to trust Him, that He will be able to "make us perfect in every good work to do his will, working in us that which is well pleasing in his sight, through Jesus Christ; to whom be glory for ever and ever. Amen!"

A QUIET HEART *by Elisabeth Elliot*

"Lord, you have assigned me my portion and my cup; you have made my lot secure."　　　　　PSALM 16:5, NIV

*J*esus slept on a pillow in the midst of a raging storm. How could He? The terrified disciples, sure that the next wave would send them straight to the bottom, shook Him awake with rebuke. How could He be so careless of their fate?

He could because He slept in the calm assurance that His Father was in control. His was a quiet heart. We see Him move serenely through all the events of His life—when He was reviled, He did not revile in return. When He knew that He would suffer many things and be killed in Jerusalem, He never deviated from His course. He had set His face like flint. He sat at supper with one who would deny Him and another who would betray Him, yet He was able to eat with them, willing even to wash their feet. Jesus in the unbroken intimacy of His Father's love, kept a quiet heart.

. . .Keep a quiet heart! Our enemy delights in disquieting us. Our Savior and Helper delights in quieting us. "As a mother comforts her child, so will I comfort you" is His promise (Isaiah 66:13, NIV). The choice is ours. It depends on our willingness to see everything in God, receive all from His hand, accept with gratitude just the portion and the cup He offers.

DUST AND DIETY *by John T. Seamands*

"And be not conformed to this world: but be ye transformed by the renewing of your mind, that ye may prove what is that good, and acceptable, and perfect, will of God."

ROMANS 12:2

*T*he great evangelist Dwight L. Moody once said, "I have had more trouble with myself than with any other man I ever met." Most of us in our moments of utter honesty could, no doubt, make a similar confession.

There is one part of us that honestly intends to be clean and kind and truthful and forgiving; and there is another part of us that is the source of thoughts we ought not to have and dreams of which we are ashamed, and prompts us to say things we are later sorry for.

The mind is the key to the man, and the way to become a completely transformed person is by the refashioning of the mind.

We may compare the human mind to a factory, the machinery of which is turning over day and night, 24 hours a day. The mind is always at work, even while we are asleep. It takes the thoughts that we feed into it during our waking hours as raw material, and works on them all the time. If we go to sleep with thoughts of anxiety and fear in our minds, we will be doubly fearful and anxious when we awaken. But if we go to sleep with thoughts of confidence and peace and the power of God to meet our needs, we will awaken with a deepened sense of adequacy and ability to meet our needs. That's why it is so valuable to have a prayer, or quote some scripture, or think some noble, positive thoughts before dropping off to sleep.

In order to become fully transformed persons there must be the conversion of the conscious mind, and that takes place when we initially come to Christ in repentance and decide we are going to follow Him. But more than that, we will never be delivered from inner conflict and find supreme joy in the Christian life until we go on to the conversion of the deep mind.

OCTOBER 22ND

CAUTION! GOD AT WORK *by Hannah Whitall Smith*

"For we know that the whole creation groaneth and travaileth in pain together until now. And not only they, but ourselves also, which have the firstfruits of the Spirit, even we ourselves groan within ourselves, waiting for the adoption, to wit, the redemption of our body." ROMANS 8:22, 23

$\mathcal{J}$t was no mere figure of speech when our Lord in that wonderful Sermon on the Mount said to His disciples: "Be ye therefore perfect even as your Father in heaven is perfect." He meant, of course, according to our measure, but He meant that reality of being conformed to His image to which we have been predestined. And in the Epistle to the Hebrews we are shown how it is to be brought about. "Now the God of peace, that brought again from the dead our Lord Jesus, that great shepherd of the sheep, through the blood of the everlasting covenant, Make you perfect in every good work to do his will; working in you that which is well pleasing in his sight, through Jesus Christ; to whom be glory for ever and ever. Amen."

It is to be by His working in us, and not by our working in ourselves, that this purpose of God in our creation is to be accomplished; and if it should look as regards some of us that we are too far removed from any conformity to the image of Christ for such a transformation ever to be wrought, we must remember that our Maker is not finished making us yet. The day will come, if we do not hinder, when the work begun in Genesis shall be finished in Revelation, and the whole Creation, as well as ourselves, shall be delivered from the bondage of corruption into the glorious liberty of the children of God.

"For we know that the whole creation groaneth and travaileth in pain together until now. And not only they, but ourselves also, which have the firstfruits of the Spirit, even we ourselves groan within ourselves, waiting for the adoption, to wit, the redemption of our body."

OCTOBER 23RD

A PALACE FOR GOD *by Ken Abraham*

"Jesus answered and said unto him, 'If a man love me, he will keep my words: and my Father will love him, and we will come unto him, and make our abode with him.' "

John 14:23

$\mathcal{T}$ he great English writer C. S. Lewis knew well the temptations to judge ourselves and each other by false standards. He also understood the balance between our perseverance and God's patience with our imperfections:

"On the one hand, God's demand for perfection need not discourage you in the least in your present attempts to be good, or even in your present failures. Each time you fall He will pick you up again. And He knows perfectly well that your own efforts are never going to bring you anywhere near perfection. On the other hand, you must realize from the outset that the goal toward which He is beginning to guide you is absolute perfection; and no power in the whole universe, except you yourself, can prevent Him from taking you to the goal."

Borrowing from George MacDonald, another great writer, Lewis continued:

"Imagine yourself as a living house. God comes in to rebuild that house. At first, perhaps, you can understand what He is doing. He is getting the drains right and stopping the leaks in the roof and so on; you knew that those jobs needed doing and so you are not surprised. But presently He starts knocking the house about in a way that hurts abominably and does not seem to make sense.

"What on earth is He up to? The explanation is that He is building quite a different house from the one you thought of. . . You thought you were going to be made into a decent little cottage: but He is building a palace.

"He intends to come and live in it himself.

"If you think that you don't deserve God's grace, you are right. But then again, neither do the rest of us."

OCTOBER 24TH

HOLINESS UNTO THE LORD *by Captain E. G. Garré*

"And every man that hath this hope in him purifieth himself, even as he is pure."   1 JOHN 3:3

*T*he one great characteristic of John Hyde was holiness. I do not mention prayerfulness now, for prayer was his life work. I do not especially call attention to soul-winning, for his power as a soul-winner was due to his Christ-likeness. God says, "without holiness no man shall see the Lord."

His life was a witness to the power of Jesus' Blood to cleanse from all sin. "There is no power on the world so irrepressible as the power of personal holiness." A man's gifts may lack opportunity. The spiritual power of a consecrated will needs no opportunity, and can enter where doors are shut. In this strange and tangled business of human life there is no energy that so steadily does its work as the mysterious, un-conscious, silent, unobtrusive, impenetrable influence which comes from a man who has done with all self-seeking. And herein lay John Hyde's mystical power and great influence. Multitudes have been brought to their knees by prayer he uttered when filled with the Spirit.

OCTOBER 25TH

GUIDE OTHERS TO GLORY
by Edith Dean/Susanna Wesley

"Giving no offence in any thing. . . But in all things approving ourselves as the minsters of God, in much patience, in afflictions, in necessities, in distresses. . . By pureness, by knowledge, by longsuffering, by kindness, by the Holy Ghost, by love unfeigned."　　　　2 CORINTHIANS 6:3, 4, 6

$\mathcal{T}$ he training Susanna Wesley gave her children is indicated by this letter she wrote her eldest son Samuel, who also became a preacher:

Consider well what a separation from the world, what purity, what devotion, what exemplary virtue, are required in those who are to guide others to glory. . . . I would advise you to arrange your affairs by a certain method, by which means you will learn to improve every precious moment. . . . Begin and end the day with Him who is the Alpha and Omega, and if you really experience what it is to love God, you will redeem all the time you can for His more immediate service.

Endeavor to act upon principle and do not live like the rest of mankind, who pass through the world like straws upon a river, which are carried which way the stream or wind drive them. . . .Get as deep as an impression on your mind as is possible of the constant presence of the great and holy God. He is about our beds and about our paths and spies out all our ways. Whenever you are tempted to the commission of any sin, or the omission of any duty, pause and say to yourself, What am I about to do? God sees me.

Susanna Wesley's story is one of uncommon misery, hardship and failure. Spiritually, however, it is a life of true riches, glory and victory, for she never lost her high ideals nor her sublime faith. During a severe trial, she went to her room and wrote:

Though man is born to trouble, yet I believe there is scarce a man to be found upon earth but, take the whole course of his life, hath more mercies than afflictions, and much more pleasure than pain. All my sufferings, by the admirable management of Omnipotent Goodness, have concurred to promote my spiritual and eternal good. . . Glory be to thee, O Lord!

OCTOBER 26TH

VISION BY PERSONAL PURITY *by Oswald Chambers*

"Blessed are the pure in heart: for they shall see God."
MATTHEW 5:8

*P*urity is not innocence, it is much more. Purity is the outcome of sustained spiritual sympathy with God. We have to grow in purity. The life with God may be right and the inner purity remain unsullied, and yet every now and again the bloom on the outside may be sullied. God does not shield us from this possibility, because in this way we realize the necessity of maintaining the vision by personal purity. If the spiritual bloom of our life with God is getting impaired in the tiniest degree, we must leave of everything and get it put right. Rcmember that vision depends on character—the pure in heart see God.

God makes us pure by His sovereign grace, but we have something to look after, this bodily life by which we come in contact with other people and with other points of view, it is these that are apt to sully. Not only must the inner sanctuary be kept right with God, but the outer courts as well are to be brought into perfect accord with the purity God gives us by His grace. The spiritual understanding is blurred immediately the outer court is sullied. If we are going to retain personal contact with the Lord Jesus Christ, it will mean there are some things we must scorn to do or to think, some legitimate things we must scorn to touch.

A practical way of keeping personal purity unsullied in relation to other people is to say to yourself—That man, that woman, perfect in Christ Jesus! That friend, that relative, perfect in Christ Jesus!

CAN YOU BE HOLY? *by Ken Abraham*

"Be ye holy in all manner of conversation; Because it is written, 'Be ye holy; for I am holy. . . . Pass the time of your sojourning here in fear.' "   1 PETER 1:15–17

*B*elieve that God can make you holy here and now. Many devout Christians hope to become holy some day, if not here on earth, hopefully in heaven. But the Spirit of God impressed Peter in those first few years after Pentecost to exhort us: "Be holy yourselves also in all your behavior; because it is written, 'You shall be holy, for I am holy. . .' conduct yourselves in fear [holy, reverential awe] during the time of your stay upon earth. . ." (1 Peter 1:15–17). Clearly, Peter is implying that holiness is something to be pursued in this lifetime, not simply in the life to come.

John Wesley often asked his audiences such penetrating questions as:

1. Have you received the Holy Spirit's fullness since you have believed?
2. Will you ever need Him more than you do right now?
3. Will you ever be "more ready" to receive Him than right now?
4. Will God ever be "more ready" to fill you with His Holy Spirit than He is right now?

If you answered no to any of the above questions, then begin your quest for holiness by believing that God can deliver you from the bondage of sin: He can cleanse your heart, mind, and mouth; and He can fill you with His Holy Presence—right now.

NATURAL HOLINESS *by Joy Dawson*

"Seeing ye have purified your souls in obeying the truth through the Spirit unto unfeigned love of the brethren, see that ye love one another with a pure heart fervently."

1 PETER 1:22

*J*esus is in the house of a Pharisee having a meal, and an ex-prostitute hears He's there. (See Luke 7:36–50.) She seizes the opportunity of getting close to Him, away from the inevitable crowds that always followed Him.

She gate-crashes the party and immediately proceeds to open up her alabaster flask of ointment. Then she demonstratively bursts into tears, which splash over His feet. Undaunted by the cold, critical stares of the Pharisee host, she uses her long hair to mop up the tear stains, and unashamedly kisses His feet and then anoints them with the ointment.

She lavishly expresses the devotion and gratitude of her heart to the only One who has ever shown her such love, such forgiveness, such mercy, such recognition, such respect, and who has given her such peace of mind. Does all this display of affection faze Jesus? Is He embarrassed? No! He's totally relaxed. With calm authority, He rebukes the religious host and praises the repentant woman from the streets.

None of this should really surprise us when we understand that one of the purposes of Jesus Christ's leaving heaven and coming to this earth was to show us how to live. For that reason, we can see He was demonstrating through the relationship with this woman that true holiness and naturalness go hand in hand.

In fact, only really holy people are free to be really natural.

They have nothing to hide.
There is no need to act.
There is nothing to cover up.

WHAT DID I DO TO DESERVE THIS?
by Ken Abraham

"But we all, with open face beholding as in a glass the glory of the Lord, are changed into the same image from glory to glory, even as by the Spirit of the Lord."

2 CORINTHIANS 3:18

*U*ntil you understand that your relationship with God is a blood-covenant relationship, you will be trapped in a performance-oriented, defective concept of Christianity. Instead of recognizing that He gives His grace freely to you, you will be constantly attempting to prove to God that you merit His favor.

Mephibosheth must have known that feeling of helplessness. After all, what could he possibly do for the king? He was crippled in both feet. When David imposed his loving grace upon Mephibosheth, all he could do was admit his absolute helplessness and accept the king's unmerited but boundless love and grace.

Don't you hate that? I do. Accepting God's grace comes hard to me, not that I'd want to stand in His presence for a milli-second on my own merit. It's just that, well, I feel so helpless in His presence and I'm a performance-oriented sort of guy. Although I know better and have even written books advising others in this area, if I am not extremely careful, I find that I begin to base my self-image on what I do or what I have accomplished.

297

I must constantly remind myself that it is not what I do for Jesus that gets me into heaven; it is what He has already done on the cross.

Yes, I do things for Him out of a heart of love, attitude of gratitude and a desire to please Him. But I no longer do these things as I once did—to gain His approval. As a Christian, I live my life from His approval, not for His approval. What a difference!

OCTOBER 30TH

GOD ENLIGHTENS MY DARKNESS
compiled by Mary W. Tileston

"The LORD my God will enlighten my darkness."

PSALM 18:28

When we in darkness walk,
  Nor feel the heavenly flame,
Then is the time to trust our God,
  And rest upon His name.

A. M. TOPLADY

*H*e has an especial tenderness of love towards thee for that thou art in the dark and hast no light, and His heart is glad when thou dost arise and say, "I will go to my Father." For He sees thee through all the gloom through which thou canst not see Him. Say to Him, "My God, I am very dull and low and hard; but Thou are wise and high and tender, and Thou art my God. I am Thy child. Forsake me not." Then fold the arms of thy faith, and wait in quietness until light goes up in the darkness. Fold the arms of thy Faith, I say, but not of thy Action: bethink thee of something that thou oughtest to do, and go and do it, if it be but the sweeping

of a room, or the preparing of a meal, or a visit to a friend;
heed not thy feelings: do thy work.

GEORGE MACDONALD

PREPARING HIS SERVANTS *by John Henry Jowett*

*"Nathanael saith unto him, 'Whence knowest thou me?' Jesus
answered and said unto him, 'Before that Philip called thee,
when thou wast under the fig tree, I saw thee.' "*   JOHN 1:48

*O*ur Lord does not stumble upon His disciples by accident. His discoveries aren't surprises. He knows where His
nuggets lie. Before He calls to service He has been secretly
preparing the servant. "I girded thee, though thou hast not
known Me."

He knew all about Simon. "Thou art Simon"—just a lis-
tener, not yet a strong, bold doer: a man of many opinions
not yet consolidated into the truth of experimental convictions. "Thou shalt be called Peter." Simon become Peter!
Loose gravel become hard rock! Hear-says become the "ver-
ilies" of unshakable experience! The Lord proclaims our
glorious possibilities.

And He knew all about Nathanael. "When thou wast
under the fig-tree I saw thee." "In that secret meditation of
thine, when thy wishes and desires were being born, I saw
thee!" "When others saw nothing, I had fellowship with thee
in the secret place."

And He knows all about thee and me. "I know My sheep."
We do not take Him by surprise. He does not come in late, and
find the performance half over. He is in at our beginnings,
when grave issues are being born. "I am Alpha."

NOVEMBER

LIFE UNTO DEATH *by William A. Quale*

"For I am persuaded, that neither death, nor life, . . .shall be able to separate us from the love of God, which is in Christ Jesus our Lord." ROMANS 8:38, 39

November is the month of leaf fall. Not that this month monopolizes that melancholy poetry. October is much given to it. But November has that for a business. If, when November puts lean finger across the lips and stumbles out in the dark to die, any leaves are left dangling on a naked branch, it is because the leaf has inherent tenacities which are wholly out of the usual. Some leaves refuse to fall until Spring comes and thrusts them off to make way for the greenery of the year new born. Not death but life kills some forest leaves. But November is assiduous to strip the finery from every tree. And November winds use the bare twigs as the strings of a harp to make a song of lamentation. The cottonwoods stand stripped to the skin like a naked swimmer; and November winds use the bare twigs as the strings of a harp on which to make November threnody.

You can see through the underwood far as the eye can travel through the pillars of the trees. Of the leaves we say: "After life's fitful fever they sleep well."

300

THE MERCY OF COMFORT *by Charles Dickens*

". . .And I will have mercy upon her that had not obtained mercy."
HOSEA 2:23

*O*f all the people who came to him, none were so full of grief and distress, as one man who was a Ruler or Magistrate over many people, and he wrung his hands, and cried, and said, "Oh Lord, my daughter—my beautiful, good, innocent little girl, is dead. Oh come to her, come to her, and lay Thy blessed hand upon her, and I know she will revive, and come to life again, and make me and her mother happy. Oh Lord we love her so, we love her so! And she is dead!"

Jesus Christ went out with him, and so did his disciples and went to his house, where the friends and neighbours were crying in the room where the poor dead little girl lay, and where there was soft music playing; as there used to be, in those days, when people died. Jesus Christ, looking on her, sorrowfully, said—to comfort her poor parents—"She is not dead. She is asleep." Then he commanded the room to be cleared of the people that were in it, and going to the dead child, took her by the hand, and she rose up, quite well, as if she had only been asleep. Oh what a sight it must have been to see her parents clasp her in their arms, and kiss her, and thank God, and Jesus Christ his son, for such great Mercy!

ENDURING FAITH *by Ken Abraham*

"Know therefore that the LORD thy God, he is God, the faithful God, which keepeth covenant and mercy with them that love him and keep his commandments to a thousand generations."   DEUTERONOMY 7:9

*J*f God has placed a dream in your heart, do not give up. Be diligent. Endure even in the dungeons of life.

Our generation knows little about endurance; we are so accustomed to instant gratification. Endurance does not mean, "I'll just hang in there until Jesus comes." Endurance means, "I believe that what God said He would do, He will, in fact, do!" Endurance means that you can say with the ancient prophet Habakkuk,

> "Though the fig tree should not blossom, and there be
>   no fruit on the vines,
> though the yield of the olive should fail, and the fields
>   produce no food,
> though the flocks should be cut off from the fold, and
>   there be no cattle in
> the stalls, yet I will exalt in the LORD, I will rejoice in
>   the God of my salvation.
> The LORD GOD is my strength, and He has made my
>   feet like hinds' feet,
> and makes me walk on my high places."
>   HABAKKUK 3:17–19

That is what endurance is all about!

Your days of preparation may even now be nearing an end. The delay you have endured has not been an accident, but was according to His plan and for His purposes. Soon the Lord will be standing outside your dream or the vision He has given you, and you will hear, "Come forth!"

Perhaps you have been a friend of Jesus' for a long time, but recently you feel you have been spiritually dead, a form wrapped in the grave clothes of doubt, discouragement, depression and disillusionment. Today, hear His voice as He speaks to you, "My child, come forth!"

NOVEMBER 4TH

SICKNESS AMONG CHRIST'S FRIENDS
by John Henry Jowett

" '. . .Lord, behold, he whom thou lovest is sick.' When Jesus heard that, he said, 'This sickness is not unto death, but for the glory of God, that the Son of God might be glorified thereby.' "   JOHN 11:3, 4

*A*nd so sickness can enter the circle of the friends of the Lord. "He whom Thou lovest is sick." My sicknesses do not mean that I have lost His favour. The shadow is His, as well as the sunshine. When He removes from the glare of boisterous health it may be because of some spiritual fern which needs the ministry of the shade. "This sickness is. . .for the glory of God." Something beautiful will spring out of the shadowed seclusion, something which shall spread abroad the name and fame of God.

And, therefore, I do not wonder at the Lord's delay. He did not hasten away to the sick friend: "He abode two days still in the same place where he was." Shall I put it like this: the awakening bulbs were not yet ready for the brighter light—just a little more shade! We are impatient to get healthy; the Lord desires that we become holy. Our physical sickness is continued in order that we may put on spiritual strength.

And there are others besides sick Lazarus concerned in the sickness: "I am glad for your sakes I was not there." The disciples were included in the divine scheme. Their spiritual welfare was to be affected by it. Let me ever remember that the circle affected by sickness is always wider than the patient's bed. And may God be glorified in all!

NOVEMBER 5TH

THE POWER OF WORSHIP *by Jack Hayford*

"Speaking to yourselves in psalms and hymns and spiritual songs, singing and making melody in your heart to the Lord; Giving thanks always for all things unto God and the Father in the name of our Lord Jesus Christ."

EPHESIANS 5:19, 20

*W*hat can we do when life seems hard, defeating, unfulfilling and aimless? Well, we can be honest in our prayers, as the psalmist was. We can cry to God, as in Psalm 90:13, "Return, O Lord! How long? And have compassion on Your servants."

Can you see what is happening here? This writer isn't crying out in dark unbelief, but in the light of hope. In short, he is *worshiping*. The fact his heart isn't overflowing with blessing or abundance is no hindrance to his worship.

Even in the dark times, we must realize the vast power of worship to give our lives meaning and purpose. Worshiping God even amid despair is a way to defy the Adversary and declare our valuing of the good—the best—in life: The Lord!

There is no more worthy purpose to praise; no more worthy time for it!

UNUTTERABLE LOVE *by Ken Abraham*

"If we confess our sins, he is faithful and just to forgive us our sins, and to cleanse us from all unrighteousness."
1 JOHN 1:9

*T*he grand privilege and obligation of a Christian is that Christ can fill your heart so full of His holy love, you won't be able to contain it all. It was an explosion of this love in the heart of Samuel Logan Brengle that launched him into a life of holiness.

In his book *When the Holy Ghost Is Come*, Brengle described his experience:

"I had been searching the Scriptures, ransacking my heart, humbling my soul, and crying to God almost day and night for a pure heart and the baptism with the Holy Ghost, when one glad, sweet day (it was January 9, 1885) this text suddenly opened to my understanding: 'If we confess our sins, He is faithful and just to forgive our sins, and to cleanse us from all unrighteousness': and I was enabled to believe without any doubt that the precious Blood cleansed my heart, even mine, from all sin. Shortly after that, while reading these words of Jesus to Martha: 'I am the resurrection and the life; he that believeth in me, though he were dead, yet shall he live: And whosoever liveth and believeth in me shall never never die' (John 11:24, 26)—instantly my heart was melted like wax before fire; Jesus Christ was revealed to my spiritual consciousness, revealed in me, and my soul was filled with unutterable love. I walked in a heaven of love. Then one day, with amazement, I said to a friend: 'This is the perfect love about which the Apostle John wrote; but it is beyond all I dreamed of. In it is personality. This love thinks, wills, talks with me, corrects me, instructs and teaches me.' And then I knew that God the Holy Ghost was in this love and this love was God, for 'God is love.' "

NOVEMBER 7TH

THE BLESSING OF SURRENDER *by Andrew Murray*

". . .Now yield your members servants to righteousness unto holiness." ROMANS 6:19

There was in our company a godly worker who has much to do in training workers, and I asked him what he would say was the great need of the Church, and the message that ought to be preached. He answered very quietly and simply and determinedly: "Absolute surrender to God is the one thing." The words struck me as never before. And that man began to tell how, in the workers with whom he had to deal, he finds that if they are sound on that point, even though they be backward, they are willing to be taught and helped, and they always improve; whereas, others who are not sound there very often go back and leave the work. The condition for obtaining God's full blessing is absolute surrender to Him.

THE SELF-LESS LIFE *by Andrew Murray*

". . .So now also Christ shall be magnified in my body, whether it be by life, or by death." PHILIPPIANS 1:20

*H*ave you believed that Almighty God is able so to reveal Christ in your heart, so to let the Holy Spirit rule in you, that the self-life shall not have power or dominion over you? Have you coupled the two together, and with tears of penitence and with deep humiliation and feebleness, cried out: *O God, it is impossible to me; man cannot do it, but, glory to Thy name, it is possible with God?* Have you claimed deliverance? Come and do it tonight. I want you to put yourselves afresh in absolute surrender into the hands of a God of infinite love; and as infinite as His love is His power to do it.

"CAN GOD?" *by Mrs. Mary E. Cowman*

"Yea, they spake against God; they said, 'Can God furnish a table in the wilderness?' " PSALM 78:19

*"C*AN GOD?" Oh, fatal question! It shut Israel out of the land of Promise. And we are in danger of making the same mistake. Can God find me a situation, or provide food for my children? Can God keep me from yielding to that besetting sin? Can God extricate me from this terrible snare in which I am entangled? We look at the difficulties, the surges that are

rolling high, and we say, "If Thou canst do anything, help us!"

They said, "Can God?" It hurt and wounded God deeply. Say no more, "Can God?" Rather say this, "God Can!" That will clear up many a problem. That will bring you through many a difficulty in your life.

There is no strength in unbelief.

Has the life of God's people reached the utmost limit of what God can do for them? Surely not! God has new places, and new developments, and new resources. He can do new things, Unheard-of hidden things, hidden things! Let us enlarge our hearts and not limit Him. "When thou didst terrible things which we looked not for, thou camest down, the mountains flowed down at thy presence" (Isaiah 64:3).

We must desire and believe. We must ask and expect that God will do unlooked-for things! We must set our faith on a God of Whom men do not know what He hath prepared for them that wait for Him. The Wonder-doing God. . .must be the God of our confidence.

ANDREW MURRAY

The Wonder-doing God can surpass all our expectation!

NOVEMBER 10TH

AT HIS TABLE *by Brother Lawrence*

"Thou preparest a table before me in the presence of mine enemies: thou anointest my head with oil; my cup runneth over." PSALM 23:5

I think it proper to inform you after what manner I consider myself before God, whom I behold as my King.

I consider myself as the most wretched of men, full of

sores and corruption, and who has committed all sorts of crimes against his King. Touched with a sensible regret, I confess to Him all my wickedness, I ask His forgiveness, I abandon myself in His hands that He may do what He pleases with me. The King, full of mercy and goodness, very far from chastising me, embraces me with love, makes me eat at His table, serves me with His own hands, gives me the key of His treasures; He converses and delights Himself with me incessantly, in a thousand and a thousand ways, and treats me in all respects as His favorite. It is thus I consider myself from time to time in His holy presence.

NOVEMBER 11TH

OUR SAVIOUR *by Charles Dickens*

"The Lord is nigh unto them that are of a broken heart; and saveth such as be of a contrite spirit."   PSALM 34:18

*O*ne of the Pharisees begged Our Saviour to go into his house, and eat with him. And while our Saviour sat eating at the table, there crept into the room a woman of that city who had led a bad and sinful life, and was ashamed that the Son of God should see her; and yet she trusted so much to His goodness, and His compassion for all who, having done wrong were truly sorry for it in their hearts, that, by little and little, she went behind the seat on which He sat, and dropped down at His feet, and wetted them with her sorrowful tears; then she kissed them and dried them on her long hair, and rubbed them with some sweet-smelling ointment she had brought with her in a box. Her name was Mary Magdalene. Jesus said, "As God forgives this woman so much sin, she will love Him, I hope, the more." And He said to her, "God forgives you!"

THE PATHETIC MULTITUDE *by John Henry Jowett*

"I have compassion on the multitude, because they have now been with me three days, and have nothing to eat: And if I send them away fasting to their own houses, they will faint by the way: for divers of them came from far."

Mark 8:2, 3

*M*y Lord has "compassion upon the multitude." And (shall I reverently say it?) His compassion was part of His passion. His pity was always costly. It culminated upon Calvary, but it was bleeding all along the road! It was a fellow-feeling with all the pangs and sorrows of the race. And a pity that bleeds is a pity that heals. "In His love and in His pity He redeemed us."

And the multitude is round about us still, and the people are in peril of fainting by the way. There is the multitude of misfortune, the children of disadvantage, who never seem to have come to their own. And there is the multitude of outcasts, the vast army of publicans and sinners. And there are the bewildering multitudes of Africa, and India, and China, and they have nothing to eat!

How do I regard them? Do I share the compassion of the Lord? Do I exercise a sensitive and sanctified imagination, and enter somewhat into the pangs of their cravings? My Lord calls for my help. "How many loaves have ye?" "Bring out all you have! Consecrate your entire resources! Put your all upon the altar of sacrifice!" And in reply to the call can I humbly and trustfully say, "O, Lamb of God, I come!"

OUR PROVISION *by Charles Dickens*

"Behold the fowls of the air: for they sow not, neither do they reap, . . .yet your heavenly Father feedeth them. Are ye not much better than they?"   MATTHEW 6:26

*J*esus going with his disciples over a sea, called the Sea of Tiberias and sitting with them on a hillside, saw great numbers of these poor people waiting below, and said to the apostle Philip, "Where shall we buy bread, that they may eat and be refreshed, after their long journey?" Philip answered, "Lord, two hundred pennyworth of bread would not be enough for so many people, and we have none." "We have only," said another apostle—Andrew, Simon Peter's brother—"five small barley loaves, and two little fish, belonging to a lad who is among us. What are they, among so many!" Jesus Christ said, "Let them all sit down!" They did; there being a great deal of grass in that place. When they were all seated, Jesus took the bread, and looked up to Heaven, and blessed it, and broke it, and handed it in pieces to the apostles, who handed it to the people. And of those five little loaves, and two fish, five thousand men, besides women, and children, ate, and had enough; and when they were all satisfied, there were gathered up twelve baskets full of what was left. This was another of the Miracles of Jesus Christ.

FORGOTTEN IN PLENTY,
REMEMBERED IN POVERTY *by Jill Briscoe*

"Give, and it shall be given unto you; good measure, pressed down, and shaken together, and running over, shall men give into your bosom. . . ."   LUKE 6:38

"*W*hat do you have in the house?" (Elisha asked the poor widow).

"Nothing," she replied. "Absolutely nothing! Nothing to sell, nothing to eat, nothing to burn on the fire, nothing to sleep on. Nothing! I have borrowed from my neighbors and my friends, but now they want their money, and I have none."

"Think," the prophet urged. "Are you sure there's nothing in the house?"

"Just a little pot of oil," she replied.

Elisha smiled. "Forgotten in plenty, remembered in your poverty. Omnipotence's provision has been there all the time!" he murmured. The little widow gazed at him wonderingly, and Elisha began to explain what she must do. . .

Turning to the amazed children who had watched the whole glorious turn of events, their mother began to give them orders. "We are going to reach out to our neighbors," (the widow) announced. . . "Run now and ask for empty vessels—get many of them!"

"When you learn to pour yourself out into the empty vessels all around you and lose your own problems in seeking to 'be' the answer to theirs, then you will be able to rejoice in My fullness," Elisha said to the little widow, as she busily kept filling vessel after vessel that her sons brought to her.

"Is it magic, mummy?" the little boys asked wonderingly.

The little lady laughed. "It's greater than magic," she

said. "I'm simply obeying the Word of God, given to me by the man of God, about the provision of God, and I'm learning that the oil flows according to my faith!"

THE VOCATION OF THE NATURAL LIFE
by Oswald Chambers

"But when it pleased God. . .to reveal his Son in me."
GALATIANS 1:15, 16

The call of God is not a call to any particular service; my interpretation of it may be because contact with the nature of God has made me realize what I would like to do for Him. The call of God is essentially expressive of His nature; service is the outcome of what is fitted to my nature. The vocation of the natural life is stated by the apostle Paul—"When it pleased God. . .to reveal his Son in me that I *might preach* him. . ."

Service is the overflow of superabounding devotion; but, profoundly speaking, there is no *call* to that, it is my own little actual bit and is the echo of my identification with the nature of God. Service is the natural part of my life. God gets me into a relationship with Himself whereby I understand His call, then I do things out of sheer love for Him on my own account. To serve God is the deliberate love-gift of a nature that has heard the call of God. Service is expressive of that which is fitted to my nature: God's call is expressive of His nature; consequently when I receive His nature and hear His call, the voice of the Divine nature sounds in both and the two work together. The Son of God reveals Himself in me, and I serve Him in the ordinary ways of life out of devotion to Him.

NO PREJUDICE *by Charles Dickens*

"For there is no respect of persons with God."
ROMANS 2:11

*J*esus Christ chose Twelve poor men to be his companions. These twelve are called the Apostles or Disciples, and He chose them from among Poor Men, in order that the Poor might know—always after that; in all years to come—that Heaven was made for them as well as for the rich, and that God makes no difference between those who wear good clothes and those who go barefoot and in rags. The most miserable, the most ugly, deformed, wretched creatures that live, will be bright Angels in Heaven if they are good here on earth. Never forget this, when you are grown up. Never be proud or unkind, my dears, to any poor man, woman, or child. If they are bad, think that they would have been better, if they had had kind friends, and good homes, and had been better taught. So, always try to make them better by kind persuading words; and always try to teach them and relieve them if you can. And when people speak ill of the Poor and Miserable, think how Jesus Christ went among them and taught them, and thought them worthy of His care. And always pity them yourselves, and think as well of them as you can.

A MODERN-DAY PROPHET
by Brother Andrew

"Blessed is he that readeth, and they that hear the words of this prophecy, and keep those things which are written therein: for the time is at hand."　　REVELATION 1:3

If we want to change the world for God, we must start by listening to his Word as given in the Scriptures.

Many times in the Old Testament I read, "And the word of the Lord came unto" a certain prophet. The job of the prophets was to listen to what God was saying and then to declare it, in both word and deed, wherever God told them to go. Most of the prophets in the Bible were not specially trained or highly educated men who received a call during their last year of seminary. By and large they were ordinary people—like you and me—who were following God in their everyday lives. And yet when they spoke God's message, they were able to raise up and bring down entire kingdoms. Their ministry came to have great impact.

To be prophetic today does not require us to have an audience with world leaders. It simply means carrying out Jesus' Great Commission to "go and make disciples of all nations" (Matthew 28:19). We do this in response to the prompting of the Holy Spirit through the Scriptures.

Since the Old Testament prophets didn't have the Bible, they had to hear their message directly from God. Today we can look to his written Word to know him and his will for us. As we saturate ourselves in the Scriptures and in prayer, our relationship with Christ deepens. And through the Bible he will begin to impress upon us just how and where he wants us to share his message.

Lord, cause me to hear your Word for my life today. And lead me to the places and people who need to receive that Word.

THE HIGH PLACES OF LOVE *by Hannah Hurnard*

"And God is able to make all grace abound toward you; that ye, always having all sufficiency in all things, may abound to every good work." 2 CORINTHIANS 9:8

Hear the summons night and day
    Calling us to come away.
From the heights we leap and flow
    To the valleys down below.
Always answering to the call,
    To the lowest place of all.
Sweetest urge and sweetest pain,
    To go low and rise again.

"That is very puzzling," said Much-Afraid. "Let us go down lower still, the water seems to be singing so gladly, because it is hurrying to go down to the lowest place, and yet you are calling me to the Highest Places. What does it mean?"

"The High Places," answered the Shepherd, "are the starting places for the journey down to the lowest place in the world. When you have hinds' feet and can go 'leaping on the mountains and skipping on the hills,' you will be able, as I am, to run down from the heights in gladdest self-giving and then go up to the mountains again. You will be able to mount to the High Places swifter than eagles."

NOVEMBER 19TH

THE GREATNESS OF DOING *by Brother Lawrence*

"But ye, brethren, be not weary in well doing."
2 THESSALONIANS 3:13

*T*hat we ought, once and for all, heartily to put our whole trust in God, and make a total surrender of ourselves to Him, secure that He would not deceive us.

That we ought not to be weary of doing little things for the love of God, who regards not the greatness of the work, but the love with which it is performed. That we should not wonder if, in the beginning, we often failed in our endeavors, but that at last we should gain a habit, which will naturally produce its acts in us, without our care, and to our exceeding great delight.

NOVEMBER 20TH

MISSED OPPORTUNITIES *by Corrie ten Boom*

"I will restore to you the years that the locust hath eaten. . . "
JOEL 2:25

*M*issed opportunities!
If only. . .

It is good to regret missed opportunities, but quite wrong to be miserable about them. You cannot look back across your past life without seeing things to regret. That is as it should be. But we have to draw a subtle distinction between a legitimate regret and a wrong condition of heart. Give God your "if onlies."

Think of those laborers in the vineyard in the parable which Jesus told in Matthew 20:1–16. They all received the same wages, although some had worked the whole day and some had worked for only an hour. Compare that to a person's life. Some people enter the Kingdom right at the end of their lives. They may regret all those years when they were not serving Christ. But the important thing is that they are in the Kingdom. The thing that matters first of all, if you are a Christian, is not what you once were but what you are now.

Lord Jesus, I give my "if onlies" to You. Make me a faithful laborer here and now.

NOVEMBER 21ST

THERE IS NO OTHER WAY *by Elisabeth Elliot*

"'Obey my voice, and I will be your God, and ye shall be my people: and walk ye in all the ways that I have commanded you; that it may be well unto you.'"   JEREMIAH 7:23

*I*n order to get to a place called Laity Lodge in Texas you have to drive into a riverbed. The road takes you down a steep, rocky hill into a canyon and straight into the water. There is a sign at the water's edge which says, "Yes. You drive in the river."

One who has made up his mind to go to the uttermost with God will come to a place as unexpected and perhaps looking as impossible to travel as that riverbed looks. He may glance around for an alternative route, but if he wants what God promises His faithful ones, he must go straight into the danger. There is no other way.

The written word is our direction. Trust it. Obey it. Drive in the river and get to Laity Lodge. Moses said to

318

Israel, "I offer you the choice of life or death, blessing or curse. Choose life and then you and your descendants will live; love the Lord your God, obey him, and hold fast to him: that is life for you."

When you take the risk of obedience, you find solid rock beneath you—markers, evidence that someone has traveled this route before. "The Lord your God will cross over at your head. . .he will be with you; he will not fail you or forsake you. Do not be discouraged or afraid" (Deuteronomy 30: 19–20; 31:3, 8 NEB). It's what the old gospel song puts so simply:

Trust and obey, for there's no other way
To be happy in Jesus but to trust and obey.
JOHN H. SAMMIS

NOVEMBER 22ND

AN ENLARGED HEART *by F. B. Meyer*

"I am the Lord thy God which teacheth thee to profit, which leadeth thee by the way that thou shouldest go."
ISAIAH 48:17

*T*he Spirit of Jesus waits to be to you, O pilgrim, what He was to Paul. Only be careful to obey his least prohibitions, and where, after believing prayer, there are no apparent hindrances, believe that you are on the way everlasting, and go forward with an enlarged heart. *Teach me to do Thy will, for Thou art my God: Thy Spirit is good, lead me into the land of uprightness.* Do not be surprised if the answer comes in closed doors. But when doors are shut right and left, an open road is sure to lead to Troas. There Luke awaits, and visions will point the way, where vast opportunities stand open, and faithful friends are waiting.

ADDING *by A. B. Simpson*

"But seek ye first the kingdom of God, and his righteousness; and all these things shall be added unto you."

MATTHEW 6:33

*F*or every heart that is seeking anything from the Lord this is a good watch-word. That very thing, or the desire for it, may unconsciously separate us from the Lord or at least from the singleness of our purpose toward Him. The thing we desire may be a right thing, but we may desire it in a distrustful and selfish spirit. Let us commit it to Him and believe for it; but let us, at the same time, keep our purpose fixed on His will and glory.

Let us claim even His promised blessings, not for themselves or ourselves, but for Him. Then shall it be true, "Delight thyself also in the Lord; and he shall give thee the desires of thine heart" (Psalm 37:4). All other things but Himself God will "add." But they must always be added, never first. Then shall we be able to believe for them without doubt, when we claim them for Him and not for ourselves. It is only when we are Christ's that all things are ours.

Lord, help me this day to seek Thee first, and be more desirous to please Thee and have Thy will than to possess any other blessing.

THANKSGIVING *by Donald Grey Barnhouse*

"Enter into his gates with thanksgiving, and into his courts with praise: be thankful unto him, and bless his name."

PSALM 100:4

I was once invited to a luncheon where thirty or forty Christians—ministers and laymen—were gathered together for discussion of a certain problem of Christian work.

A well-known layman was asked to return thanks before the meal. I have heard the blessing asked hundreds of times, but suddenly my attention was aroused. The man who was praying said, "We thank Thee for all these gifts, for our food, for our water. . ."

Thank God for the water. . . I have asked the blessing before thousands of meals, but that day for the first time, I thanked the Lord in spirit and in truth for common ordinary water, and for the Living Water. I then began to think of other common things for which we never thank God, and began thanking Him.

What are you really thankful for? Do you realize that God tells us we are to be thankful for everything?

If difficulties reach us personally, we should take the attitude which the Spirit taught Paul when he said, "Most gladly therefore will I rather glory in my infirmities, that the power of Christ may rest upon me" (2 Cor. 12:9). Since we know that all things work together for the good of those who love the Lord (Rom. 8:28), we must take the attitude of thankfulness for anything that the Lord sends to us.

Thanksgiving Day for the true Christian is something far deeper and far wider than the joy of autumn harvest blessings. Thanksgiving Day for the Christian is an entrance into the

321

deepest thoughts of God, so that we may say, "Yes, Father, I am learning to be thankful for everything!"

IS THANKSGIVING ALWAYS POSSIBLE?
by Donald Grey Barnhouse

"And let them sacrifice the sacrifices of thanksgiving, and declare his works with rejoicing."　　　PSALM 107:22

*G*od's definite will for the believer is that he shall be a fountain of praise and that his life shall be in thanksgiving to God at all times and in all circumstances.

The Lord God, who is the Author of all our blessings, appreciates, desires, and even seeks our praise and thanksgiving. "Whoso offereth praise glorifieth me" (Ps. 50:23).

And the Psalmist also said, "Every day will I bless thee, and I will praise thy name for ever and ever" (Ps. 145:2).

We are to thank God in all things; the Lord knows what is best for us, and He is ordering the course of our life, bringing the details to pass in the time and manner of His desire. He has never made a mistake, and what He allows to come into the life of His child is for the good of that child and for the glory of God. Any chastisement that ever reaches us comes for our profit, that we might be partakers of His holiness (Heb. 12:10).

One of the great preachers of the past, the saintly Rutherford, went through persecutions beyond the lot of most men. Yet at the end of his life he could write:

Deep waters crossed life's pathway,
　　The hedge of thorns was sharp;

Now these all lie behind me,
On, for a well-tuned harp!

It is wonderful that a man who has been through sufferings akin to those of Job should cry out in desire for a heart to praise the Lord. Such desire is proof of confidence and trust in the Father, for it is the acknowledgement that He does all things well. Thanksgiving in all things, this is the will of God.

NOVEMBER 26TH

TRIALS MAKE ROOM FOR CONSOLATION
by Charles H. Spurgeon

"For as the sufferings of Christ abound in us, so our consolation also aboundeth by Christ." 2 CORINTHIANS 1:5

*H*ere is a blessed proportion. The Ruler of Providence bears a pair of scales—in this side He puts His people's trials, and in that He puts their consolations. When the scale of trial is nearly empty, you will find the scale of consolation just as heavy. When the black clouds gather most, the light is the more brightly revealed on us. When the night lowers and the tempest is coming on, the Heavenly Captain is always closest to His crews. It is a blessed thing that when we are most cast down, then it is that we are most lifted up by the consolations of the Spirit. One reason is, because trials make more room for consolation. Great hearts can only be made by great troubles. The spade of trouble digs the reservoir of comfort deeper, and makes more room for consolation. God comes into our heart—He finds it full—He begins to break our comforts and to make it empty; then there is more room for grace. The humbler a man lies, the more comfort he will always have, because he will be more fitted to receive it. Another reason why we are often most happy in our troubles, is this—then we have the closest dealings with God. When the barn is full, man can live without God; when the purse is bursting with gold, we try to do without so much prayer. But once take our gourds away, and we want our God; once cleanse the idols out of the house, then we are compelled to honour Jehovah. "Out of the depths have I cried unto thee, O Lord." There is no cry so good as that which comes from the bottom of the mountains; no prayer half so hearty as that which comes up from the depths of the soul, through deep trials and afflictions. Hence they bring us to God, and we are happier; for nearness to God is happiness. Come, troubled believer, fret not over your heavy troubles, for they are the herald of weighty mercies.

NOVEMBER 27TH

TRUST IN THE LORD *compiled by Mary W. Tileston*

"Trust in the LORD, and do good; so shalt thou dwell in the land, and verily thou shalt be fed."   PSALM 37:3

Build a little fence of trust
    Around to-day;
Fill the space with loving work,
    And therein stay;
Look not through the sheltering bars
    Upon to-morrow,
God will help thee bear what comes,
    Of joy or sorrow.

MARY FRANCES BUTTS

$\mathcal{L}$et us bow our souls and say, "Behold the handmaid of the Lord!" Let us lift up our hearts and ask, "Lord, what wouldst thou have me to do?" Then light from the opened heaven shall stream on our daily task, revealing the grains of gold, when yesterday all seemed dust; a hand shall sustain us and our daily burden, so that, smiling at yesterday's fears, we shall say, "This is easy, this is light"; every "lion in the way," as we come up to it, shall be seen chained, and leave open the gates of the Palace Beautiful; and to us, even to us, feeble and fluctuating as we are, ministries shall be assigned, and through our hands blessings shall be conveyed in which the spirit of just men make perfect might delight.

ELIZABETH CHARLES

NOVEMBER 28TH

DAILY BREAD *compiled by Mary W. Tileston*

"Thou openest thine hand, and satisfiest the desire of every living thing."   PSALM 145:16

> What Thou shalt to-day provide,
>   Let me as a child receive;
> What to-morrow may betide,
>   Calmly to Thy wisdom leave.
> 'Tis enough that thou wilt care;
>   Why should I the burden bear?

JOHN NEWTON

$\mathcal{H}$ave we found that anxiety about possible conse-quences increased the clearness of our judgment, made us wiser and braver in meeting the present, and arming ourselves for the future? . . . If we had prayed for this day's bread, and left the next to itself, if we had not huddled our days together, not allotting to each its appointed task, but ever deferring that to the future, and drawing upon the future for its own troubles, which must be met when they come whether we have anticipated them or not, we should have found a simplicity and honesty in our lives, a capacity for work, an enjoyment in it, to which we are now, for the most part, strangers.

F. D. MAURICE

NOVEMBER 29TH

THE FATHER'S INTEREST *by Andrew Murray*

". . .Our Father which art in heaven, Hallowed be thy name. Thy kingdom come. Thy will be done. . . ."

LUKE 11:2

*T*here are two sorts of prayer: personal and intercessory. The latter ordinarily occupies the lesser part of our time and energy. This may not be. Christ has opened the school of prayer specially to train intercessors for the great work of bringing down, by their faith and prayer, the blessings of His work and love on the world around. There can be no deep growth in prayer unless this be made our aim. The little child may ask of the father only what it needs for itself; and yet it soon learns to say, "Give some for sister too." But the grown-up son, who only lives for the father's interest and takes charge of the father's business, asks more largely, and gets all that is asked. And Jesus would train us to the blessed life of consecration and service, in which our interests are all subordinate to the Name, and the Kingdom, and the Will of the Father.

326

RECEIVE YE! *by Andrew Murray*

". . .He breathed on them, and saith unto them, 'Receive ye the Holy Ghost.' "   JOHN 20:22

*F*ather in heaven! Thou didst send Thy Son to reveal Thyself to us, Thy Father-love, and all that that love has for us. And He has taught us, that the gift above all gifts which Thou wouldest bestow in answer to prayer is, the Holy Spirit.

O my Father! I come to Thee with this prayer; there is nothing I would—may I not say, I do—desire so much as to be filled with the Spirit, the Holy Spirit. The blessings He brings are so unspeakable, and just what I need. He sheds abroad Thy love in the heart, and fills it with Thyself. I long for this. He breathes the mind and life of Christ in me, so that I live as He did, in and for the Father's love. I long for this. He endues with power from on high for all my walk and work. I long for this. O Father! I beseech Thee, give me this day the fullness of Thy Spirit.

Father! I ask this, resting on the words of my Lord: "HOW MUCH MORE THE HOLY SPIRIT." I do believe that Thou hearest my prayer; I receive now what I ask; Father! I claim and I take it: the fullness of Thy Spirit as mine. I receive the gift this day again as a faith gift; in faith I reckon my Father works through the Spirit all He has promised. The Father delights to breathe His Spirit into His waiting child as he tarries in fellowship with Himself. Amen.

DECEMBER

THE CHRIST OF CHRISTMAS *by William A. Quale*

". . .Your sorrow shall be turned into joy."   JOHN 16:20

*B*efore Christ came it was only a month of icy Winter fierce in onset of frost and snow and raging icy wind, but since his coming December, however angry its beginning, its ending has always been in a burst of laughter. When December is at its frozen noon all of a sudden mirth invades this spacious Winter and voice of man and woman, youth and maid, schoolboy and little toddling child, leaps to a song, and the icy church bells sing a carol and Christmas chimneys have radiant light. People forget their weeping or are ashamed to invade Christmas with their tears. December has been silenced of his boisterous anger by the more boisterous good nature of the whole world of happy hearts. December himself learns a Christmas tune and sings with tempestuous mirth a melody, the burden of which I catch to be: "Merry Christmas, Peace on Earth, good will to men. Christ is come and has changed my Winter into laughing Spring. I am less December now than June. My flowers are children's smiling faces and my birds' singing is the Christmas laughter of such hearts as have heard that in Bethlehem a child is born and the angels sing and I, December of the frozen heart, have caught the angels' tune, Praise! Praise!"

THE COLD SNOWS *by Charles H. Spurgeon*

"Thou hast made summer and winter."   PSALM 74:17

*M*y soul, begin this wintry month with thy God. The cold snows and the piercing winds all remind thee that He keeps His covenant with day and night, and tends to assure thee that He will also keep that glorious covenant which He has made with thee in the person of Christ Jesus. He who is true to His Word in the revolutions of the seasons of this poor sin-polluted world, will not prove unfaithful in His dealings with His own well-beloved Son.

Winter in the soul is by no means a comfortable season, and if it be upon thee just now it will be very painful to thee; but there is this comfort, namely, that the Lord makes it. He sends the sharp blasts of adversity to nip the buds of expectation; He scattereth the frost like ashes over the once verdany meadows. He does it all; He is the great Winter King, and rules in the realms of frost, and therefore thou canst not murmur. Frosts kill noxious insects, and put a bound to raging diseases; they break up the clods, and sweeten the soil. O that such good results would always follow our winters of affection!

How we prize the fire just now! How pleasant is its cheerful glow! Let us in the same manner prize our Lord, Who is the constant source of warmth and comfort in every time of trouble. Let us draw nigh to Him, and in Him find joy and peace in believing. Let us wrap ourselves in the warm garments of His promises, and go forth to labours which befit the season, for it were ill to be as the sluggard who will not plough by reason of the cold; for he shall beg in summer and have nothing.

COMFORT MY PEOPLE *by Hannah Whitall Smith*

"Comfort ye, comfort ye my people, saith your God."
ISAIAH 40:1

*T*he true commission in my opinion is to be found in Isaiah 40:1, 2: "Comfort ye, comfort ye my people, saith your God. Speak ye comfortably to Jerusalem, and cry unto her, that her warfare is accomplished, that her iniquity is pardoned: for she hath received of the Lord's hand double for all her sins." "Comfort ye my people" is the divine command; do not scold them. If it is the Gospel you feel called to preach, then see to it that you do really preach Christ's Gospel and not man's. Christ comforts, man scolds. Christ's Gospel is always good news, and never bad news. Man's gospel is generally a mixture of a little good news and a great deal of bad news; and, even where it tries to be good news, it is so hampered with "ifs" and "buts," and with all sorts of man-made conditions, that it utterly fails to bring any lasting joy or comfort.

HOW MUCH MORE? *by Andrew Murray*

"Or what man is there of you, whom if his son ask bread, will he give him a stone? Or if he ask a fish, will he give him a serpent? . . .how much more shall your Father which is in heaven give good things to them that ask him?"

MATTHEW 7:9–11

$\mathcal{I}$n these words our Lord proceeds further to confirm what He had said of the certainty of an answer to prayer. To remove all doubt, and show us on that sure ground His promise rests, He appeals to what every one has seen and experienced here on earth. We are all children, and know what we expected of our fathers. We are fathers, or continually see them; and everywhere we look upon it as the most natural thing there can be, for a father to hear his child. And the Lord asks us to look up from earthly parents, of whom the best are but evil, and to calculate HOW MUCH MORE the heavenly Father will give good gifts to them that ask Him. Jesus would lead us up to see, that as much greater as God is than sinful man, so much greater our assurance ought to be that He will more surely than any earthly father grant our childlike petitions. As such greater as God is than man, so much surer is it that prayer will be heard with the Father in heaven than with a father on earth.

GOD *by T. C. Horton & Charles E. Hurlburt*

"But unto the Son he saith, 'Thy throne, O God, is for ever and ever.' "　　　　　　　　　　　　　　HEBREWS 1:8

*H*ere we have the Alpine height in titles for our Lord, "Thy throne, O God!" All other names and titles are inferior to this. When He was born in a manger, God was there. When He worked at the carpenter's trade, God was there at work. When He associated with the fishermen, it was God who was their companion. When He spoke, God spoke. When He died on the cross, it was God Himself who poured out His Life. When He comes "with a shout," it will be the voice of God that calls us to be with Him forever. It is God the Son who holds the sceptre and rules the worlds, and we will rule and reign with Him. *Oh, God our Saviour and Coming King, hasten Thy coming, and help us to help Thee hasten that day, for Thine own name's sake. Amen.*

KNOWING HIM *by Charles Dickens*

"That I may know him, and the power of his resurrection. . ."　　　　　　　　　　　　　　PHILIPPIANS 3:10

*M*y dear children, I am very anxious that you should know something about the History of Jesus Christ. For everybody ought to know about Him. No one ever lived, who was so good, so kind, so gentle, and so sorry for all people who did wrong, or were in anyway ill or miserable, as He was. And as He is now in Heaven, where we hope to go, and all to meet each other after we are dead, and there be happy always together, you never can think what a good place Heaven is, without knowing who He was and what He did.

DECEMBER 7TH

MY LITTLE CHRISTMAS TREE *by Vance Havner*

". . .Because I live, ye shall live also."   JOHN 14:19

*W*ell, it won't be long until they'll be singing "It's Beginning to Look a Lot Like Christmas" but the blessed season won't find us here. All that is left is the little tree and me. One day after Sara left for heaven I got the precious momento out and it still stands bravely though stooped with age. The tiny tinsel angel on it is bowed and not so bright. We're somewhat alike, I'm afraid, but come Christmas I'm going to set it on the table again. There'll be a vacant chair across from me for it will be Sara's first Christmas in heaven. But the little tree and I will muster all the courage possible and with my creaky old voice I might even try a verse of "Joy To The World." I'm rejoicing in the coronation of the dearest one I've known, promotion from pain and grief to the courts of heaven. I'm not hiding the little tree among my souvenirs as a sad reminder of days forever past. As long as it can stand I'll set it up as a symbol of victory ahead.

Run up your flag, my dear sorrowing one, and wave your banner! If your life is hid with Christ in God together with your loved one, it matters not on which side of death you stand, you are both somewhere and God has bound Himself by His word to bring you together again. Don't become the victim of tender memories or worship at their shrine, but let them whet your expectation for better times ahead. ". . .because I live, ye shall live also" (John 14:19). "I will come again and receive you unto myself" (14:3). And with Him will be those who reached the Father's house ahead of us. We shall be raised together with them who are asleep in Jesus to meet the Lord in the air and so shall we ever be with the Lord. What a day, what a day that will be!

LONELINESS IS A GIFT *by Tim Hansel*

"And, behold, I am with thee, and will keep thee in all places whither thou goest, and will bring thee again into this land; for I will not leave thee, until I have done that which I have spoken to thee of." GENESIS 28:15

*L*oneliness is a gift from God. A gift that opens up our heart to yearn for His peace. It is a longing for a deeper experience of His presence. When we want God more than anything—more than success, more than peace, more than health—then we truly know how to pray; then we discover Him in fullness.

God made us for Himself. We were designed for a relationship with the Father and, believe it or not, loneliness is one of the most powerful ways for us to fully understand and experience that. Sometimes the problem is that we are too full of ourselves—perhaps because we don't truly believe that God is enough, that His reality is sufficient on a daily, practical level. So we pursue our distractions and are on the way to becoming "functional atheists," no longer believing that God can fill our empty hearts.

God has spoken very boldly about his desire to be a presence in our lives. If I want to heal the ache and loneliness in my own life, one of the things I need to do is get away alone with God. The paradoxical "answer" to loneliness is aloneness. . .with God. In the silence God will speak to you most powerfully. Too often His words to us get muffled, lost, or covered by the crowd of many noises both inside and outside of us. We must have a quiet heart in order to hear God's distinctive message to us.

Loneliness is not a time of abandonment. It just feels that way. It's actually a time of encounter at new levels with the only One who can really heal that empty place in our hearts.

Although I know all too well the terrible ache of loneliness, I also know that the wilderness is a place of great adventure.

Lean into your loneliness. God is shouting to you. Can you hear Him calling you by name?

DECEMBER 9TH

A FRIEND THAT STICKETH CLOSER
THAN A BROTHER
by T. C. Horton & Charles E. Hurlburt

"A man that hath friends must show himself friendly: and there is a friend that sticketh closer than a brother."

PROVERBS 18:24

Stay, lonely pilgrim, searching long for fellowship. Stop here and find "A FRIEND." "There is a Friend," though all the world deny it. One who is always true and faithful. One who never leaves and ne'er forsakes. No brother will, or can, abide as He. Will you be friend to Jesus, as He is friend to

335

thee? *We worship Thee, we trust all to Thee, and take from Thee all peace, all grace, all needed power to do and be what pleaseth Thee, our never-absent FRIEND. Amen.*

DECEMBER 10TH

THE GIFT OF GOD
by T. C. Horton & Charles E. Hurlburt

"Jesus answered and said unto her, 'If thou knewest the gift of God, and who it is that saith unto thee, Give me to drink; thou wouldest have asked of him, and he would have given thee living water.'" JOHN 4:10

*H*ere is that wonderful scene at the well of Samaria. The Lord has gone out of his way to meet the poor, sinful woman who has come to the well at a time when other women would not come; heavy-hearted, hopeless, but One loved her with a holy love. He is there and reveals Himself as the "Gift of God." He is God's gift to us. What is our gift to Him? May we yield ourselves, and all we are and have to Him! May we imitate the Samaritan woman and go forth with the message: Come, see a Man-God's Gift. Amen.

MESSIAH *by T. C. Horton & Charles E. Hurlburt*

"The woman saith unto him, 'I know that Messias cometh, which is called Christ: when he is come, he will tell us all things.'"   JOHN 4:25

*T*here is no book like the Bible and there never can be. Christ's interview with the woman at the well and His revelation of Himself is unique and contrary to any conception that could have been made of Him. The Samaritans, as did the Jews, anticipated a Christ (An Anointed One). This was the promise given in Deuteronomy 18:18. This woman was the last one we would have chosen for such a revelation—but her soul was filled at once with the Spirit of life and hope, and her lips bore a testimony—humiliating to herself—but bringing salvation to a multitude. Oh, that our lips might bear such convincing, convicting and converting testimony.

Lord, make us like this Samaritan woman! Amen.

ONE THING NEEDFUL *by Andrew Murray*

". . .Behold, I will pour out my spirit unto you, I will make known my words unto you."   PROVERBS 1:23

*F*or every need of the spiritual life this is the one thing needful: the Holy Spirit. All the fullness is in Jesus; the fullness of grace and truth, out of which we receive grace for grace. The Holy Spirit is the appointed conveyancer, whose special work it is to make Jesus and all there is in Him for us ours in personal appropriation, in blessed experience. He is the Spirit of life in Christ Jesus; as wonderful as the life is, so wonderful is the provision by which such an agent is provided to communicate it to us. If we but yield ourselves entirely to the disposal of the Spirit, and let Him have His way with us, He will manifest the life of Christ within us. He will do this with a Divine power, maintaining the life of Christ in us in uninterrupted continuity. Surely, if there is one prayer that should draw us to the Father's throne and keep us there, it is this: for the Holy Spirit, whom we as children have received, to stream into us and out from us in greater fullness.

CHRISTMAS CHEER *by John Henry Jowett*

". . .Good will toward men."   LUKE 2:14

*T*he heavens are not filled with hostility. The sky does not express a frown. When I look up I do not contemplate a face of brass, but the face of infinite good will. Yet when I was a child, many a picture has made me think of God as suspicious, inhumanly watchful, always looking round the corner to catch me at the fall. That "eye," placed in the sky of many a picture, and placed there to represent God, filled my heart with a chilling fear. That God was to me a magnified policeman, watching for wrong-doers, and ever ready for the infliction of punishment. It was all a frightful perversion of the gracious teaching of Jesus.

Heaven overflows with good will toward men! Our God not only wishes good, he wills it! "He gave His only begotten Son," as the sacred expression of His infinite good will.

He has good will toward thee and me, and mine and thine.
Let that holy thought make our Christmas cheer.

GOD MANIFESTED IN THE FLESH
by T. C. Horton & Charles E. Hurlburt

*"And without controversy great is the mystery of godliness:
God was manifest in the flesh, justified in the Spirit, seen of
angels, preached unto the Gentiles, believed on in the world,
received up into glory."*　　　　　　　　　　1 TIMOTHY 3:16

*H*ere is a sermon of marvelous mystery. In a few
words we have given to us the magnitude of the mission of
Christ in leaving the glory and coming to this earth, clothed
in the garments of flesh; accomplishing His Divine mission
of redemption while in human form; leaving His witnesses
to His crucifixion, resurrection and ascension to His high
and holy place in glory. We should stand with uncovered
heads and with hearts beating in adoration, worship Him as
the Holy Spirit of God emphasizes to us this great truth: He
came, He died, He lives in us and He lives in the glory, and
we will dwell forever with Him.

　　*Holy Spirit, help us to magnify and glorify the God-
man. Amen.*

NO FEAR IN LOVE *by Hannah Hurnard*

"There is no fear in love; but perfect love casteth out fear. . ."
1 JOHN 4:18

*A*rt thou fearful love will fail?
   Foolish thought and drear,
"God is love" and must prevail,
   Love casts out all fear!
We have seen his lovely plan
   In God's Son made Son of Man.

Holy love could not create
   Save for love's sake sweet,
Therefore we his creatures wait
   Union made complete.
When love's perfect work is done,
   God and man will be at one.
We may know that God is love,
   Know his Father's heart,
He hath spoken from above
   And our doubts depart.
We have seen what hath sufficed
   In the face of Jesus Christ.

THE JOY OF JESUS *by R. T. Kendall*

"Blessed is the people that know the joyful sound: they shall walk, O LORD, in the light of thy countenance. In thy name shall they rejoice all the day: and in thy righteousness shall they be exalted."   PSALM 89:15, 16

*I*f you think you are going to be happy when Jesus comes the second time, let me tell you that it will be but like crumbs from the table compared to the joy our Lord will have on that day. Parents, what makes you happy on Christmas Day? Is it not seeing your children happy? This is what makes Christmas Christmas, is it not? When I watch my son or daughter open a present that they had hoped for, and I see their joy, it is my joy. I delight in just seeing their faces. And that is what makes our Lord's joy complete. His joy comes not only from what he did or from pleasing his Father but also from seeing the expressions on our faces when we see him.

What was it like on Easter morning when Jesus first appeared to Mary Magdalene? Do you know why he appeared to her first? I suspect that Mary Magdalene took it the hardest when Jesus was betrayed and crucified. Oh, the joy Jesus felt when he could see her as she wrapped her arms around him. He had to say, "Stop clinging to me." There was the joy that Jesus felt when he could say to Peter, "It's all right." For Jesus knew how Peter felt when he wept his heart out (Matt. 26:75). Jesus wanted to go to Peter and say, "It's okay." There were those disciples in the upper room. They had forsaken the Lord in the last hour; now they heard that he was alive and they were so ashamed. But what joy Jesus had in going to the disciples to say, "Peace. Peace.

341

It's all right. It's okay." And when they saw Jesus meant it—that he held no grudges, but absolutely and totally forgave them—what joy they felt! What joy he felt in seeing them accept his forgiveness!

DECEMBER 17TH

CALL HIS NAME JESUS *by Matthew Henry*

"And she shall bring forth a son, and thou shalt call his name JESUS: for he shall save his people from their sins."
MATTHEW 1:21

*J*esus is the same name as Joshua. JESUS is the Greek form of the Hebrew word Joshua, which means "The LORD is Salvation," or "The LORD saves." There were two of that name in the Old Testament who were both illustrious types of Christ: Joshua who was Israel's captain at their first settlement in Canaan, and Joshua who was their high priest at their second settlement after the captivity (Zech. 6:11, 12). Christ is our Joshua; both the Captain of our salvation, and the High Priest of our profession. Joshua had been called Hosea, but Moses prefixed the first syllable of the name Jehovah, and made it Jehoshua (Num. 13:16), to intimate that the Messiah, who was to bear that name, should be Jehovah. Christ came to save His people, not in their sins, but from their sins; to purchase for them, not a liberty to sin, but a liberty from sins, to redeem them from all iniquity (Tit. 2:14); and to redeem them from among men (Rev. 14:4) to Himself.

FEAR NOT *by Hannah Whitall Smith*

"Now our Lord Jesus Christ himself, and God, even our Father, which hath loved us, and hath given us everlasting consolation and good hope through grace, Comfort your hearts, and stablish you in every good word and work."

2 THESSALONIANS 2:16, 17

*T*he only gospel that, to my thinking, can rightly be called the Gospel is that one proclaimed by the angel to the frightened shepherds, who were in the fields keeping watch over their flocks by night: "Fear not," said the angel, "for behold I bring you good tidings of great joy, which shall be to all people. For unto you is born this day in the city of David, a Saviour which is Christ the Lord."

Never were more comfortable words preached to any congregation. And if only all the preachers in all the pulpits would speak the same comfortable words to the people; and if all the congregations, who hear these words, would believe them, and would take the comfort of them, there would be no more uncomfortable Christians left anywhere. And over all the whole land would be fulfilled the apostle's prayer for the Thessalonians: "Now our Lord Jesus Christ himself, and God, even our Father, which hath loved us, and hath given us everlasting consolation and good hope through grace, Comfort your hearts, and stablish you in every good word and work."

ANGELS WE HAVE HEARD ON HIGH
by Kenneth W. Osbeck

"And, lo, the angel of the Lord came upon them, and the glory of the Lord shone round about them: and they were sore afraid. And the angel said unto them, 'Fear not: for, behold, I bring you good tidings of great joy, which shall be to all people.' "   Luke 2:9, 10

*A*s vast numbers of angels swiftly descended toward earth through the star sprinkled sky, the leading angel halted them with a sign. They hovered with folded wings over a silent field near Bethlehem. "There they are," said the leading angel, "the humble shepherds who have been chosen by God to recieve our message. It will be the most wonderful news that mortal man has ever received. Are you ready with your great angelic chorus?"

The leading angel drifted slightly downward so that he could be seen by the brilliance of the light. "Do not be afraid. I bring you good news of great joy that will be for all the people. Today in the town of David a Savior has been born to you; He is Christ the Lord."

Instantly surrounding the angel was the brilliant heavenly host, and echoing through the sky was the most beautiful singing that the shepherds had ever heard, exulting and praising God for the long-awaited gift of His Son. They made haste to see the Savior with their own eyes.

The Bible teaches that angels are the ministering servants of God and that they are continually being sent to help and protect us, the heirs of salvation. Certainly their most important task, however, was this momentous occasion announcing Christ's arrival on earth!

THE LORD OF WORKING MEN *by John Henry Jowett*

"Glory to God in the highest, and on earth peace, good will toward men."　　　　　　　　　　　　　　　LUKE 2:14

*A*nd so the good news was told to shepherds, to working men who were toiling in the fields. The coming King would hallow the common work of man, and in His love and grace all the problems of labour would find a solution.

The Lord of the Christmas-tide throws a halo over common toil. Even Christian people have not all learnt the significance of the angels' visit to the lonely shepherds. Some of us can see the light resting upon a bishop's crosier, but we cannot see the radiance on the ordinary shepherd's staff. We can discern the hallowedness of a priest's vocation, but we see no sanctity in the calling of the grocer, or of the scavenger in the street. We can see the nimbus on the few, but not on the crowd; on the unusual, but not upon the commonplace. But the very birth-hour of Christianity irradiated the humble doings of humble people. When the angels went to the shepherds, common work was encircled with an immortal crown.

And it is in the Lord Jesus that all labour troubles are to be put to rest. If we work from any other centre we shall arrive at confusion confounded. "I have the keys."

THE LORD OF STUDENTS *by John Henry Jowett*

"When they saw the star, they rejoiced with exceeding great joy."   MATTHEW 2:10

*A*nd so the good news came to "wise men," shall we say to students, busying themselves with the vast and intricate problems of the mind. And the evangel offered the students mental satisfaction, bringing the interpreting clue, beaming upon them with the guiding ray which would lead them into perfect noon.

Yes, our wise men must find the key of wisdom in the Lord. In a wiser sense than the meaning of the original word it is true that "the fear of the Lord is the beginning of wisdom." To seek mental satisfaction and leave out Jesus is like trying to make a garden and leave out the sun. "Without Me ye can do nothing," not even in the unravelling of the problems which beset and besiege the mind.

If my mental pilgrimage is to be as "a shining light shining more and more even unto perfect day," I must begin with Jesus, and pay homage to His Kingly and incomparable glory. I must lay my treasures at His feet, "gold, and frankincense, and myrrh." Then will He lead me "into all truth," and "the truth shall make me free."

DECEMBER 22ND

THE KING OF KINGS: IN A STABLE
by Charles Dickens

"But made himself of no reputation, and took upon him the form of a servant, and was made in the likeness of men: And being found in fashion as a man, he humbled himself, and became obedient unto death, even the death of the cross."
PHILIPPIANS 2:7, 8

*H*e was born, a long, long time ago—nearly Two Thousand years ago—at a place called Bethlehem. His father and mother lived in a city called Nazareth, but they were forced, by business, to travel to Bethlehem. His father's name was Joseph, and his mother's name was Mary. And the town being very full of people, also brought there by business, there was no room for Joseph and Mary in the Inn or in any house; so they went into a Stable to lodge, and in this stable Jesus Christ was born. There was no cradle or anything of that kind there, so Mary laid her pretty little boy in what is called the Manger, which is the place the horses eat out of. And there he fell asleep.

LOVE'S RICHEST MEANING *by James Dobson*

"For where your treasure is, there will your heart be also."
MATTHEW 6:21

*T*he springtime of that year had set my dad thinking about the brevity of life and the certainty of old age ahead. The poem which follows is entitled, "Your Birthday," and it made my mother cry.

'Tis true for us the summer too is gone
Now whiplashed winds arise and further on
The ice and sleet and cold in grim assault
to pierce us through
Does fall in springtime frighten you?

Impotent shines the April sun so fair
To melt the wisps of frost within your hair
My dear, I know you feel the threatening gloom
But I'm with you
And hand in hand we'll face the winter, too.

Isn't that a beautiful expression of love in its richest meaning? My dad has promised to stand shoulder to shoulder with my mother, even when assaulted by whiplashed winds and threatening gloom. His commitment is not based on ephemeral emotions or selfish desires. It is supported by an uncompromising will. Don't you see that this "oneness" of spirit is what women seek in their husbands? We human beings can survive the most difficult of circumstances if we are not forced to stand alone.

What do women want from their husbands? It is not a

bigger home or a better dishwasher or a newer automobile. Rather, it is the assurance that "hand in hand we'll face the best and worst that life has to offer—together."

AWAY IN A MANGER *by Kenneth W. Osbeck*

"And she brought forth her firstborn son, and wrapped him in swaddling clothes, and laid him in a manger; because there was no room for them in the inn." Luke 2:7

*T*he shepherds had an angel
  The wise men had a star
But what have I, a little child,
  To guide me home from far,
Where glad stars sing together
  And singing angels are?
Christ watches me, His little lamb,
  Cares for me day and night,
That I may be His own in heaven;
  So angels clad in white
Shall sing their "Glory, glory,"
  For my sake in the height.

CHRISTINA ROSSETTI

How important it is that we take time to help our children see beyond the glitter of the Christmas season and teach them the true meaning of Christ's birth. The most thrilling story ever known to man began in Bethlehem at Christmas.

Use this season to enjoy times of family worship. Include the reading of the Christmas story—Luke 2:1–20 (perhaps

349

from different versions), share personal insights from the story, dramatize the various events, sing and play the carols, pray together, and discuss how the family could share their joy with others.

O COME LET US ADORE HIM
by Mrs.Charles E. Cowman

". . .And they shall call his name Emmanuel. . .God with us."
MATTHEW 1:23

A few years ago a striking Christmas card was published, with the title, "If Christ had not come." It was founded upon our Saviour's words, "If I had not come." The card represented a clergyman falling into a short sleep in his study on Christmas morning and dreaming of a world into which Jesus had never come.

A ring at the door-bell, and a messenger asked him to visit a poor dying mother. He hastened with the weeping child and as he reached the home he sat down and said, "I have something here that will comfort you." He opened his Bible to look for a familiar promise, but it ended at Malachi, and there was no gospel and no promise of hope and salvation, and he could only bow his head and weep with her in bitter despair.

Two days afterward he stood beside her coffin and conducted the funeral service, but there was no message of consolation, no word of a glorious resurrection, no open Heaven, but only "dust to dust, ashes to ashes," and one long eternal farewell. He realized at length that "He had not," and burst into tears and bitter weeping in his sorrowful dream.

Suddenly he woke with a start, and a great shout of joy and praise burst from his lips as he heard his choir singing in his church close by.

Let us be glad and rejoice today, because "He has come." And let us remember the annunciation of the angel, "Behold I bring you good tidings of great joy, which shall be to all people, for unto you is born this day in the city of David a Saviour, which is Christ the Lord" (Luke 2:10, 11).

DECEMBER 26TH

THE GREATEST MIRACLE *by James Stalker*

"And in that same hour he cured many of their infirmities and plagues. . . ."   LUKE 7:21

*T*he miracles of Christ were the natural outflow of the divine fulness which dwelt in Him. God as in Him, and His human nature was endowed with the Holy Ghost without measure. It was natural, when such a Being was in the world, that mighty works should manifest themselves in Him. He was Himself the great miracle, of which His particular miracles were merely sparks or emanations. He was the great interruption of the order of nature, or rather a new element which had entered into the order of nature to enrich and ennoble it, and His miracles entered with Him, not to disturb, but to repair its harmony. Therefore all His miracles bore the stamp of His character. They were not mere exhibitions of power, but also of holiness, wisdom and love.

351

THE LIVING CHRIST *by Andrew Murray*

"Howbeit when he, the Spirit of truth, is come, he will guide you into all truth. . ."   JOHN 16:13

*T*he Holy Spirit was given for this one purpose—that the glorious redemption and life in Christ might with divine power be conveyed and communicated to us. We have the Holy Spirit to make the living Christ, in all His saving power, and in the completeness of His victory over sin, ever present within us. It is this that constitutes Him the Comforter: with Him we need never mourn an absent Christ. Let us therefore, as often as we read, or meditate, or pray in connection with this abiding in Christ, reckon upon it as a settled thing that we have the Spirit of God Himself within us, teaching, and guiding, and working. Let us rejoice in the confidence that we must succeed in our desires, because the Holy Spirit is working all the while with secret but divine power in the soul that does not hinder Him by its unbelief.

AS YOUR WISDOM *by Andrew Murray*

"But of him are ye in Christ Jesus, who of God is made unto us wisdom, and righteousness, and sanctification, and redemption."   1 CORINTHIANS 1:30

*J*esus Christ is not only Priest to purchase, and King to secure, but also Prophet to reveal to us the salvation which God hath prepared for them that love Him. Just as at the creation the light was first called into existence, that in it all God's other works might have their life and beauty, so in our text wisdom is mentioned first as the treasury in which are to be found the three precious gifts that follow. The life is the light of man; it is in revealing to us, and making us behold the glory of God in His own face, that Christ makes us partakers of eternal life. It was by the tree of knowledge that sin came; it is through the knowledge that Christ gives that salvation comes. He is made of God unto us wisdom. In Him are hid all the treasures of wisdom and knowledge.

HE IS WISDOM *by Jill Briscoe*

"Christ. . .is made unto us wisdom. . ."
         1 CORINTHIANS 1:30

*T*he earthly King and Queen of Hearts in Proverbs knew very well that "the fear of the Lord is the beginning of knowledge" (Proverbs 1:7). The King of Hearts in heaven promises an ongoing revelation of wisdom because He is wisdom, and is a giving God. "Christ. . .is made unto us wisdom. . ." (1 Corinthians 1:30), Paul tells us. That ongoing revelation will never stop. What's more, He promises that what we know of Him down here is only the beginning. "Eye hath not seen, nor ear heard, neither have entered into the heart of man, the things which God hath prepared for them that love him," He promises in 1 Corinthians 2:9. That's why eternity will be so necessary. That's how long it's going to take to know all there is to know about our wise and wonderful heavenly King of Hearts. "The fear of the Lord is clean, enduring for ever. . ." sings the psalmist in 19:9. Yes, wisdom lasts forever.

THE DEEP *by Mrs. Charles E. Cowman*

"Launch out into the deep. . ."   LUKE 5:4

*H*ow deep He does not say. The depth into which we launch will depend upon how perfectly we have given up the shore, and the greatness of our need, and the apprehension of our possibilities. The fish were to be found in the deep, not in the shallow water.

So with us; our needs are to be met in the deep things of God. We are to launch out into the deep of God's Word, which the Spirit can open up to us in such crystal fathomless meaning that the same words we have accepted in times past will have an ocean meaning in them, which renders their first meaning to us very shallow.

Into the deep of the atonement, until Christ's precious blood is so illuminated by the Spirit that it becomes an omnipotent balm, and food and medicine for the soul and body.

Into the deep of the Father's will, until He becomes a bright, dazzling, sweet, fathomless summer sea, in which we bathe and bask and breathe, and lose ourselves and our sorrows in the calmness and peace of His everlasting presence.

Into the deep of the Holy Spirit, until He becomes a bright marvelous answer to prayer, the most careful and tender guidance, the most thoughtful anticipation of our needs, the most accurate and supernatural shaping of our events.

Into the deep of God's purposes and coming kingdom, until the Lord's coming and His millennial reign are opened up to us; and beyond these the bright entrancing ages on ages unfold themselves, until the mental eye is dazed with light, and the heart flutters with inexpressible anticipations of its joy with Jesus and the glory to be revealed.

DECEMBER 31ST

INNER PEACE *by Oswald Chambers*

"Peace I leave with you, my peace I give unto you: not as the world giveth, give I unto you. Let not your heart be troubled, neither let it be afraid." JOHN 14:27

"Thou wilt keep him in perfect peace, whose mind is stayed on thee: because he trusteth in thee" (Isaiah 26:3). The peace of God is not the peace of stoicism or passivity. It is the most intense activity. Some people say that they are tired of life; they mean to say that they are tired of dying. They are tired of the spiritual death that stops activity. They are tired of life getting so sluggish.

What does Jesus say? "I have come that ye might have life and that ye might have it more abundantly; but ye will not come to me that ye might have it." Everything in this natural world is pitted against you, and unless you have His life you will never have real peace.

May the Lord have a NEW YEAR in you!

Lord, thank You for inner peace in the midst of a troubled world.

INDEX OF AUTHORS

ABRAHAM, KEN,
1/24, 4/26, 9/6, 10/27, 11/6, *Positive Holiness;*
5/24, *Stand Up and Fight Back;*
3/26, 5/21, 6/16, 7/7, 9/20, 10/23, 10/29, 11/3,
The Disillusioned Christian

ALLEN, JAMES,
2/26, *As a Man Thinketh*

ANDREW, BROTHER,
4/29, 4/30, 11/17, *The Calling*

ARTHUR, KAY,
3/12, 3/16, "Because the Lord Is My Shepherd",
5/25, *Lord, Is It Warfare? Teach Me To Stand;*
9/21, *Lord, I Want to Know You*

AUGUSTINE, ST.,
2/20, 5/3, *Confessions of St. Augustine*

BAGSTER, SAMUEL,
8/3, 8/5, 8/13, *Daily Light from the Bible*

BARNHOUSE, DONALD GREY,
8/4, 8/9, 11/24, 11/25, *Illustrating Great Themes of
Scripture*

BONHOEFFER, DIETRICH,
2/17, *The Cost of Discipleship*

BOOTH, CATHERINE,
  see DEAN, EDITH

BOUNDS, E.M.,
  3/4, *Purpose in Prayer*

BRISCOE, JILL,
  2/23, 6/23, 6/30, 12/29, *Queen of Hearts;*
  11/14, *Prime Rib and Apple*

BRUCE, DR. F.F.,
  10/3, *The Tyndale New Testament Commentaries:*
    Romans

BUNYAN, JOHN, *see* HARDING, WILLIAM

CAMPOLO, DR. ANTHONY,
  see GAITHER, GLORIA

CHAMBERS, OSWALD,
  1/27, 2/29, 3/2, 8/23, 12/31, *Devotions For a Deeper*
    Life;
  5/28, 6/6, 10/12, 10/26, 11/15, *My Utmost for His*
    Highest

CHESHAM, SALLIE,
  3/21, *Peace Like a River*

COLSON, CHARLES,
  6/9, *Life Sentence*

COWMAN, MRS. CHARLES E.,
  1/15, 2/10, 7/2, 9/26, 11/9, *Springs in the Valley;*
  1/4, 3/3, 3/17, 4/7, 4/17, 9/30, *Consolation;*
  6/2, 12/25, 12/30, *Streams in the Desert*

CROSBY, FANNY,
    see RUFFIN, BERNARD

CUNNINGHAM, LOREN,
    3/11, 3/14, *Is That Really You, God?*

DAWSON, JOY,
    10/17, 10/28, *Intimate Friendship*

DEAN, EDITH/BOOTH, CATHERINE,
    8/29, *Great Women of the Christian Faith*

DEAN, EDITH/WESLEY, SUSANNA,
    8/7, 10/25, *Great Women of the Christian Faith*

DICK, DAN,
    8/8, *Daily Praise From the Bible*

DICKENS, CHARLES,
    4/20, 4/21, 4/22, 6/12, 6/24, 6/26, 9/7,
    9/16, 9/17, 9/27, 11/2, 11/11, 11/13, 11/16,
    12/6, 12/22, *The Life of Our Lord*

DOBSON, DR. JAMES,
    7/20, 12/23, *What Wives Wish Their Husbands
        Knew About Women*
        (*also see* GAITHER, GLORIA)
DRUMMOND, HENRY,
    2/3, 6/22, *The Greatest Thing In the World*

DUEWEL, WESLEY L.,
    5/16, 5/18, *Mighty Prevailing Prayer*

ELLIOT, ELISABETH,
    1/14, 3/20, 6/27, 8/27, 10/20, 11/21, *A Quiet Heart;*
    1/2, 1/18, 4/3, *Discipline: The Glad Surrender*

FINNEY, CHARLES G.,
7/5, *Charles G. Finney: An Autobiography*

GAITHER, GLORIA,
7/22, *What My Parents Did Right*

GAITHER, GLORIA/CAMPOLO, DR. ANTHONY,
7/24, *What My Parents Did Right*

GAITHER, GLORIA/DOBSON, DR. JAMES,
6/29, *What My Parents Did Right*

GAITHER, GLORIA/TADA, JONI EARECKSON,
7/21, *What My Parents Did Right*

GARRÉ, CAPTAIN E.G.,
4/23, 5/15, 5/17, 9/15, 10/7, 10/24, *Praying Hyde: The Life of John "Praying" Hyde*

GRAHAM, RUTH BELL,
7/18, *Sitting By My Laughing Fire*

HANSEL, TIM,
3/10, 3/18, 5/12, 12/8, *Through the Wilderness of Loneliness*

HARDING, WILLIAM/BUNYAN, JOHN,
5/4, *John Bunyan*

HAVNER, VANCE,
7/14, 12/7, *Though I Walk Through the Valley*

HAYFORD, JACK,
7/9, 7/10, *Taking Hold of Tomorrow;*
1/22, 2/8, 7/16, 11/5, *A Heart of Praise*

360

HENRY, MATTHEW,
   12/17, *The Matthew Henry Study Bible*

HORTON, T.C./HURLBURT, CHARLES E.,
   1/17, 3/22, 3/28, 4/24, 5/14, 8/10, 8/15, 8/18, 10/13,
   12/5, 12/9, 12/10, 12/11, 12/14, *The Wonderful
   Names of Our Wonderful Lord*

HURNARD, HANNAH,
   1/7, 3/9, 5/30, 8/26, 11/18, *Hinds' Feet on High
   Places;*
   2/6, 2/11, 5/7, 6/25, 8/26, 8/30, 12/15, *Mountains of
   Spices*

JOWETT, JOHN HENRY,
   1/6, 2/5, 2/9, 3/13, 3/24, 4/13, 4/14, 4/15, 5/8, 6/3,
   6/7, 6/19, 7/8, 7/28, 9/5, 9/25, 10/9, 10/11, 10/31,
   11/4, 11/12, 12/13, 12/20, 12/21, *My Daily Meditation*

KENDALL, R.T.,
   1/8, 1/16, 1/29, 3/19, 3/29, 5/11, 6/11, 6/14,
   9/19, 10/10, 12/16,
   God Meant It for Good

LAWRENCE, BROTHER,
   2/4, 2/12, 4/9, 5/6, 5/26, 7/4, 8/14, 11/10, 11/19,
   The Practice of the Presence of God

LEWIS, C.S.,
   2/7, *Mere Christianity*

MACDONALD, GAIL & GORDON,
   2/24, 3/15, 7/23, *If Those Who Reach*

MACDONALD, GEORGE,
   2/18, 4/18, 6/13, *Creation in Christ*

MANNING, BRENNAN,
   1/30, *The Lion and the Lamb*

MARSHALL, CATHERINE,
   4/2, *A Closer Walk*

MEYER, F.B.,
   10/4, *Five "Musts" of the Christian Life;*
   1/28, 9/22, 11/22, *Paul*

MOODY, D.L.,
   1/10, 1/26, 2/22, 6/10, 7/26, 9/10,
      Moody's Anecdotes

MURRAY, ANDREW,
   1/11, 3/25, 4/11, 5/19, 10/18, 11/7, 11/8,
      Absolute Surrender;
   1/19, 1/21, 2/13, 2/21, 4/28, 7/27, 8/17, 9/4,
   9/24, 10/2, 10/5, 11/29, 11/30, 12/4, 12/12,
      With Christ in the School of Prayer;
   4/4, 4/25, 4/27, 9/9, 12/27, 12/28, *Abide in Christ*

OGILVIE, LLOYD JOHN,
   1/9, 3/5, *Why Not Accept Christ's Healing*

OSBECK, KENNETH W.,
   7/12, 7/17, 8/2, 8/6, 8/11, 12/19, 12/24,
      Amazing Grace

PACKER, J.I.,
   1/31, 2/15, 5/29, 8/22, *Keep In Step With the Spirit*

QUALE, WILLIAM A.,
   1/1, 2/1, 3/1, 4/1, 5/1, 6/1, 7/1, 8/1, 9/1, 10/1, 11/1,
   12/1, *God's Calendar*

...HILL, LEONARD,
  6/18, *Meat For Men;*
  8/20, 8/21, *Revival God's Way*

REDPATH, ALAN,
  5/31, 6/8, *Victorious Christian Living Studies*

ROGERS, JANICE,
  see CUNNINGHAM, LOREN

RUFFIN, BERNARD/CROSBY, FANNY,
  5/9, 7/13, *Fanny Crosby*

SCHAEFFER, EDITH,
  2/25, 7/19, *Forever Music;*
  7/11, 7/15, *The Life of Prayer*

SEAMANDS, JOHN T.,
  10/21, *On Tiptoe With Joy*

SIMPSON, A.B.,
  1/20, 1/23, 2/2, 2/27, 2/28, 7/3, 7/29, 7/31, 8/28, 9/23,
    9/28, 11/23, *Days of Heaven on Earth*

SMITH, HANNAH WHITALL,
  1/12, 2/19, 5/5, 5/27, 7/25, 10/22, 12/3, 12/18,
    God of All Comfort;
  3/7, 5/2, 6/17, 6/28, 10/19, *The Christian's Secret of A
    Happy Life*

SMITH, MALCOLM,
  3/27, 6/20, 10/15, *Spiritual Burnout*

SPURGEON, CHARLES H.,
  1/3, 4/12, 5/23, 9/12, *Evening By Evening*
  2/16, 3/23, 4/8, 4/16, 4/19, 5/20, 6/4, 6/15, 6/
  9/11, 9/14, 9/29, 10/8, 11/26, 12/2,
    Morning By Morning

STALKER, JAMES,
  6/5, 9/8, 12/26, *The Life of Christ*

TADA, JONI EARECKSON,
  see GAITHER, GLORIA

TCHIVIDJIAN, GIGI GRAHAM,
  5/10, *Weather of the Heart*

TEN BOOM, CORRIE,
  3/6, 3/30, 4/6, 4/10, 5/13, 10/16, 11/20,
    Each New Day

TILESTON, MARY W.,
  1/5, 1/25, 2/14, 3/8, 4/5, 5/22, 7/30, 8/25, 8/31,
  9/18, 10/6, 10/14, 10/30, 11/27, 11/28,
    Daily Strength for Daily Needs

TORREY, R. A.,
  9/2, 9/3, *How To Pray*

TOZER, A. W.,
  7/6, 8/12, 8/16, 8/19, 8/24, *Renewed Day by Day*

YANCEY, PHILIP,
  1/13, 3/31, 9/13, *Finding God in Unexpected Places*

INDEX OF BIBLICAL REFERENCES

GENESIS
1:1 1/14
1:4 1/3
1:14 1/1
1:26, 31 2/25
18:19 9/23
24:49 5/12
28:15 12/8
35:3 7/8

EXODUS
3:14 9/26
14:13 5/20
16:4 9/9
20:3 6/19
33:14 7/14
35:35 2/26

LEVITICUS
19:18 10/9

DEUTERONOMY
4:9 7/28
6:6, 7 6/29
7:9 11/3
11:19 7/22
33:27 7/26

JOSHUA
1:11, 13 7/9
3:17 5/31
6:20 5/27

1 SAMUEL
7:12 1/4
18:14 6/7

2 SAMUEL
15:15 1/5
22:47 3/28

EZRA
8:22 8/31

NEHEMIAH
8:10 3/25

JOB
23:10 9/30

PSALMS
4:1 6/24
5:1–3 4/2
8:1, 3, 4 7/15
9:1, 2 7/18
9:10 6/27
10:17 2/24
16:5 NIV 10/20
16:11 3/27
18:2 3/7, 6/28
18:28 10/30
19:1, 2 7/12
19:14 10/17
23:1 3/13, 10/13
23:3 1/17
23:4 3/16

23:5 11/10
24:10 4/24
30:5 3/1
32:6 8/17
32:8 1/7
32:11 8/19
34:1, 4 8/2
34:17 3/4
34:18 11/11
34:18, 19 3/11
37:3 11/27
37:4 1/25, 7/7
39:1 10/6
40:3 8/5
42:7 1/28
48:14 3/10, 5/30
50:15 9/21
51:1 10/15
51:6 10/10
56:3, 4 8/4
63:3, 4 8/3
71:5 5/9
72:6 3/22
73:26 6/20
74:17 12/2
78:19 11/9
81:2 8/8
86:12 8/6
89:15, 16 12/16
90:12 9/25
91:4 5/3
95:6, 7 1/22
96: 11, 12 7/11

100:2 5/23
100:4 11/24
103:11 4/6
103:12 10/16
104:1 5/1
104:3 6/17
105:3 4/5
107:22 11/25
118:14 3/24
119:18 3/15
127:3 7/19
130:6 2/11
138:7, 8 3/9
138:8 9/19
145:1, 3 2/8
145:16 11/28
146:2 8/11
148:8 3/3
150:6 8/1

PROVERBS
1:23 12/12
3:1, 2 4/3
4:1 7/21
4:4, 5 8/7
11:25 3/23
14:21 2/7
16:9 3/14
17:6 7/20
18:24 12/9
22:6 7/25
31:28 7/24

ECCLESIASTES
3:1 1/2
3:11 4/1
5:18 9/8

SONG OF SOLOMON
3:1 9/29

ISAIAH
14:3 7/30
26:3 7/31
40:1 12/3
40:31 5/2, 7/3
48:17 11/22
49:15, 16 4/11
53:5 4/16
55:9 6/11
55:13 4/17
58:7 3/31

JEREMIAH
29:11 2/19, 3/26
31:3 6/21
7:23 5/22, 11/21

LAMENTATIONS
3:22, 23 2/9

HOSEA
2:23 11/2

JOEL
2:25 11/20

JONAH
4:9 10/8

MALACHI
2:6 7/10

MATTHEW
1:21 12/17
1:23 12/25
2:10 12/21
3:16, 17; 4:1 3/18
5:8 10/26
5:16 9/17
5:23, 24 10/11
6:9 1/19
6:25 9/18
6:26 11/13
6:33 7/27, 11/23
7:9–11 12/4
9:37, 38 4/30, 9/15
11:28 9/10
16:19 3/5
17:20 9/24
18:4 6/13
18:18, 20 10/5
18:21, 22 2/13
20:1 9/7
25:21 6/30
25:40 8/29
26:39 6/15
27:46 4/18

MARK
6:50 3/2
8:2, 3 11/12
11:22 2/16
14:7 8/28

LUKE
1:37 1/11
2:7 12/24
2:9, 10 12/19
2:14 12/13, 12/20
5:4 12/30
5:5, 6 9/27
6:27 2/17
6:38 11/14
6:41 10/14
7:21 12/26
9:24 1/16
10:2 10/2
10:27 2/6
10:40 9/12
11:2 11/29
11:13 2/21
12:34 2/4
17:21 6/22
18:1 7/2
21:28 9/22
22:40 4/13
23:18–21 4/14
24:5, 6 4/21

JOHN
1:48 10/31

2:5 9/5
3:7 4/8
3:29 5/28
4:10 12/10
4:11 6/6
4:14 2/10, 6/5
4:25 12/11
4:28, 29 10/4
7:37 6/4
11:3, 4 11/4
12:32 1/12
13:5 4/12
13:35 2/22, 8/26
14:9 5/5
14:12 4/28
14:17 1/31
14:19 12/7
14:23 10/23
14:27 5/10, 12/31
15:1, 2 9/1
15:2 6/2
15:4 9/2
15:5 9/4
15:7 1/27, 9/3
15:11 2/2, 8/20
15:14 2/29
16:7 1/21
16:13 12/27
16:20 12/1
18:25 4/15
20:21 RSV 5/13
20:22 11/30

ACTS
1:9 4/10
4:32 10/7
7:9 5/11
16:25, 26 8/9
17:28 8/14
19:2 1/24

ROMANS
2:11 11/16
4:21 6/16
5:11 8/22
5:8 4/20
6:13 5/19
6:19 11/7
8:2 1/30
8:15 7/5
8:22, 23 10/22
8:25 1/9
8:28 3/29, 9/20
8:29 1/29
8:32 2/15
8:37 2/28, 3/17
8:38, 39 11/1
10:14 RSV 3/30
10:17 1/13, 8/30
11:33 2/20
12:1 5/15
12:2 5/6, 10/21
12:10 5/8, 10/1

1 CORINTHIANS
1:30 12/28, 12/29

3:3 10/12
8:6 8/16
10:12 6/10
12:4–6 10/3
13:8 NIV 6/23

2 CORINTHIANS
1:5 11/26
3:17 7/4
3:18 5/26, 10/29
4:3, 4 5/16
4:9 1/23
4:11 4/7
5:1 8/27
6:2 4/4
6:3, 4, 6 10/25
9:7 9/16
9:8 11/18
12:9 6/8, 9/14

GALATIANS
1:15, 16 11/15
2:20 4/25, 9/6
5:22 5/7
6:9 7/1

EPHESIANS
2:10 9/13
3:17–19 4/9
4:24 5/29
5:19 8/24
5:19, 20 11/5
5:20 8/12

6:5 1/18
6:11 3/6, 5/24
6:11 5/25
6:12 5/18

PHILIPPIANS
1:20 11/8
2:5 10/18
2:7, 8 12/22
3:10 12/6
3:16 9/28
4:6 1/20
4:6 8/13
4:6, 7 3/20
4:8 8/23
4:9 4/29
4:11 2/1, 9/11

COLOSSIANS
1:16 7/17
1:27 2/23, 4/27
3:15 3/21

1 THESSALONIANS
4:17, 18 6/1

2 THESSALONIANS
2:16, 17 12/18
3:13 11/19
3:16 6/26

1 TIMOTHY
2:5 8/18
3:16 12/14

2 TIMOTHY
2:21 5/17
3:15 5/21

HEBREWS
1:8 12/5
2:10 5/14
4:15 3/19
4:16 5/4
11:1 1/10, 4/22
11:24, 25 1/15
11:25 1/8
11:6–8 1/6
11:8 7/29
12:1 3/8
12:2 8/21
12:10 6/14
12:29 2/18
13:20 3/12

JAMES
4:8 6/18
5:16 2/27

1 PETER
1:15–17 10/27
1:18, 19 4/23
1:19 4/19
1:22 10/28
3:8 8/25
5:6 6/9, 6/12

2 PETER
1:4 1/26
1:19 8/10
3:18 8/15

1 JOHN
1:7 4/26
1:9 11/6
3:3 10/24
3:18 7/23
4:7 6/25
4:7–8 2/5
4:12 2/14
4:16 2/3
4:18 12/15

JUDE
21 2/12
24 10/19

REVELATION
1:3 11/17
22:2 6/3
22:17 7/6

ACKNOWLEDGEMENTS

Barbour Publishing,, Inc. expresses their appreciation to all those who generously gave permission to reprint copyrighted material. Diligent effort has been made to identify, locate, contact, and secure permission to use copyrighted material. If any permissions or acknowledgments have been inadvertently omitted or if such permissions were not received by the time of publication, the publisher would sincerely appreciate receiving complete information so that correct credit can be given in future editions. "No Limits", "Take My Life and Let It Be", "The Secret to Spiritual Success", "Can You Be Holy?", "Unutterable Love" by Abraham, Ken, *Positive Holiness*, Fleming H. Revell, a division of Baker Book House, Grand Rapids, MI 49516. Used by permission. "We're in for a Fight" from *Stand Up and Fight Back*, by Ken Abraham. Copyright 1993, Servant Publications, Ann Arbor, MI 48107. Used by permission. "Keep Your Eyes on Jesus", "From Disillusioned to Dis-Illusioned", "Assuming a Promise", "Living with Your Dreams", "Bricks and Books", "A Palace for God", "What Did I Do to Deserve This?", "Enduring Faith" from *The Disillusioned Christian* by Ken Abraham, Thomas Nelson Publishers, Nashville, TN 37214. Used by permission. "The Paralysis of Analysis", "The Calling", "A Modern-Day Prophet" from *The Calling* by Brother Andrew. Copyright 1996, Moorings, a division of Random House, Inc., Nashville, TN 37214. Used by permission. "The Great Shepherd", "The Shepherd's Staff" by Kay Arthur, "Because the Lord is My Shepherd"; published by Precept Ministries, Copyright 1991. "Equipped to Win" by Kay Arthur, *Lord, Is It Warfare? Teach Me to Stand;* published by Multnomah Press, Copyright 1991. "Trouble or Triumph" by Kay Arthur, *Lord, I Want to Know You;* published by Multnomah Press, Copyright 1992. "Singing for Holiness", "Southern Exposure", "Thanksgiving", "Is Thanksgiving Always Possible?" by Donald Grey Barnhouse, *Illustrating Great Themes of Scripture*, Copyright 1996, Fleming H. Revell, a division of Baker Book House, Grand Rapids, MI 49516.